Artificial Intelligence

ARTIFICIAL INTELLIGENCE

Dr. S. Chandra

PRASHANT PUBLISHING HOUSE
DELHI-110094

Published by :

Prashant Publishing House

C-34, 28 Foota Road, Gali-3,
West Karwal Nagar, Delhi-110094
Phone : 011-22963970, Mob. : 9810396373
e-mail.: prashantpublishinghouse@gmail.com

Artificial Intelligence

First Published 2019

ISBN 978-93-88526-04-3

PRINTED IN INDIA

Published by Mr. R.K. Jha M/s Prashant Publishing House and Published at H.S. Offset House Press, Delhi.

Contents

Preface

Artificial Intelligence is defined as the science of making computers do things that require intelligence when done by humans. Artificial Intelligence has had some success in limited, or simplified, domains. Knowledge Management provides a balance of conceptual and practical aspects of knowledge management offering the opportunity for students and practitioners to understand and effectively consider knowledge management approaches in their organizations.

Artificial Intelligence (AI) is the name that has been given to the field of computer science devoted to making machines do things that would require intelligence if done by humans (to paraphrase Minsky). Some are even ambitious enough to say that the goal of AI is to create minds in machines. But it has proven exceedingly difficult to even define words like "intelligence" and "mind", much less achieve computer implementation. The results of the 40-year history of AI have dampened the spirits of legions of would-be enthusiasts.

Artificial neural network types vary from those with only one or two layers of single direction logic, to complicated multi–input many directional feedback loop and layers. On the whole, these systems use algorithms in their programming to determine control and organization of their functions. Some may be as simple, one neuron layer with an input and an output, and others can mimic complex systems such as dANN, which can mimic chromosomal DNA through sizes at cellular level, into artificial organisms and simulate reproduction, mutation and population sizes. Most systems use "weights" to change the parameters of the throughput and the varying connections to the neurons. Artificial neural networks can be autonomous and learn by input from outside "teachers" or even self-teaching from written in rules.

The chip design of the nanocomputer would be best suited to have a carbon base which is both self-testing and reconfigurable. Because we know that faults will be at levels upwards of 10% for any chip built in the nanometre range, it will be necessary for these features to be part of any solution we choose. Also, it's important to remember the breadth of our failure rate. A Nanocomputer will contain not just one billion but several billion chips. If we have a computer with 5 billion chips, we will have 500 million chips which are defective with a 10% error rate. It will be an important cost factor to be able to repair these chips after they have been fabricated.

This is a reference book. All the matter is just compiled and edited in nature, taken from the various sources which are in public domain.

With its application oriented approach and inclusion of recent topics, the book would also be useful to postgraduate students and researchers in this field.

—*Editor*

1

Introduction

Artificial intelligence (AI) is the intelligence of machines and the branch of computer science that aims to create it. AI textbooks define the field as "the study and design of intelligent agents" where an intelligent agent is a system that perceives its environment and takes actions that maximize its chances of success. John McCarthy, who coined the term in 1956, defines it as "the science and engineering of making intelligent machines." The field was founded on the claim that a central property of humans, intelligence—the sapience of *Homo sapiens*—can be so precisely described that it can be simulated by a machine. This raises philosophical issues about the nature of the mind and the ethics of creating artificial beings, issues which have been addressed by myth, fiction and philosophy since antiquity. Artificial intelligence has been the subject of optimism, but has also suffered setbacks and, today, has become an essential part of the technology industry, providing the heavy lifting for many of the most difficult problems in computer science.

AI research is highly technical and specialized, deeply divided into subfields that often fail to communicate with each other. Subfields have grown up around particular institutions, the work of individual researchers, the solution of specific problems, longstanding differences of opinion about how AI should be done and the application of widely differing tools. The central problems of AI include such traits as reasoning, knowledge, planning, learning, communication, perception and the ability to move and manipulate objects. General intelligence (or "strong AI") is still among the field's long term goals.

Thinking machines and artificial beings appear in Greek myths, such as Talos of Crete, the bronze robot of Hephaestus and Pygmalion's Galatea. Human likenesses believed to have intelligence were built in every major civilization: animated cult images were worshipped in Egypt and Greece and humanoid automatons were built by Yan Shi, Hero of Alexandria and Al-Jazari. It was also widely believed that artificial beings had been created by Jâbir ibn Hayyân, Judah Loew and Paracelsus. By the 19th and 20th centuries, artificial beings had become a common feature in fiction, as in Mary Shelley's *Frankenstein* or Karel Èapek's *R.U.R. (Rossum's Universal Robots).* Pamela McCorduck argues that all of these are examples of an ancient urge, as she describes it, "to forge the gods". Stories of these creatures and their fates discuss many of the same hopes, fears and ethical concerns that are presented by artificial intelligence. Mechanical or "formal" reasoning has been developed by philosophers and mathematicians since antiquity. The study of logic led directly to the invention of the programmable digital electronic computer, based on the work of mathematician Alan Turing and others. Turing's theory of computation suggested that a machine, by shuffling symbols as simple as "0" and "1", could simulate any conceivable act of mathematical deduction. This, along with recent discoveries in neurology, information theory and cybernetics, inspired a small group of researchers to begin to seriously consider the possibility of building an electronic brain.

The field of AI research was founded at a conference on the campus of Dartmouth College in the summer of 1956. The attendees, including John McCarthy, Marvin Minsky, Allen Newell and Herbert Simon, became the leaders of AI research for many decades. They and their students wrote programmes that were, to most people, simply astonishing: computers were solving word problems in algebra, proving logical theorems and speaking English. By the middle of the 1960s, research in the U.S. was heavily funded by the Department of Defense and laboratories had been established around the world. AI's founders were profoundly optimistic about the future of the new field: Herbert Simon predicted that "machines will be capable, within twenty years, of doing any work a man can do" and Marvin Minsky agreed, writing that "within a generation ... the problem of creating 'artificial intelligence' will substantially be solved". They had failed to recognize the difficulty of some of the problems they faced. In 1974, in response to the criticism of England's Sir James Lighthill and ongoing pressure from Congress to fund more productive projects, the U.S. and British governments cut off all undirected, exploratory research in AI. The next few years, when funding for projects was hard to find, would later be called an "AI winter".

In the early 1980s, AI research was revived by the commercial success of expert systems, a form of AI programme that simulated the knowledge and analytical skills of one or more human experts. By 1985 the market for AI had reached over a billion dollars. At the same time, Japan's fifth generation computer project inspired the U.S and British governments to restore funding for academic research in the field. However, beginning with the collapse of the Lisp Machine market in 1987, AI once again fell into disrepute, and a second, longer lasting AI winter began.

In the 1990s and early 21st century, AI achieved its greatest successes, albeit somewhat behind the scenes. Artificial intelligence is used for logistics, data mining, medical diagnosis and many other areas throughout the technology industry. The success was due to several factors: the increasing computational power of computers, a greater emphasis on solving specific subproblems, the creation of new ties between AI and other fields working on similar problems, and a new commitment by researchers to solid mathematical methods and rigorous scientific standards. On 11 May 1997, Deep Blue became the first computer chess-playing system to beat a reigning world chess champion, Garry Kasparov. In 2005, a Stanford robot won the DARPA Grand Challenge by driving autonomously for 131 miles along an unrehearsed desert trail. In February 2011, in a Jeopardy! quiz show exhibition match, IBM's question answering system, Watson, defeated the two greatest Jeopardy! champions, Brad Rutter and Ken Jennings, by a significant margin.

The leading-edge definition of artificial intelligence research is changing over time. One pragmatic definition is: "AI research is that which computing scientists do not know how to do cost-effectively today." For example, in 1956 optical character recognition (OCR) was considered AI, but today, sophisticated OCR software with a context-sensitive spell checker and grammar checker software comes for free with most image scanners. No one would any longer consider already-solved computing science problems like OCR "artificial intelligence" today. Low-cost entertaining chess-playing software is commonly available for tablet computers. DARPA no longer provides significant funding for chess-playing computing system development. The child's XBox 360 gaming system November 2010 Kinect 3D-body-motion interface uses algorithms that emerged from lengthy AI research, but few consumers realize the technology source. AI applications are no longer the exclusive domain of Department of defense R&D, but are now common place consumer items and inexpensive intelligent toys. In common usage, the term "AI" no longer seems to apply to off-the-shelf solved computing-science problems, which may have originally emerged out of years of AI research.

BACKGROUND

Artificial Intelligence is defined as the science of making computers do things that require intelligence when done by humans. AI has had some success in limited, or simplified, domains. However, the five decades since the inception of AI have brought only very slow progress, and early optimism concerning the attainment of human-level intelligence has given way to an appreciation of the profound difficulty of the problem.Quite simple human behaviour can be intelligent yet quite complex behaviour performed by insects is unintelligent. Consider the behaviour of the digger wasp, *Sphex ichneumoneus*.

When the female wasp brings food to her burrow, she deposits it on the threshold, goes inside the burrow to check for intruders, and then if the coast is clear carries in the food. The unintelligent nature of the wasp's behaviour is revealed if the watching experimenter moves the food a few inches while the was is inside the burrow checking. On emerging, the wasp repeats the whole procedure: she carries the food to the threshold once again, goes in to look around, and emerges. She can be made to repeat this cycle of behaviour upwards of forty times in succession.

Mainstream thinking in psychology regards human intelligence not as a single ability or cognitive process but rather as an array of separate components. Research in AI has focussed chiefly on the following components of intelligence: learning, reasoning, problem-solving, perception, and language-understanding.

Simplest learning

The simplest is learning by trial-and-error. For example, a simple programme for solving mate-in-one chess problems might try out moves at random until one is found that achieves mate. The programme remembers the successful move and next time the computer is given the same problem it is able to produce the answer immediately.

The simple memorising of individual items—solutions to problems, words of vocabulary, etc.—is known as rote learning. Rote learning is relatively easy to implement on a computer. More challenging is the problem of implementing what is called generalisation. Learning that involves generalisation leaves the learner able to perform better in situations not previously encountered.

A programme that learns past tenses of regular English verbs by rote will not be able to produce the past tense of *e.g.* "jump" until presented at least once with "jumped", whereas a programme that is able to generalise from examples can learn the "add-ed" rule, and so form the past tense of "jump" in the absence of any previous encounter with this verb. Sophisticated modern techniques enable programmes to generalise complex rules from data.

HISTORY OF ARTIFICIAL INTELLIGENCE

The history of artificial intelligence began in antiquity, with myths, stories and rumors of artificial beings endowed with intelligence or consciousness by master craftsmen; as Pamela McCorduck writes, AI began with "an ancient wish to forge the gods." The seeds of modern AI were planted by classical philosophers who attempted to describe the process of human thinking as the mechanical manipulation of symbols. This work culminated in the invention of the programmable digital computer in the 1940s, a machine based on the abstract essence of mathematical reasoning. This device and the ideas behind it inspired a handful of scientists to begin seriously discussing the possibility of building an electronic brain. The field of artificial intelligence research was founded at a conference on the campus of Dartmouth College in the summer of 1956. Those who attended would become the leaders of AI research for decades. Many of them predicted that a machine as intelligent as a human being would exist in no more than a generation and they were given millions of dollars to make this vision come true.

Eventually it became obvious that they had grossly underestimated the difficulty of the project. In 1973, in response to the criticism of Sir James Lighthill and ongoing pressure from congress, the U.S. and British Governments stopped funding undirected research into artificial intelligence. Seven years later, a visionary initiative by the Japanese Government inspired governments and industry to provide AI with billions of dollars, but by the late 80s the investors became disillusioned and withdrew funding again. This cycle of boom and bust, of "AI winters" and summers, continues to haunt the field. Undaunted, there are those who make extraordinary predictions even now. Progress in AI has continued, despite the rise and fall of its reputation in the eyes of government bureaucrats and venture capitalists. Problems that had begun to seem impossible in 1970 have been solved and the solutions are now used in successful commercial products. However, no machine has been built with a human level of intelligence, contrary to the optimistic predictions of the first generation of AI researchers. "We can only see a short distance ahead," admitted Alan Turing, in a famous 1950 paper that catalyzed the modern search for machines that think. "But," he added, "we can see much that must be done."

Precursors

McCorduck (2004) writes "artificial intelligence in one form or another is an idea that has pervaded Western intellectual history, a dream in urgent need of being realized," expressed in humanity's myths, legends, stories, speculation and clockwork automatons.

AI in Myth, Fiction and Speculation

Mechanical men and artificial beings appear in Greek myths, such as the golden robots of Hephaestus and Pygmalion's Galatea. In the Middle Ages, there were rumors of secret mystical or alchemical means of placing mind into matter, such as Jâbir ibn Hayyân's *Takwin*, Paracelsus' homunculus and Rabbi Judah Loew's Golem. By the 19th century, ideas about artificial men and thinking machines were developed in fiction, as in Mary Shelley's *Frankenstein* or Karel Èapek's *R.U.R. (Rossum's Universal Robots)*, and speculation, such as Samuel Butler's "Darwin among the Machines." AI has continued to be an important element of science fiction into the present.

ARTIFICIAL INTELLIGENCE OUTLINE AND HISTORY

Artificial Intelligence (AI) is the name that has been given to the field of computer science devoted to making machines do things that would require intelligence if done by humans (to paraphrase Minsky). Some are even ambitious enough to say that the goal of AI is to create minds in machines. But it has proven exceedingly difficult to even define words like "intelligence" and "mind", much less achieve computer implementation. The results of the 40-year history of AI have dampened the spirits of legions of would-be enthusiasts. The most "glamorous" contemporary computer applications are GUI or Java programmes, not AI. Artificial Intelligence has been divided into those concerned with processing of symbolic information and those concerned with Neural Networks. But the Symbolic AI camp has made every effort to exclude Neural Networks from the definition of AI, and the field of "Connectionism" is increasingly regarded as a somewhat independent discipline. Marvin Minsky has said that Neural Networks are "too stupid" to be considered Artificial Intelligence. Symbolic AI itself is divided into two subgroups, one primarily concerned with logic, and the other concerned with heuristics ("rule-of-thumb" methods).

Artificial Intelligence as a field dates from the summer of 1956 when a conference on the subject was organized by John McCarthy at Dartmouth College in New Hampshire. In attendance were the four "founding fathers" of AI: John McCarthy, Marvin Minsky, Herbert Simon and Allen Newell. Herbert Simon was a political scientist who was interested in the way decisions are made in bureaucracies. He found that "management manuals" are often used by organizations to provide solutions to problems — and he became interested in the compilation and application of the problem-solving procedures of these manuals — a "heuristic" approach.

Simon teamed-up with mathematician Allen Newell to create the world's first AI programme: "Logic Theorist". Combining logic with "search tree" heuristics, Logic Theorist proved 38 of the first 52 theorems of Russell and Whitehead's *Principal Mathematica*. The proof for one of these theorems was even more elegant that the one given in *Principal*. At the Dartmouth conference, Simon and Newell distinguished themselves by being the only participants who already had a working AI programme.

John McCarthy induced the conference participants to support the term "Artificial Intelligence" to describe their discipline. Discussion centered on the idea that intelligence is based on internal representations of information, corresponding symbols, and the processing of information and symbols. In this view, intelligence transcends any specific hardware (or "wetware", as brains are often called). McCarthy believed that the key to AI was being "able to write out the rules that would let a computer think the way we do". He was one of the foremost proponents of the "logic" school, and he attempted to implement machine intelligence through predicate calculus. McCarthy is also the creator of LISP (LISt Processing) language, the most widely-used computer language in AI research in North America. LISP is intended to reproduce what is regarded as the associative features of thought. LISP is based on Alonzo Church's "Lambda Calculus", which can apply functions to functions as readily as it can apply functions to numbers or characters. LISP programming is notoriously recursive (ie, using functions that call themselves).

Marvin Minsky is probably the most famous of the four "founding fathers" of AI. He is particularly well-known among cryonicists because he sponsored Eric Drexler's PhD thesis and wrote the forward to *Engines of Creation*. Minsky cofounded the MIT AI Lab with McCarthy in 1958. McCarthy left in 1962 to start AI research at Stanford, leaving Minsky to "rule the roost" in AI at MIT for many, many years.

In the early days of computing science there were, on the one side, a small group of enthusiasts with unbounded visions of what computers could do. To many, the automating of all mental activities — and ultimately the automation of mind — seemed only a few years away. On the other side was the general public, who (in pre-PC times) had a gross ignorance and no small amount of fear about the capabilities of computers. Managers, professionals and others feared for their jobs. IBM researchers were developing programmes which could play chess, play checkers and prove geometry theorems, but the effect of this work on marketing was not seen to be favourable.

IBM dropped its game-playing and theorem-proving research and adopted the posture that computers can not steal jobs because they are only moronic devices for number-crunching, data-manipulation and word-processing. IBM's pragmatic marketing position has proven prophetic in light of widespread PC use and what many people believe to be forty years of failed attempts to achieve Artificial Intelligence.

Several attempt have been made to create programme "agents" in "Micro Worlds", where simple language could be applied to a limited field of discourse. One of the most ambitious of such projects was a system by Terry Winograd that represented a robot named SHRDLU. The robot would manipulate coloured blocks and pyramids in response to English-like commands, and could give simple explanations when quizzed about its actions (like how to build a steeple). The programme consisted of many fragments that acted as independent agents. This approach is more "heuristic" than logical, and it typifies Minsky's approach to AI.

In theory, a "Micro World" could be expanded continuously until the robot's "universe of discourse" overlapped the human universe of discourse — and the robot was a genuinely sentient being. In practice, scaling-up a "Micro World" has proven exceedingly difficult. Minsky directed such a project at MIT which got bigger and bigger until there were so many programmes which had been written by so many people — and the system was so large — that no one understood it. It was abandoned in 1971. Later, Minsky wrote *The Society Of Mind* in which he attempted to decompose the human mind into a "society" of independent "agents", none of which could be called intelligent. Minsky's thesis is that this is the way that real minds work — and it is the way that machine minds will be built.

In the early 1970s the language PROLOG (PROgramming in LOGic) became the favoured AI language outside the United States (LISP was too firmly established in the US). PROLOG is a "higher-level" language that allows the programmer to specify what is to be done, rather than how, due to PROLOG's mechanisms for manipulating logical statements.

The late 1970s and early 1980s witnessed a huge surge in corporate interest and capital into the area of AI known as "expert systems". These systems consist of a knowledge base of "if-then" rules, accumulated from human experts. A car diagnosis system, for example, might contain the rule "If the engine won't turn-over, thencheck the battery strength". And "If the engine won't turn-over and the battery strength is high, then check the spark plugs". Expert systems incorporated the value of knowledge as well as logic in problem-solving, and had the promise of being as useful as human experts.

The first expert system was DENDRAL, a system for narrowing-down the possible chemical structure of a compound based on formula, spectral information and the encoded wisdom of chemists. DENDRAL proved its success by deducing the structure of Di-n-decyl $C_{20}H_{22}$ from 11 million possible combinations.

But as the system accumulated more knowledge it became too difficult to expand and maintain. MYCIN was a better-designed expert system that more cleanly separated the rules (knowledge-base) from the logic used to apply the rules. MYCIN diagnosed infectious blood diseases on the basis of blood tests, bacterial cultures and other information. Other expert systems were developed which proved to be of benefit for certain specialized applications. But knowledge-engineering — transferring human expert knowledge to expert computer systems — proved to be far more difficult than anyone anticipated. The systems required continual revision to avoid obsolescence. And too often they made gross mistakes that no one with "common sense" would make. The expert system "boom" was followed by an expert system "bust".

Computer systems designed to translate from one human language to another have proven exceedingly difficult to build, for the same reason that computer systems built to understand human language have foundered. Word meanings are context-dependent. The phrase "That is a big drop" has a different meaning in an optometrist's office than it has on the edge of a cliff.

A sentence like "Still waters run deep" is even more challenging, not simply because it is metaphorical, but because every word in the sentence can:

- Have multiple meanings and
- Be used in more than one part-of-speech. Semantics governs syntax, which can make parsing sentences unfathomable for computer programmes.

Based on the assumption that common-sense understanding necessarily must be built upon a large knowledge-base, Doug Lenat has begun a $25 million project to create a computer-system with an enormous amounts of knowledge. Cyc (short for encyclopedia) collects knowledge in "frames" (collections of facts and rules) in a feeding process that is expected to take two person-centuries, and include 100 million frames.

Cyc is capable of "meditating" on its knowledge, searching for analogies. Lenat claims that Cyc will eventually be able to educate itself (by reading and having discussions with "tutors") rather than having to be "spoon fed" its knowledge. But McCarthy thinks Cyc has inadequate logic, and Minsky doesn't think Cyc has a wide-enough variety of procedures to do much with its information.

The Artificial Life community has expanded on the "Micro World" concept by creating Micro Worlds in which the artificial creatures experience "pleasure and pain", have needs and must adapt. In these "Micro Worlds" there is not only a universe of discourse, but a universe of values (motives, "feelings"). In S.W. Wilson's Animat system, the creatures adapt by learning what rules "work" and what rules don't. Genetic algorithms provide a basis for "learning".

AI "founding father" Allen Newell has designed the SOAR system, a collection of psychological mechanisms based on his book *Unified Theories Of Cognition*. SOAR uses representations and ends-means analysis for problem-solving. A "problem" is, by definition, a discrepancy between an existing condition and a goal condition. As with the Artificial Life systems, SOAR presumes that an intelligent system must be "motivated" by goal-states — and the sophisticated heuristic search strategies of ends-means analysis are used to achieve those states. "Learning" occurs in the process.

AUTOMATONS

Realistic humanoid automatons were built by craftsman from every civilization, including Yan Shi, Hero of Alexandria, Al-Jazari and Wolfgang von Kempelen. The oldest known automatons were the sacred statues of ancient Egypt and Greece. The faithful believed that craftsman had imbued these figures with very real minds, capable of wisdom and emotion—Hermes Trismegistus wrote that "by discovering the true nature of the gods, man has been able to reproduce it."

Formal Reasoning

Artificial intelligence is based on the assumption that the process of human thought can be mechanized. The study of mechanical—or "formal"—reasoning has a long history. Chinese, Indian and Greek philosophers all developed structured methods of formal deduction in the first millennium BCE. Their ideas were developed over the centuries by philosophers such as Aristotle (who gave a formal analysis of the syllogism), Euclid (whose *Elements* was a model of formal reasoning), al-Khwrizm+ (who developed algebra and gave his name to "algorithm") and European scholastic philosophers such as William of Ockham and Duns Scotus. Majorcan philosopher Ramon Llull (1232–1315) developed several *logical machines* devoted to the production of knowledge by logical means; Llull described his machines as mechanical entities that could combine basic and undeniable truths by simple logical operations, produced by the machine by mechanical meanings, in such ways as to produce all the possible knowledge. Llull's work had a great influence on Gottfried Leibniz, who redeveloped his ideas.

In the 17th century, Leibniz, Thomas Hobbes and René Descartes explored the possibility that all rational thought could be made as systematic as algebra or geometry. Hobbes famously wrote in *Leviathan*: "reason is nothing but reckoning".

Leibniz envisioned a universal language of reasoning (his *characteristica universalis*) which would reduce argumentation to calculation, so that "there would be no more need of disputation between two philosophers than between two accountants. For it would suffice to take their pencils in hand, down to their slates, and to say each other (with a friend as witness, if they liked): *Let us calculate.*" These philosophers had begun to articulate the physical symbol system hypothesis that would become the guiding faith of AI research. In the 20th century, the study of mathematical logic provided the essential breakthrough that made artificial intelligence seem plausible. The foundations had been set by such works as Boole's *The Laws of Thought* and Frege's *Begriffsschrift*. Building on Frege's system, Russell and Whitehead presented a formal treatment of the foundations of mathematics in their masterpiece, the *Principia Mathematica* in 1913.

Inspired by Russell's success, David Hilbert challenged mathematicians of the 1920s and 30s to answer this fundamental question: "can all of mathematical reasoning be formalized?" His question was answered by Gödel's incompleteness proof, Turing's machine and Church's Lambda calculus. Their answer was surprising in two ways. First, they proved that there were, in fact, limits to what mathematical logic could accomplish. But second (and more important for AI) their work suggested that, within these limits, *any* form of mathematical reasoning could be mechanized. The Church-Turing thesis implied that a mechanical device, shuffling symbols as simple as 0 and 1, could imitate any conceivable process of mathematical deduction. The key insight was the Turing machine—a simple theoretical construct that captured the essence of abstract symbol manipulation. This invention would inspire a handful of scientists to begin discussing the possibility of thinking machines.

Computer Science

Calculating machines were built in antiquity and improved throughout history by many mathematicians, including (once again) philosopher Gottfried Leibniz. In the early 19th century,

Charles Babbage designed a programmable computer (the Analytical Engine), although it was never built. Ada Lovelace speculated that the machine "might compose elaborate and scientific pieces of music of any degree of complexity or extent". (She is often credited as the first programmer because of a set of notes she wrote that completely detail a method for calculating Bernoulli numbers with the Engine.) The first modern computers were the massive code breaking machines of the Second World War (such as Z3, ENIAC and Colossus). The latter two of these machines were based on the theoretical foundation laid by Alan Turing and developed by John Von Neumann.

The Birth of Artificial Intelligence 1943-1956

In the 1940s and 50s, a handful of scientists from a variety fields (mathematics, psychology, engineering, economics and political science) began to discuss the possibility of creating an artificial brain. The field of artificial intelligence research was founded as an academic discipline in 1956.

Cybernetics and Early Neural Networks

The earliest research into thinking machines was inspired by a confluence of ideas that became prevalent in the late 30s, 40s and early 50s. Recent research in neurology had shown that the brain was an electrical network of neurons that fired in all-or-nothing pulses. Norbert Wiener's cybernetics described control and stability in electrical networks. Claude Shannon's information theory described digital signals (i.e., all-or-nothing signals). Alan Turing's theory of computation showed any form computation could be described digitally. The close relationship between these ideas suggested that it might be possible to construct an electronic brain. Examples of work in this vein includes robots such as W. Grey Walter's turtles and the Johns Hopkins Beast. These machines did not use computers, digital electronics or symbolic reasoning; they were controlled entirely by analog circuitry. Walter Pitts and Warren McCulloch analyzed networks of idealized artificial neurons and showed how they might perform simple logical functions. They were the first to describe what later researchers would call a neural network. One of the students inspired by Pitts and McCulloch was a young Marvin Minsky, then a 24 year old graduate student. In 1951 (with Dean Edmonds) he built the first neural net machine, the SNARC. Minsky was to become one of the most important leaders and innovators in AI for the next 50 years.

Game AI

In 1951, using the Ferranti Mark 1 machine of the University of Manchester, Christopher Strachey wrote a checkers programme and Dietrich Prinz wrote one for chess. Arthur Samuel's checkers programme, developed in the middle 50s and early 60s, eventually achieved sufficient skill to challenge a respectable amateur. Game AI would continue to be used as a measure of progress in AI throughout its history.

Turing's Test

In 1950 Alan Turing published a landmark paper in which he speculated about the possibility of creating machines with true intelligence. He noted that "intelligence" is difficult to define and devised his famous Turing Test. If a machine could carry on a conversation (over a teletype) that was indistinguishable from a conversation with a human being, then the machine could be called "intelligent." This simplified version of the problem allowed Turing to argue convincingly that a "thinking machine" was at least *plausible* and the paper answered all the most common objections to the proposition. The Turing Test was the first serious proposal in the philosophy of artificial intelligence.

Symbolic Reasoning and the Logic Theorist

When access to digital computers became possible in the middle fifties, a few scientists instinctively recognized that a machine that could manipulate numbers could also manipulate symbols and that the manipulation of symbols could well be the essence of human thought. This was a new approach to creating thinking machines. In 1955, Allen Newell and (future Nobel Laureate) Herbert Simon created the "Logic Theorist" (with help from J. C. Shaw). The programme would eventually prove 38 of the first 52 theorems in Russell and Whitehead's *Principia Mathematica*, and find new and more elegant proofs for some. Simon said that they had "solved the venerable mind/body problem, explaining how a system composed of matter can have the properties of mind." (This was an early statement of the philosophical position John Searle would later call "Strong AI": that machines can contain minds just as human bodies do.)

Dartmouth Conference 1956: the Birth of AI

The Dartmouth Conference of 1956 was organized by Marvin Minsky, John McCarthy and two senior scientists: Claude Shannon and Nathan Rochester of IBM. The proposal for the conference included this assertion: "every aspect of learning or any other feature of intelligence can be so precisely described that a machine can be made to simulate it". The participants included Ray Solomonoff, Oliver Selfridge, Trenchard More, Arthur Samuel, Allen Newell and Herbert Simon, all of whom would create important programmes during the first decades of AI research. At the conference Newell and Simon debuted the "Logic Theorist" and McCarthy persuaded the attendees to accept "Artificial Intelligence" as the name of the field. The 1956 Dartmouth conference was the moment that AI gained its name, its mission, its first success and its major players, and is widely considered the birth of AI.

The Golden Years 1956-1974

The years after the Dartmouth conference were an era of discovery, of sprinting across new ground. The programmes that were developed during this time were, to most people, simply "astonishing": computers were solving algebra word problems, proving theorems in geometry and learning to speak English. Few at the time would have believed that such "intelligent" behaviour by machines was possible at all. Researchers expressed an intense optimism in private and in print, predicting that a fully intelligent machine would be built in less than 20 years. Government agencies like ARPA poured money into the new field.

The Work

There were many successful programmes and new directions in the late 50s and 1960s. Among the most influential were these:

Reasoning as Search

Many early AI programmes used the same basic algorithm. To achieve some goal (like winning a game or proving a theorem), they proceeded step by step towards it (by making a move or a deduction) as if searching through a maze, backtracking whenever they reached a dead end. This paradigm was called "reasoning as search". The principal difficulty was that, for many problems, the number of possible paths through the "maze" was simply astronomical (a situation known as a "combinatorial explosion"). Researchers would reduce the search space by using heuristics or "rules of thumb" that would eliminate those paths that were unlikely to lead to a solution. Newell and Simon tried to capture a general version of this algorithm in a programme called the "General Problem Solver". Other "searching" programmes were able to accomplish impressive tasks like solving problems in geometry and algebra, such as Herbert Gelernter's Geometry Theorem Prover (1958) and SAINT, written by Minsky's student James Slagle (1961). Other programmes searched through goals and subgoals to plan actions, like the STRIPS system developed at Stanford to control the behaviour of their robot Shakey.

PROBLEMS OF AI

The general problem of simulating (or creating) intelligence has been broken down into a number of specific sub-problems. These consist of particular traits or capabilities that researchers would like an intelligent system to display. The traits described below have received the most attention.

Deduction, Reasoning, Problem Solving

Early AI researchers developed algorithms that imitated the step-by-step reasoning that humans were often assumed to use when they solve puzzles, play board games or make logical deductions. By the late 1980s and '90s, AI research had also developed highly successful methods for dealing with uncertain or incomplete information, employing concepts from probability and economics. For difficult problems, most of these algorithms can require enormous computational resources — most experience a "combinatorial explosion": the amount of memory or computer time required becomes astronomical when the problem goes beyond a certain size. The search for more efficient problem solving algorithms is a high priority for AI research. Human beings solve most of their problems using fast, intuitive judgments rather than the conscious, step-by-step deduction that early AI research was able to model. AI has made some progress at imitating this kind of "sub-symbolic" problem solving: embodied agent approaches emphasize the importance of sensorimotor skills to higher reasoning; neural net research attempts to simulate the structures inside human and animal brains that give rise to this skill.

Knowledge Representation

Knowledge representation and knowledge engineering are central to AI research. Many of the problems machines are expected to solve will require extensive knowledge about the world. Among the things that AI needs to represent are: objects, properties, categories and relations between objects; situations, events, states and time; causes and effects; knowledge about knowledge (what we know about what other people know); and many other, less well researched domains. A complete representation of "what exists" is an ontology (borrowing a word from traditional philosophy), of which the most general are called upper ontologies.

Among the Most Difficult Problems in Knowledge Representation Are:

Default Reasoning and the Qualification Problem

Many of the things people know take the form of "working assumptions." For example, if a bird comes up in conversation, people typically picture an animal that is fist sized, sings, and flies. None of these things are true about all birds. John McCarthy identified this problem in 1969 as the qualification problem: for any commonsense rule that AI researchers care to represent, there tend to be a huge number of exceptions. Almost nothing is simply true or false in the way that abstract logic requires. AI research has explored a number of solutions to this problem.

The Breadth of Commonsense Knowledge

The number of atomic facts that the average person knows is astronomical. Research projects that attempt to build a complete knowledge base of commonsense knowledge (e.g., Cyc) require enormous amounts of laborious ontological engineering — they must be built, by hand, one complicated concept at a time. A major goal is to have the computer understand enough concepts to be able to learn by reading from sources like the internet, and thus be able to add to its own ontology.

The Subsymbolic form of Some Commonsense Knowledge

Much of what people know is not represented as "facts" or "statements" that they could express verbally. For example, a chess master will avoid a particular chess position because it "feels too exposed" or an art critic can take one look at a statue and instantly realize that it is a fake. These are intuitions or tendencies that are represented in the brain non-consciously and sub-symbolically. Knowledge like this informs, supports and provides a context for symbolic, conscious knowledge. As with the related problem of sub-symbolic reasoning, it is hoped that situated AI or computational intelligence will provide ways to represent this kind of knowledge.

Planning

Intelligent agents must be able to set goals and achieve them. They need a way to visualize the future (they must have a representation of the state of the world and be able to make predictions about how their actions will change it) and be able to make choices that maximize the utility (or "value") of the available choices. In classical planning problems, the agent can assume that it is the only thing acting on the world and it can be certain what the consequences of its actions may be. However, if this is not true, it must periodically check if the world matches its predictions and it must change its plan as this becomes necessary, requiring the agent to reason under uncertainty. Multi-agent planning uses the cooperation and competition of many agents to achieve a given goal. Emergent behaviour such as this is used by evolutionary algorithms and swarm intelligence.

Learning

Machine learning has been central to AI research from the beginning. In 1956, at the original Dartmouth AI summer conference, Ray Solomonoff wrote a report on unsupervised probabilistic machine learning: "An Inductive Inference Machine". Unsupervised learning is the ability to find patterns in a stream of input. Supervised learning includes both classification and numerical regression. Classification is used to determine what category something belongs in, after seeing a number of examples of things from several categories. Regression takes a set of numerical input/output examples and attempts to discover a continuous function that would generate the outputs from the inputs. In reinforcement learning the agent is rewarded for good responses and punished for bad ones. These can be analyzed in terms of decision theory, using concepts like utility. The mathematical analysis of machine learning algorithms and their performance is a branch of theoretical computer science known as computational learning theory.

TECHNIQES

The subject of artificial intelligence spans a wide horizon. It deals with the various kinds of knowledge representation schemes, different techniques of intelligent search, various methods for resolving uncertainty of data and knowledge, different schemes for automated machine learning and many others. Among the application areas of AI, we have Expert systems, Game-playing, and Theorem-proving, Natural language processing, Image recognition, Robotics and many others.

The subject of artificial intelligence has been enriched with a wide discipline of knowledge from Philosophy, Psychology, Cognitive Science, Computer Science, Mathematics and Engineering.

Subject

The subject of artificial intelligence was originated with game-playing and theorem-proving programmes and was gradually enriched with theories from a number of parent disciplines. As a young discipline of science, the significance of the topics covered under the subject changes considerably with time.

Concept of Learning

The concept of learning is illustrated here with reference to a natural problem of learning of pronunciation by a child from his mother. The hearing system of the child receives the pronunciation of the character 'A' and the voice system attempts to imitate it. The difference of the mother's and the child's pronunciation, hereafter called the error signal, is received by the child's learning system auditory nerve, and an actuation signal is generated by the learning system through a motor nerve for adjustment of the pronunciation of the child. The adaptation of the child's voice system is continued until the amplitude of the error signal is insignificantly low. Each time the voice system passes through an adaptation cycle, the resulting tongue position of the child for speaking 'A' is saved by the learning process. The learning problem discussed above is an example of the well-known parametric learning, where the adaptive learning process adjusts the parametres of the child's voice system autonomously to keep its response close enough to the 'sample training pattern'.

The artificial neural networks, which represent the electrical analogue of the biological nervous systems, are gaining importance for their increasing applications in supervised (parametric) learning problems. Besides this type, the other common learning methods, which we do unknowingly, are inductive and analogy-based learning. In inductive learning, the learner makes generalizations from examples. For instance, noting that 'cuckoo flies', 'parrot flies' and 'sparrow flies', the learner generalizes that 'birds fly'. On the other hand, in analogy-based learning, the learner, for example, learns the motion of electrons in an atom analogously from his knowledge of planetary motion in solar systems.

Representation

The reasoning problem, one has to reach a pre-defined goal state from one or more given initial states. So, the lesser the number of transitions for reaching the goal state, the higher the efficiency of the reasoning system. Increasing the efficiency of a reasoning system thus requires minimization of intermediate states, which indirectly calls for an organized and complete knowledge base. A complete and organized storehouse of knowledge needs minimum search to identify the appropriate knowledge at a given problem state and thus yields the right next state on the leading edge of the problem-solving process. Organization of knowledge, therefore, is of paramount importance in knowledge engineering. A variety of knowledge representation techniques are in use in Artificial Intelligence. Production rules, semantic nets, frames, filler and slots, and predicate logic are only a few to mention. The selection of a particular type of representational scheme of knowledge depends both on the nature of applications and the choice of users.

Significance

The significant area of artificial intelligence is planning. The problems of reasoning and planning share many common issues, but have a basic difference that originates from their definitions. The reasoning problem is mainly concerned with the testing of the satisfiability of a goal from a given set of data and knowledge.

The planning problem, on the other hand, deals with the determination of the methodology by which a successful goal can be achieved from the known initial states. Automated planning finds extensive applications in robotics and navigational problems, some of which will be discussed shortly.

Acquisition of Knowledge

Acquisition of knowledge is equally hard for machines as it is for human beings. It includes generation of new pieces of knowledge from given knowledge base, setting dynamic data structures for existing knowledge, learning knowledge from the environment and refinement of knowledge. Automated acquisition of knowledge by machine learning approach is an active area of current research in Artificial Intelligence.

Intelligent Search: Search problems, which we generally encounter in Computer Science, are of a deterministic nature, *i.e.*, the order of visiting the elements of the search space is known. For example, in depth first and breadth first search algorithms, one knows the sequence of visiting the nodes in a tree. However, search problems, which we will come across in AI, are non-deterministic and the order of visiting the elements in the search space is completely dependent on data sets.

Logic Programming

One outgrowth of such attempts is propositional logic, which deals with a set of binary statements (propositions) connected by Boolean operators. The logic of propositions, which was gradually enriched to handle more complex situations of the real world, is called predicate logic. One classical variety of predicate logic-based programmes is Logic Programme. PROLOG, which is an abbreviation for PROgramming in LOGic, is a typical language that supports logic programmes. Logic Programming has recently been identified as one of the prime area of research in AI.

The ultimate aim of this research is to extend the PROLOG compiler to handle spatio-temporal models and support a parallel programming environment. Building architecture for PROLOG machines was a hot topic of the last decade.

Soft Computing

Soft computing is 'an emerging approach to computing, which parallels the remarkable ability of the human mind to reason and learn in an environment of uncertainty and imprecision'. It, in general, is a collection of computing tools and techniques, shared by closely related disciplines that include fuzzy logic, artificial neural nets, genetic algorithms, belief calculus, and some aspects of machine learning like inductive logic programming. These tools are used independently as well as jointly depending on the type of the domain of applications.

Imprecision and Uncertainty

Data and knowledgebases in many typical AI problems, such as reasoning and planning, are often contaminated with various forms of incompleteness. The incompleteness of data, hereafter called imprecision, generally appears in the database for i) lack of appropriate data, and ii) poor authenticity level of the sources. The incompleteness of knowledge, often referred to as uncertainty, originates in the knowledge base due to lack of certainty of the pieces of knowledge Reasoning in the presence of imprecision of data and uncertainty of knowledge is a complex problem.

Various tools and techniques have been devised for reasoning under incomplete data and knowledge. Some of these techniques employ i) stochastic ii) fuzzy and iii) belief network models. In a stochastic reasoning model, the system can have transition from one given state to a number of states, such that the sum of the probability of transition to the next states from the given state is strictly unity.

In a fuzzy reasoning system, on the other hand, the sum of the membership value of transition from the given state to the next state may be greater than or equal to one. The belief network model updates the stochastic/fuzzy belief assigned to the facts embedded in the network until a condition of equilibrium is reached, following which there would be no more change in beliefs. Recently, fuzzy tools and techniques have been applied in a specialized belief network, called a fuzzy Petri net, for handling both imprecision of data and uncertainty of knowledge by a unified approach.

NATURAL LANGUAGE PROCESSING

Natural language processing gives machines the ability to read and understand the languages that humans speak. Many researchers hope that a sufficiently powerful natural language processing system would be able to acquire knowledge on its own, by reading the existing text available over the internet. Some straightforward applications of natural language processing include information retrieval (or text mining) and machine translation.

Motion and Manipulation

The field of robotics is closely related to AI. Intelligence is required for robots to be able to handle such tasks as object manipulation and navigation, with sub-problems of localization (knowing where you are), mapping (learning what is around you) and motion planning (figuring out how to get there).

Perception

Machine perception is the ability to use input from sensors (such as cameras, microphones, sonar and others more exotic) to deduce aspects of the world. Computer vision is the ability to analyze visual input. A few selected subproblems are speech recognition, facial recognition and object recognition.

Social Intelligence

Emotion and social skills play two roles for an intelligent agent. First, it must be able to predict the actions of others, by understanding their motives and emotional states. (This involves elements of game theory, decision theory, as well as the ability to model human emotions and the perceptual skills to detect emotions.) Also, for good human-computer interaction, an intelligent machine also needs to *display* emotions. At the very least it must appear polite and sensitive to the humans it interacts with. At best, it should have normal emotions itself.

Creativity

A sub-field of AI addresses creativity both theoretically (from a philosophical and psychological perspective) and practically (via specific implementations of systems that generate outputs that can be considered creative, or systems that identify and assess creativity). A related area of computational research is Artificial Intuition and Artificial Imagination.

General Intelligence

Most researchers hope that their work will eventually be incorporated into a machine with *general* intelligence (known as strong AI), combining all the skills above and exceeding human abilities at most or all of them. A few believe that anthropomorphic features like artificial consciousness or an artificial brain may be required for such a project. Many of the problems above are considered AI-complete: to solve one problem, you must solve them all. For example, even a straightforward, specific task like machine translation requires that the machine follow the author's argument (reason), know what is being talked about (knowledge), and faithfully reproduce the author's intention (social intelligence). Machine translation, therefore, is believed to be AI-complete: it may require strong AI to be done as well as humans can do it.

APPROACHES

There is no established unifying theory or paradigm that guides AI research. Researchers disagree about many issues. A few of the most long standing questions that have remained unanswered are these: should artificial intelligence simulate natural intelligence, by studying psychology or neurology? Or is human biology as irrelevant to AI research as bird biology is to aeronautical engineering? Can intelligent behaviour be described using simple, elegant principles (such as logic or optimization)? Or does it necessarily require solving a large number of completely unrelated problems? Can intelligence be reproduced using high-level symbols, similar to words and ideas? Or does it require "sub-symbolic" processing? John Haugeland, who coined the term GOFAI, also proposed that AI should more properly be referred to as synthetic intelligence, a term which has since been adopted by some non-GOFAI researchers.

Theories

In the quest to create intelligent machines, the field of Artificial Intelligence has split into several different approaches based on the opinions about the most promising methods and theories. These rivaling theories have lead researchers in one of two basic approaches; bottom-up and top-down.

Bottom-up theorists believe the best way to achieve artificial intelligence is to build electronic replicas of the human brain's complex network of neurons, while the top-down approach attempts to mimic the brain's behaviour with computer programmes.

Parallel Computation

The human brain is made up of a web of billions of cells called neurons, and understanding its complexities is seen as one of the last frontiers in scientific research. It is the aim of AI researchers who prefer this bottom-up approach to construct electronic circuits that act as neurons do in the human brain. Although much of the working of the brain remains unknown, the complex network of neurons is what gives humans intelligent characteristics. By itself, a neuron is not intelligent, but when grouped together, neurons are able to pass electrical signals through networks. The neuron "firing", passing a signal to the next in the chain.

Research has shown that a signal received by a neuron travels through the dendrite region, and down the axon. Separating nerve cells is a gap called the synapse. In order for the signal to be transferred to the next neuron, the signal must be converted from electrical to chemical energy. The signal can then be received by the next neuron and processed. Based on experiments with neurons, McCulloch and Pitts showed that neurons might be considered devices for processing binary numbers.

An important back of mathematic logic, binary numbers (represented as 1's and 0's or true and false) were also the basis of the electronic computer. A century earlier the true/false nature of binary numbers was theorized in 1854 by George Boole in his postulates concerning the Laws of Thought. Boole's principles make up what is known as Boolean algebra, the collection of logic concerning AND, OR, NOT operands.

Boole also assumed that the human mind works according to these laws, it performs logical operations that could be reasoned. Ninety years later, Claude Shannon applied Boole's principles in circuits, the blueprint for electronic computers. Boole's contribution to the future of computing and Artificial Intelligence was immeasurable, and his logic is the basis of neural networks.

McCulloch and Pitts, using Boole's principles, wrote a paper on neural network theory. The thesis dealt with how the networks of connected neurons could perform logical operations. It also stated that, one the level of a single neuron, the release or failure to release an impulse was the basis by which the brain makes true/false decisions. Using the idea of feedback theory, they described the loop which existed between the senses —> brain —> muscles, and likewise concluded that Memory could be defined as the signals in a closed loop of neurons. Although we now know that logic in the brain occurs at a level higher then McCulloch and Pitts theorized, their contributions were important to AI because they showed how the firing of signals between connected neurons could cause the brains to make decisions. McCulloch and Pitt's theory is the basis of the artificial neural network theory.

Using this theory, McCulloch and Pitts then designed electronic replicas of neural networks, to show how electronic networks could generate logical processes. They also stated that neural networks may, in the future, be able to learn, and recognize patterns. The results of their research and two of Weiner's books served to increase enthusiasm, and laboratories of computer simulated neurons were set up across the country. Two major factors have inhibited the development of full scale neural networks.

Because of the expense of constructing a machine to simulate neurons, it was expensive even to construct neural networks with the number of neurons in an ant. Although the cost of components have decreased, the computer would have to grow thousands of times larger to be on the scale of the human brain. The second factor is current computer architecture. The standard Von Neuman computer, the architecture of nearly all computers, lacks an adequate number of pathways between components. Researchers are now developing alternate architectures for use with neural networks.

Even with these inhibiting factors, artificial neural networks have presented some impressive results. Frank Rosenblatt, experimenting with computer simulated networks, was able to create a machine that could mimic the human thinking process, and recognize letters. But, with new top-down methods becoming popular, parallel computing was put on hold. Now neural networks are making a return, and some researchers believe that with new computer architectures, parallel computing and the bottom-up theory will be a driving factor in creating artificial intelligence.

Expert Systems

Because of the large storage capacity of computers, expert systems had the potential to interpret statistics, in order to formulate rules. An expert system works much like a detective solves a mystery. Using the information, and logic or rules, an expert system can solve the problem.

Games

On game with strong AI ties is chess. World-champion chess playing programmes can see ahead twenty plus moves in advance for each move they make. In addition, the programmes have an ability to get progress ably better over time because of the ability to learn. Chess programmes do not play chess as humans do. In three minutes, Deep Thought (a master programme) considers 126 million moves, while human chess master on average considers less than 2 moves. Herbert Simon suggested that human chess masters are familiar with Favourable board positions, and the relationship with thousands of pieces in small areas.

Computers on the other hand, do not take hunches into account. The next move comes from exhaustive searches into all moves, and the consequences of the moves based on prior learning. Chess programmes, running on Cray super computers have attained a rating of senior master, in the range of Gary Kasparov, the Russian world champion.

Frames

On method that many programmes use to represent knowledge are frames. Pioneered by Marvin Minsky, frame theory revolves around packets of information. For example, say the situation was a birthday party. A computer could call on its birthday frame, and use the information contained in the frame, to apply to the situation. The computer knows that there is usually cake and presents because of the information contained in the knowledge frame. Frames can also overlap, or contain sub-frames.

Cybernetics and Brain Simulation

In the 1940s and 1950s, a number of researchers explored the connection between neurology, information theory, and cybernetics. Some of them built machines that used electronic networks to exhibit rudimentary intelligence, such as W. Grey Walter's turtles and the Johns Hopkins Beast. Many of these researchers gathered for meetings of the Teleological Society at Princeton University and the Ratio Club in England. By 1960, this approach was largely abandoned, although elements of it would be revived in the 1980s.

Symbolic

When access to digital computers became possible in the middle 1950s, AI research began to explore the possibility that human intelligence could be reduced to symbol manipulation. The research was centered in three institutions: CMU, Stanford and MIT, and each one developed its own style of research. John Haugeland named these approaches to AI "good old fashioned AI" or "GOFAI".

Cognitive Simulation

Economist Herbert Simon and Allen Newell studied human problem solving skills and attempted to formalize them, and their work laid the foundations of the field of artificial intelligence, as well as cognitive science, operations research and management science. Their research team used the results of psychological experiments to develop programmes that simulated the techniques that people used to solve problems. This tradition, centered at Carnegie Mellon University would eventually culminate in the development of the Soar architecture in the middle 80s.

Logic Based

Unlike Newell and Simon, John McCarthy felt that machines did not need to simulate human thought, but should instead try to find the essence of abstract reasoning and problem solving, regardless of whether people used the same algorithms. His laboratory at Stanford (SAIL) focused on using formal logic to solve a wide variety of problems, including knowledge representation, planning and learning. Logic was also focus of the work at the University of Edinburgh and elsewhere in Europe which led to the development of the programming language Prolog and the science of logic programming.

"Anti-logic" or "Scruffy"

Researchers at MIT (such as Marvin Minsky and Seymour Papert) found that solving difficult problems in vision and natural language processing required ad-hoc solutions – they argued that there was no simple and general principle (like logic) that would capture all the aspects of intelligent behaviour. Roger Schank described their "anti-logic" approaches as "scruffy" (as opposed to the "neat" paradigms at CMU and Stanford). Commonsense knowledge bases (such as Doug Lenat's Cyc) are an example of "scruffy" AI, since they must be built by hand, one complicated concept at a time.

Knowledge Based

When computers with large memories became available around 1970, researchers from all three traditions began to build knowledge into AI applications. This "knowledge revolution" led to the development and deployment of expert systems (introduced by Edward Feigenbaum), the first truly successful form of AI software. The knowledge revolution was also driven by the realization that enormous amounts of knowledge would be required by many simple AI applications.

Sub-symbolic

During the 1960s, symbolic approaches had achieved great success at simulating high-level thinking in small demonstration programmes. Approaches based on cybernetics or neural networks were abandoned or pushed into the background.

By the 1980s, however, progress in symbolic AI seemed to stall and many believed that symbolic systems would never be able to imitate all the processes of human cognition, especially perception, robotics, learning and pattern recognition. A number of researchers began to look into "sub-symbolic" approaches to specific AI problems.

BOTTOM-UP, EMBODIED, SITUATED, BEHAVIOUR-BASED OR NOUVELLE AI

Researchers from the related field of robotics, such as Rodney Brooks, rejected symbolic AI and focused on the basic engineering problems that would allow robots to move and survive. Their work revived the non-symbolic viewpoint of the early cybernetics researchers of the 50s and reintroduced the use of control theory in AI.

This coincided with the development of the embodied mind thesis in the related field of cognitive science: the idea that aspects of the body (such as movement, perception and visualization) are required for higher intelligence.

Computational Intelligence

Interest in neural networks and "connectionism" was revived by David Rumelhart and others in the middle 1980s. These and other sub-symbolic approaches, such as fuzzy systems and evolutionary computation, are now studied collectively by the emerging discipline of computational intelligence.

Statistical

In the 1990s, AI researchers developed sophisticated mathematical tools to solve specific subproblems. These tools are truly scientific, in the sense that their results are both measurable and verifiable, and they have been responsible for many of AI's recent successes. The shared mathematical language has also permitted a high level of collaboration with more established fields (like mathematics, economics or operations research). Stuart Russell and Peter Norvig describe this movement as nothing less than a "revolution" and "the victory of the neats."

INTEGRATING THE APPROACHES

Intelligent Agent Paradigm

An intelligent agent is a system that perceives its environment and takes actions which maximizes its chances of success. The simplest intelligent agents are programmes that solve specific problems. More complicated agents include human beings and organizations of human beings (such as firms). The paradigm gives researchers license to study isolated problems and find solutions that are both verifiable and useful, without agreeing on one single approach.

An agent that solves a specific problem can use any approach that works — some agents are symbolic and logical, some are sub-symbolic neural networks and others may use new approaches. The paradigm also gives researchers a common language to communicate with other fields—such as decision theory and economics—that also use concepts of abstract agents. The intelligent agent paradigm became widely accepted during the 1990s.

Agent Architectures and Cognitive Architectures

Researchers have designed systems to build intelligent systems out of interacting intelligent agents in a multi-agent system. A system with both symbolic and sub-symbolic components is a hybrid intelligent system, and the study of such systems is artificial intelligence systems integration. A hierarchical control system provides a bridge between sub-symbolic AI at its lowest, reactive levels and traditional symbolic AI at its highest levels, where relaxed time constraints permit planning and world modelling. Rodney Brooks' subsumption architecture was an early proposal for such a hierarchical system.

Tools

In the course of 50 years of research, AI has developed a large number of tools to solve the most difficult problems in computer science. A few of the most general of these methods are discussed below.

Search and Optimization

Many problems in AI can be solved in theory by intelligently searching through many possible solutions: Reasoning can be reduced to performing a search. For example, logical proof can be viewed as searching for a path that leads from premises to conclusions, where each step is the application of an inference rule. Planning algorithms search through trees of goals and subgoals, attempting to find a path to a target goal, a process called means-ends analysis. Robotics algorithms for moving limbs and grasping objects use local searches in configuration space. Many learning algorithms use search algorithms based on optimization. Simple exhaustive searches are rarely sufficient for most real world problems: the search space (the number of places to search) quickly grows to astronomical numbers. The result is a search that is too slow or never completes. The solution, for many problems, is to use "heuristics" or "rules of thumb" that eliminate choices that are unlikely to lead to the goal (called "pruning the search tree"). Heuristics supply the programme with a "best guess" for what path the solution lies on. A very different kind of search came to prominence in the 1990s, based on the mathematical theory of optimization. For many problems, it is possible to begin the search with some form of a guess and then refine the guess incrementally until no more refinements can be made. These algorithms can be visualized as blind hill climbing: we begin the search at a random point on the landscape, and then, by jumps or steps, we keep moving our guess uphill, until we reach the top. Other optimization algorithms are simulated annealing, beam search and random optimization. Evolutionary computation uses a form of optimization search. For example, they may begin with a population of organisms (the guesses) and then allow them to mutate and recombine, selecting only the fittest to survive each generation (refining the guesses). Forms of evolutionary computation include swarm intelligence algorithms (such as ant colony or particle swarm optimization) and evolutionary algorithms (such as genetic algorithms and genetic programming).

Logic

Logic is used for knowledge representation and problem solving, but it can be applied to other problems as well. For example, the satplan algorithm uses logic for planning and inductive logic programming is a method for learning. Several different forms of logic are used in AI research. Propositional or sentential logic is the logic of statements which can be true or false. First-order logic also allows the use of quantifiers and predicates, and can express facts about objects, their properties, and their relations with each other. Fuzzy logic, is a version of first-order logic which allows the truth of a statement to be represented as a value between 0 and 1, rather than simply True (1) or False (0). Fuzzy systems can be used for uncertain reasoning and have been widely used in modern industrial and consumer product control systems. Subjective logic models uncertainty in a different and more explicit manner than fuzzy-logic: a given binomial opinion satisfies belief + disbelief + uncertainty = 1 within a Beta distribution. By this method, ignorance can be distinguished from probabilistic statements that an agent makes with high confidence. Default logics, non-monotonic logics and circumscription are forms of logic designed to help with default reasoning and the qualification problem. Several extensions of logic have been designed to handle specific domains of knowledge, such as: description logics; situation calculus, event calculus and fluent calculus (for representing events and time); causal calculus; belief calculus; and modal logics.

ARTIFICIAL INTELLIGENCE AND HUMAN MINDS

In 1950 Alan Turing wrote an article for the journal MIND in which he suggested a test wherein an interrogator would submit teletyped questions to both a machine and a person — and receive teletyped answers from both. Turing claimed that if the interrogator could not correctly distinguish between the person and the machine, the machine deserved to be called intelligent. Turing believed that by the year 2000, the average interrogator would be unable to determine the human more than 70% of the time in less than 5 minutes.

Despite the flaws in Turing's approach, the "Turing Test" became a focal point of discussions about machine intelligence. It avoids the necessity of definingintelligence, and relies on appearances to an "average" interrogator — under a time limit. And it places a great emphasis on a machine being able to resemble a human. In a conscious effort to expose the irrelevance of deceptive appearances, Joseph Weizenbaum wrote a programme in the mid-1960s called ELIZA, which simulates a nondirective psychotherapist. If a user would type-in "My mother is afraid of cats", the programme might respond with the phrase "Tell me more about your family". To the phrase "He works with computers" it might respond "Do machines frighten you?".

If the user entered a sentence that triggered no pre-defined answer, it might respond with "Go on" or "Earlier you talked of your mother". Ironically, Weizenbaum made every effort to make ELIZA convincing, but was irritated to learn that there were people who seriously interacted with ELIZA by confiding their problems. Weizenbaum believed that human intuition and wisdom are not "machinable", and he even objected to the goals of AI on moral grounds.

In 1980 philosopher John Searle wrote a paper describing a thought experiment of a person passing the Turing Test in Chinese. In this scenario, an English-speaking person who is ignorant of Chinese would sit in a room in which he/she would receive messages written in Chinese. Detailed scripts would describe what responses to provide. Even though the person in the "Chinese Room" might convince the Chinese interrogator that someone in the room understood Chinese, all that occurred in reality was symbol manipulation. Searle claimed that this is all computers ever do or can do — manipulate symbols without any real understanding of what those symbols mean.

Searle believes that computers will eventually be able to perform every intellectual feat of which humans are capable — and pass every Turing Test with ease — yet still be lacking in subjective consciousness. He believes that 2 different "systems", one conscious and the other unconscious, could produce identical behaviour. Searle's position has been called weak AI, and it is contrasted with strong AI: the idea that intelligent machines will eventually possess consciousness, self-awareness and emotion. (Roger Penrose denies the possibility of both strong AI and weak AI.) Searle characterizes the "strong AI" position as believing that "the mind" is "just a computer programme". Others have characterized the difference between "weak AI" and "strong AI" as the difference between a "third-person" approach to consciousness and a "first-person" approach.

Before computers, many people undoubtedly believed that arithmetic operations or the symbolic manipulations of integral calculus required intelligence. Some people still worry about the fact that computer chess-playing machines may soon be able to defeat all human opponents. But the limitations on this capability are nothing more than those of hardware to exhaustively search the consequences of millions of board positions in a short time. Is the ability of a computer to defeat any human opponent at chess any more a sign of intelligence than the ability to calculate the square root of 2 to hundreds of decimal places in less than a millisecond?

The Church-Turing Thesis essentially asserts that any algorithm can be implemented on a computer. If we can introspectively reduce any intellectual feat to a step-by-step procedure (an algorithm), then a computer can implement it. Yet computers have had the most difficulty with things that humans do without conscious thought, such as recognizing faces. Much problem-solving actually involves pattern-recognition — intuitive associations of problems with similar problems. The difficulty of experts to reduce this ability to algorithms has been one of the obstacles to implementing expert systems. Yet neural networks may eventually be capable of handling some of these tasks.

Much of what passes for creativity is simply pseudo-random association. Douglas Hofstadter wrote a programme that uses Recursive Transition Network grammar and words randomly selected from word-categories to produce surrealistic prose: "A male pencil who must laugh clumsily would quack". My programme produces phrases like: "Your eye intrigues upon delight" (my word-lists are different).

A careful analysis of so-called creative thought often reveals procedures like "find extreme examples" or "invert the situation". The presumption that computers "can only do what you tell them to do" seems contradicted by the fact that game-playing programmes frequently can defeat their creators. Deciding whether a computer programme possesses intelligence should require a clear definition of the term "intelligence" and a means to measure it. An intelligent system should be able to form internal representations of the external world, be able to learn and be able to reason ("think") about the world and itself.

So-called "IQ tests" exist for human beings, but people are reluctant to apply the same standards to machines. Descriptions of what people would call intelligence might include "common sense" plus a general ability to analyse situations and to solve problems. Often humans are called intelligent even though their abilities exist in specialized areas — and they are not seen as having "common sense". But the same allowances are not made for computers. Within humanity there is a vast range of intellectual abilities between infants and adults — or between the genius and the mentally-retarded or brain-damaged. I suspect that even so-called "third-person" criteria for intelligence covertly demand signs of subjective consciousness.

What are the signs of consciousness? Searle argued that his Chinese Room example demonstrated that it is possible to effectively manipulate symbols without understanding their meaning. Do awareness, understanding and meaningfulness require subjective consciousness? Does a spider know how a web is created? Does a beaver consciously build a dam? A frog may be aware of its surroundings, but is it conscious or intelligent? Self-awareness in the presence of a mirror has been demonstrated by chimpanzees, but not by baboons. Yet other animals may possess some form of self-awareness insofar as carnivores do not attempt to eat themselves (although this may be just a response to pain).

Using self-awareness as a criterion for intelligence may not be more defensible than "common sense". Minsky has defined self-awareness as the ability to monitor one's own processes. He believes that computers could easily monitor their own processes and explain their actions more effectively than human beings. Pattern-recognition, purpose and emotion are said to be attributes of intelligence or consciousness which cannot be reduced to algorithms. Nonetheless, neural networks can achieve pattern recognition. And computers can have a purpose or goal — to win a game of chess, for example.

It might be objected that the goals of computers are only those that have been programmed — but are not the goals of humans and animals those which have been programmed into their genes (pleasures, pains, fears, etc.)? Certain people with neurological deficits have been incapable of feeling pain. Must this reduce their consciousness or intelligence? And what is emotion? Hans Moravec says that emotions are just drives for channeling behaviour — they focus energy around goals. He imagines robots that would get a "thrill" out of pleasing their owners — and exhibit "love".

The robots could become upset when their batteries run low and would plead with their owners (or express anger) for a recharge. Does emotion require biological organs? Are other forms of feeling possible with other hardware, perhaps even silicon? The undue emphasis on "humanness" of the Turing Test is a severe limitation as a criterion for either intelligence or consciousness. Dolphins have a larger cerebral cortex than human beings, and appear to communicate with each other. If they do possess intelligence, or consciousness, it is alien to that of a human.

Aside from the fact that they don't manipulate their environment with tools, their perceptive apparatus and natural environment is somewhat different:they place more emphasis on sound (echolation) and less on vision. Bats rely on echolation even more than dolphins, and a bat with an expanded brain would doubtless have a very different understanding of the world from a human.

An even more extreme example would be an organism with an expanded brain that relies primarily on taste and smell to perceive the world. But the alienness of machine intelligence, consciousness and feeling could be even more extreme. Airplanes are not built to flap their wings, but they fly more effectively than birds. The intelligence, consciousness and feelings of machines might be too remote from our own experience for us to identify with them. If it is true that a computer can only manipulate symbols without any real understanding, how do human beings achieve understanding? Books are full of knowledge, but are not conscious or intelligent.

Computers don't simply manipulate information, they do so in a goal-directed, problem-solving manner. If knowledge is used to solve problems, isn't that an indication of knowledge being meaningful? Symbols can only be meaningfully manipulated if they are meaningfully representative of something real.

Neural networks are said to recognize patterns because they give distinctive outputs corresponding to distinctive input patterns. A computer that does integral calculus gives a distinct solution for a distinct input equation. Can an operational definition be given to "understanding", or is it to be defined only relative to a subjective consciousness? What "magic" is performed by a biological brain that cannot — in theory — be performed by a computer? Why should it be necessary to build machines from organic materials to achieve consciousness?

Symbolic AI adherents have been harshly critical of the idea that intelligence can "emerge" from a neural network. But the Cyc project's attempt to accumulate a large enough knowledge base for a computer to acquire "common sense" seems itself like it is based on "emergence". A dictionary in itself is meaningless to a person because all of the words are defined in terms of other words.

A human being associates words with objects in the environment that themselves acquire meaning through their ability to induce an emotional/physiological response (like pleasure or pain). The meaning of a kiss involves both the physical features of the kiss and emotional reactions associated with who is kissing and being kissed.

Ultimately, meaning seems like another word for "qualia" — but there is also the question of context. Words have meaning not only by virtue of their association with objects, but by association with other words — and some words function only to link words. Is "meaning" an emergent phenomenon — the product of a "critical mass" of knowledge (or of something else?)?

If emergence occurs, there can be degrees of meaning, both for individual words and for the entire context of understanding. As with the way the phenomenon of heat "emerges" from molecular motion — or a traffic jam emerges for an increasing number of vehicles.

Marvin Minsky believes that a mind can be created only by analysing "mind" into its component parts ("agents"), none of which can be intelligent themselves. To quote Minsky: "Unless we can explain the mind in terms of things that have no thoughts or feelings of their own, we'll only have gone around in a circle." But Minsky's conception of the mind as a "society" of unintelligent agents still sounds suspiciously like an "emergent" phenomenon.

I say this to emphasize the "magicalness", although I don't deny that emergent phenomena exist. Connectionists seem to assume that intelligence or consciousness will emerge from a machine that simulates brain processes well-enough (reverse engineering), while Symbolists seem to assume that a machine will become conscious or intelligent if it is given enough knowledge or problem-solving capacity. If a mind cannot be created from increasingly better simulations of mind or brain, why can't it?

In the case of subjective conscious there seems to be the serious problem of objective proof. The only subjective reality we can know about directly is our own. We conclude that other people have feelings because we can identify with their behaviour. A computer need only be a good actor to pass the Turing Test — but then, perhaps, the same can be said of other people. Why should it necessarily be true that all humans have subjective consciousness?

There is simply no way to objectively prove that a machine, an animal or even another human being has subjective consciousness. The question is unfalsifiable and therefore does not even qualify as a scientific question. More seriously, how could an Uploader feel confident that a change from wetware to hardware would not involve a loss of subjective consciousness?

If it is not possible to distinguish a system having consciousness from one that does not when the behaviour of the two systems is identical, how could an Uploader be confident of not losing "self" in the process? A hardware environment may appear to provide a cozy new home for the self — but after the Uploading, all that might be left of the person would be a simulation of the person.

Even for those who do not choose to do a full upload, there could be increasing pressures to augment one's intelligence with computer-chip add-ons to our biological brains. Those who do not do this will be "left behind" by those who do. Would these add-ons augment the "self", or is there a danger of a loss of identity/subjective consciousness? Could the testimony of others be trusted? Most seriously, how can cryonicists be sure that reconstruction by nanotechnology — or even reconstruction from a perfectly vitrified state — would not result in a simulation of ourselves (or even a very close clone) rather than a reestablishment of our subjective selves? All of our carefully-kept introspective diaries may be little more than additional information on how to produce a more convincing simulation.

But I will not end on such a cynical note. I do not believe in "magic". I believe that subjective consciousness is entirely the product of the material brain, and that to perfectly reconstruct that brain can only result in a perfect reconstruction of subjective consciousness.

Even if there can only be subjective verification of subjective states, those states can only be the product of objective material and objective processes. We are, individually (though not "scientifically"), in a position to observe both objective phenomena and subjective phenomena — and to correlate the two. Even now we can correlate PET scans with subjective processes. We may eventually learn to correlate our subjective experience with the anatomical basis of mind — and this could be the key to our survival.

ARTIFICIAL INTELLIGENCE IN MANUFACTURING

As the manufacturing industry becomes increasingly competitive, sophisticated technology has emerged to improve productivity. Artificial Intelligence in manufacturing can be applied to a variety of systems. It can recognize patterns, plus perform time consuming and mentally challenging tasks.

Artificial Intelligence can optimize your production schedule and production runs. In order for organizations to meet ever increasing customer demands, and to be able to survive in an environment where change is inevitable, it is crucial that they offer more reliable delivery dates and control their costs by analysing them on a continual basis.

For businesses, being capable of delivering high quality goods at low costs and short delivery times is akin to operating in a whirlpool environment like the Devil's Triangle, and this is no easy task for any organization. Managing so that production takes place at the right time, on the right equipment, and using the right tools will minimize any deviations in delivery dates promised to the customer. Utilizing equipment, personnel and tools to their maximal efficiency will no doubt improve any organization's competitive strength. In return, proper utilization of these capabilities will result in lower costs for the organization

Optimal scheduling of jobs on equipment, without the use of computer software, is a truly difficult undertaking. Performing planning using the "Deterministic Simulation Method" will provide you with schedules that will indicate job loads per equipment. Even in the case limited to a single piece of equipment, as the number of jobs to schedule on that equipment increases, finding the right solution in the "Possible Solutions Set" becomes next to impossible. And in the real world, the difficulties arising from the large size of the solutions set due to the recipes formed by jobs, equipment and products, and shaped by the technological restrictions, as well as the complexity in finding a close to ideal solution, are readily apparent.

Research and studies are being conducted worldwide on the subject of scheduling. Software vendors working in this area follow developments closely, and they are coming out with new products to better meet demands. "Genetic Algorithms", "Artificial Intelligence", and "Neural Networks" are some of the technologies being used for scheduling

Artificial Intelligence in Financial Services

AI has found a home in financial services and is recognized as a valuable addition to numerous business applications. Sophisticated technologies encompassing neural networks and business rules along with AI-based techniques are yielding positive results in transaction-oriented scenarios for financial services. AI has been widely adopted in such areas of risk management, compliance, and securities trading and monitoring, with an extension into customer relationship management (CRM). Tangible benefits of AI adoption include reduced risk of fraud, increased revenues from existing customers due to newer opportunities, avoidance of fines stemming from non-compliance and averted securities trade exceptions that could result in delayed settlement, if not detected.

Warren Buffet is known as the ultimate investor in this age. So good is he, in fact, that artificial intelligence software developed in Carnegie Mellon that predicts stock movements was named after him by. But can machines really take the place of human traders, much less surpass them? When Deep Blue defeated Chess Grandmaster Kasparov in 1997, AI was propelled into the limelight. Indeed, if a machine can whiz through the intricacies of the ultimate game of strategy, why not beat man in other fields as well – thereby facilitating work, decreasing costs and errors and increasing productivity and quality. This study focuses on applying AI in Finance, particularly in stock trading. In the field of Finance, artificial intelligence has long been used. Some applications of Artificial Intelligence are

- Credit authorization screening
- Mortgage risk assessment
- Project management and bidding strategy
- Financial and economic forecasting
- Risk rating of exchange-traded, fixed income investments
- Detection of regularities in security price movements
- Prediction of default and bankruptcy

- Security/and or Asset Portfolio Management.

Artificial intelligence types used in finance include neural networks, fuzzy logic, genetic algorithms, expert systems and intelligent agents. They are often used in combination with each other. When AI first appeared a decade ago, it generated mass media hype but delivered inconsistent results. A number of those who praised its ability were paralyzed in the end. One such case is Fidelity Investments. In this paper, we set the stage by describing how traditional stock trading differs from AI-powered stock trading. We define the various AI systems available and also explore the various solutions available in the market, their IT foundations and how salient they are. Then, we move into how AI systems for stock trading will affect traders, companies and individuals. Benefits, risks and competitive strategy will be defined and real-world examples cited, as grounding for our recommendations in the end. Recommendations include getting management buy-in, implementing the system and managing the whole structure to succeed.

Artificial Intelligence in Marketing

Advances in artificial intelligence (AI) eventually could turbo-boost customer analytics to give companies speedier insights into individual buying patterns and a host of other consumer habits.

Artificial intelligence functions are made possible by computerized neural networks that simulate the same types of connections that are made in the human brain to generate thought. Currently, the technology is used mostly to analyze data for genetics, pharmaceutical and other scientific research. It's seeing little use in CRM right now, though it has tremendous potential in the future

AI-enhanced analytics programs also provide survival modelling capabilities — suggesting changes to products based on use. For example, customer patterns are analysed to learn ways to extend the life of light bulbs or to help decide the correct dosage for medications.

High-tech data mining can give companies a precise view of how particular segments of the customer base react to a product or service and propose changes consistent with those findings. In addition to further exploring customers" buying patterns, analytics could help companies react much more quickly to the marketplace.

According to Meta Group vice president Liz Shahnam, intelligent agents could let companies make real-time changes to marketing campaigns. "New technologies would have the model refreshed on the fly based on each new incoming piece of customer information — reaction to the campaign — for a more targeted offer,"

Artificial Intelligence in HR

It is widely believed that the role of managers is becoming a key determinant for enterprises' competitiveness in today's knowledge economy era. Owing to fast development of information technologies (ITs), corporations are employed to enhance the capability of human resource management, which is called human resource information system (HRIS). Recently, due to promising results of artificial neural networks (ANNs) and fuzzy theory in engineering, they have also become candidates for HRIS.

The artificial intelligence (AT) field can play a role in this, especially; in assuring that the fuzzy neural network has the characteristics and functions of training, learning, and simulation to make an optimal and accurate judgment according to the human thinking model. The main purposes of the study are to discuss the appointment of managers in enterprises through fuzzy neural network, to construct a new model for evaluation of managerial talent, and accordingly to develop a decision support system in human resource selection.

Therefore, the research methods of reviewing literature, in-depth interview, questionnaire survey, and fuzzy neural network are used in the study. The fuzzy neural network is used to train the concrete database, based on 191 questionnaires from experts, for getting the best network model in different training conditions. In order to let decision-makers adjust weighted values and obtain decisive results of each phase's scores, we adopted the simple additive weighting (SAW) and fuzzy analytic hierarchy process (FAHP) methods in the study. Finally, the human resource selection system of Java user interface has been constructed by FNN in the study.

APPLICATIONS

An automated online assistant providing customer service on a web page - one of many applications of artificial intelligence. Artificial intelligence techniques are pervasive and are too numerous to list. Frequently, when a technique reaches mainstream use, it is no longer considered artificial intelligence; this phenomenon is described as the AI effect.

Competitions and Prizes

There are a number of competitions and prizes to promote research in artificial intelligence. The main areas promoted are: general machine intelligence, conversational behaviour, data-mining, driverless cars, robot soccer and games.

Platforms

A platform (or "computing platform")is defined as "some sort of hardware architecture or software framework (including application frameworks), that allows software to run." As Rodney Brooks pointed out many years ago, it is not just the artificial intelligence software that defines the AI features of the platform, but rather the actual platform itself that affects the AI that results, i.e., we need to be working out AI problems on real world platforms rather than in isolation. A wide variety of platforms has allowed different aspects of AI to develop, ranging from expert systems, albeit PC-based but still an entire real-world system to various robot platforms such as the widely available Roomba with open interface.

Philosophy

Artificial intelligence, by claiming to be able to recreate the capabilities of the human mind, is both a challenge and an inspiration for philosophy. Are there limits to how intelligent machines can be? Is there an essential difference between human intelligence and artificial intelligence? Can a machine have a mind and consciousness? A few of the most influential answers to these questions are given below.

Turing's "Polite Convention"

If a machine acts as intelligently as a human being, then it is as intelligent as a human being. Alan Turing theorized that, ultimately, we can only judge the intelligence of a machine based on its behaviour. This theory forms the basis of the Turing test.

The Dartmouth Proposal

"Every aspect of learning or any other feature of intelligence can be so precisely described that a machine can be made to simulate it." This conjecture was printed in the proposal for the Dartmouth Conference of 1956, and represents the position of most working AI researchers. Newell and Simon's physical symbol system hypothesis

"A physical symbol system has the necessary and sufficient means of general intelligent action." Newell and Simon argue that intelligences consists of formal operations on symbols. Hubert Dreyfus argued that, on the contrary, human expertise depends on unconscious instinct rather than conscious symbol manipulation and on having a "feel" for the situation rather than explicit symbolic knowledge.

Gödel's incompleteness theorem

A formal system (such as a computer program) can not prove all true statements. Roger Penrose is among those who claim that Gödel's theorem limits what machines can do.

SEARLE'S STRONG AI HYPOTHESIS

"The appropriately programmed computer with the right inputs and outputs would thereby have a mind in exactly the

same sense human beings have minds." John Searle counters this assertion with his Chinese room argument, which asks us to look *inside* the computer and try to find where the "mind" might be.

The artificial brain argument

The brain can be simulated. Hans Moravec, Ray Kurzweil and others have argued that it is technologically feasible to copy the brain directly into hardware and software, and that such a simulation will be essentially identical to the original.

Prediction

Artificial Intelligence is a common topic in both science fiction and projections about the future of technology and society. The existence of an artificial intelligence that rivals human intelligence raises difficult ethical issues, and the potential power of the technology inspires both hopes and fears. In fiction, Artificial Intelligence has appeared fulfilling many roles, including a servant (R2D2 in *Star Wars*), a law enforcer (K.I.T.T. "Knight Rider"), a comrade (Lt. Commander Data in *Star Trek: The Next Generation*), a conqueror/overlord (*The Matrix*), a dictator (*With Folded Hands*), an assassin (*Terminator*), a sentient race (*Battlestar Galactica*/Transformers), an extension to human abilities (*Ghost in the Shell*) and the savior of the human race (R. Daneel Olivaw in the *Asimov's Robot Series*).

Mary Shelley's *Frankenstein* considers a key issue in the ethics of artificial intelligence: if a machine can be created that has intelligence, could it also *feel*? If it can feel, does it have the same rights as a human? The idea also appears in modern science fiction, including the films *I Robot*, *Blade Runner* and *A.I.: Artificial Intelligence*, in which humanoid machines have the ability to feel human emotions. This issue, now known as "robot rights", is currently being considered by, for example, California's Institute for the Future, although many critics believe that the discussion is premature. The subject is profoundly discussed in the 2010 documentary film *Plug & Pray*. Martin Ford and others argue that specialized artificial intelligence applications, robotics and other forms of automation will ultimately result in significant unemployment as machines begin to match and exceed the capability of workers to perform most routine and repetitive jobs. Ford predicts that many knowledge-based occupations—and in particular entry level jobs—will be increasingly susceptible to automation via expert systems and other AI-enhanced applications.

AI-based applications may also be used to amplify the capabilities of low-wage offshore workers, making it more feasible to outsource knowledge work. Joseph Weizenbaum wrote that AI applications can not, by definition, successfully simulate genuine human empathy and that the use of AI technology in fields such as customer service or psychotherapy was deeply misguided. Weizenbaum was also bothered that AI researchers (and some philosophers) were willing to view the human mind as nothing more than a computer programme (a position now known as computationalism). To Weizenbaum these points suggest that AI research devalues human life. Many futurists believe that artificial intelligence will ultimately transcend the limits of progress. Ray Kurzweil has used Moore's law (which describes the relentless exponential improvement in digital technology) to calculate that desktop computers will have the same processing power as human brains by the year 2029. He also predicts that by 2045 artificial intelligence will reach a point where it is able to improve *itself* at a rate that far exceeds anything conceivable in the past, a scenario that science fiction writer Vernor Vinge named the "singularity".

Robot designer Hans Moravec, cyberneticist Kevin Warwick and inventor Ray Kurzweil have predicted that humans and machines will merge in the future into cyborgs that are more capable and powerful than either. This idea, called transhumanism, which has roots in Aldous Huxley and Robert Ettinger, has been illustrated in fiction as well, for example in the manga *Ghost in the Shell* and the science-fiction series *Dune*. Edward Fredkin argues that "artificial intelligence is the next stage in evolution," an idea first proposed by Samuel Butler's "Darwin among the Machines" (1863), and expanded upon by George Dyson in his book of the same name in 1998. Pamela McCorduck writes that all these scenarios are expressions of the ancient human desire to, as she calls it, "forge the gods".

APPLICATION AND USES

We have been studying this issue of AI application for quite some time now and know all the terms and facts. But what we all really need to know is what can we do to get our hands on some AI today.

First, we should be prepared for a change. Our conservative ways stand in the way of progress. AI is a new step that is very helpful to the society. Machines can do jobs that require detailed instructions followed and mental alertness. AI with its learning capabilities can accomplish those tasks but only if the worlds conservatives are ready to change and allow this to be a possibility. It makes us think about how early man finally accepted the wheel as a good invention, not something taking away from its heritage or tradition.

Secondly, we must be prepared to learn about the capabilities of AI. The more use we get out of the machines the less work is required by us. In turn less injuries and stress to human beings. Human beings are a species that learn by trying, and we must be prepared to give AI a chance seeing AI as a blessing, not an inhibition.

Finally, we need to be prepared for the worst of AI. Something as revolutionary as AI is sure to have many kinks to work out. There is always that fear that if AI is learning based, will machines learn that being rich and successful is a good thing, then wage war against economic powers and famous people? There are so many things that can go wrong with a new system so we must be as prepared as we can be for this new technology.

Whatever we teach AI, they will suggest in the future if a positive outcome arrives from it. AI are like children that need to be taught to be kind, well mannered, and intelligent.

If they are to make important decisions, they should be wise. We as citizens need to make sure AI programmers are keeping things on the level. We should be sure they are doing the job correctly, so that no future accidents occur.

Teaching Computers

The Artificial Intelligence Applications Institute has many project that they are working on to make their computers learn how to operate themselves with less human input. o have more functionality with less input is an operation for AI technology. If it isn't able or isn't reliable AUSDA will instruct you on finding alternative software which would better suit your needs.

According to AI, the software will try to provide solutions to problems like "identifying the root causes of incidents in which the use of computer software is involved, studying different software development approaches, and identifying aspects of these which are relevant to those root causes producing guidelines for using and improving the development approaches studied, and providing support in the integration of these approaches, so that they can be better used for the development and maintenance of safety critical software."

Well don't worry guys, because us nerds are looking out for you too! Just ask AIAI what they have for you and it turns up the EGRESS is right down your alley.

This is a programme which is studying human reactions to accidents. It is trying to make a model of how peoples reactions in panic moments save lives. Although it seems like in tough situations humans would fall apart and have no idea what to do, it is in fact the opposite.

Quick Decisions are usually made and are effective but not flawless. These computer models will help rescuers make smart decisions in time of need. AI can't be positive all the time but can suggest actions which we can act out and therefor lead to safe rescues. So AIAI is teaching computers to be better computers and better people. AI technology will never replace man but can be an extension of our body which allows us to make more rational decisions faster.

Apple computers

Apple Computers may not have ever been considered as the state of art in Artificial Intelligence, but a second look should be given. Not only are today's PC's becoming more powerful but AI influence is showing up in them. Who else would go surfing with you on short notice- even if it is the net. Who else would care to tell you that you have a business appointment scheduled at 8:35 and 28 seconds and would notify you about it every minute till you told it to shut up.

Even with all the abuse we give today's PC's they still plug away to make us happy. We use PC's more not because they do more or are faster but because they are getting so much easier to use. And their ease of use comes from their use of AI. All Power Macintoshes come with Speech Recognition. This implication of AI in Personal computers is still very crude but it does work given the correct conditions to work in and a clear voice.

Not to mention the requirement of at least 16Mgs of RAM for quick use. Also Apple's Newton and other hand held note pads have Script recognition. Cursive or Print can be recognized by these notepad sized devices. With the pen that accompanies your silicon note pad you can write a little note to yourself which magically changes into computer text if desired. No more complaining about sloppy written reports if your computer can read your handwriting. If it can't read it though- perhaps in the future, you can correct it by dictating your letters instead.

Macros provide a huge stress relief as your computer does faster what you could do more tediously. Macros are old but they are to an extent, Intelligent. You have taught the computer to do something only by doing it once. In businesses, many times applications are upgraded. But the files must be converted.

All of the businesses records but be changed into the new software's type. Macros save the work of conversion of hundred of files by a human by teaching the computer to mimic the actions of the programmer. Thus teaching the computer a task that it can repeat whenever ordered to do so.AI is all around us all but get ready for a change. But don't think the change will be harder on us because AI has been developed to make our lives easier.

Expert Systems

As stated an expert system is able to do the work of a professional. Moreover, a computer system can be trained quickly, has virtually no operating cost, never forgets what it learns, never calls in sick, retires, or goes on vacation. Beyond those, intelligent computers can consider a large amount of information that may not be considered by humans. But to what extent should these systems replace human experts? Or, should they at all? For example, some people once considered an intelligent computer as a possible substitute for human control over nuclear weapons, citing that a computer could respond more quickly to a threat. and many

AI developers were afraid of the possibility of programmes like Eliza, the psychiatrist and the bond that humans were making with the computer. We cannot, however, over look the benefits of having a computer expert. Forecasting the weather, for example, relies on many variables, and a computer expert can more accurately pool all of its knowledge. Still a computer cannot rely on the hunches of a human expert, which are sometimes necessary in predicting an outcome.

In conclusion, in some fields such as forecasting weather or finding bugs in computer software, expert systems are sometimes more accurate than humans. But for other fields, such as medicine, computers aiding doctors will be beneficial, but the human doctor should not be replaced. Expert systems have the power and range to aid to benefit, and in some cases replace humans, and computer experts, if used with discretion, will benefit human kind.

Game playing

You can buy machines that can play master level chess for a few hundred dollars. There is some AI in them, but they play well against people mainly through brute force computation—

looking at hundreds of thousands of positions. To beat a world champion by brute force and known reliable heuristics requires being able to look at 200 million positions per second.

Speech recognition

In the 1990s, computer speech recognition reached a practical level for limited purposes. Thus United Airlines has replaced its keyboard tree for flight information by a system using speech recognition of flight numbers and city names. It is quite convenient. On the the other hand, while it is possible to instruct some computers using speech, most users have gone back to the keyboard and the mouse as still more convenient.

Just getting a sequence of words into a computer is not enough. Parsing sentences is not enough either. The computer has to be provided with an understanding of the domain the text is about, and this is presently possible only for very limited domains.

The world is composed of three-dimensional objects, but the inputs to the human eye and computers' TV cameras are two dimensional. Some useful programmes can work solely in two dimensions, but full computer vision requires partial three-dimensional information that is not just a set of two-dimensional views. At present there are only limited ways of representing three-dimensional information directly, and they are not as good as what humans evidently use.

A "knowledge engineer" interviews experts in a certain domain and tries to embody their knowledge in a computer programme for carrying out some task. How well this works depends on whether the intellectual mechanisms required for the task are within the present state of AI. When this turned out not to be so, there were many disappointing results.

One of the first expert systems was MYCIN in 1974, which diagnosed bacterial infections of the blood and suggested treatments. It did better than medical students or practicing doctors, provided its limitations were observed. Namely, its ontology included bacteria, symptoms, and treatments and did not include patients, doctors, hospitals, death, recovery, and events occurring in time. Its interactions depended on a single patient being considered. Since the experts consulted by the knowledge engineers knew about patients, doctors, death, recovery, etc., it is clear that the knowledge engineers forced what the experts told them into a predetermined framework. In the present state of AI, this has to be true. The usefulness of current expert systems depends on their users having common sense.

Heuristic classification

One of the most feasible kinds of expert system given the present knowledge of AI is to put some information in one of a fixed set of categories using several sources of information. An example is advising whether to accept a proposed credit card purchase.

Information is available about the owner of the credit card, his record of payment and also about the item he is buying and about the establishment from which he is buying it (*e.g.*, about whether there have been previous credit card frauds at this establishment).

2

Robotics Technology

Robotics is the branch of technology that deals with the design, construction, operation, structural disposition, manufacture and application of robots. Robotics is related to the sciences of electronics, engineering, mechanics, and software. The word "robot" was introduced to the public by Czech writer Karel Èapek in his play R.U.R. (Rossum's Universal Robots), published in 1920. The term "robotics" was coined by Isaac Asimov in his 1941 science fiction short-story "Liar!"

HISTORY

Stories of artificial helpers and companions and attempts to create them have a long history. The word *robot* was introduced to the public by the Czech writer Karel Èapek in his play *R.U.R. (Rossum's Universal Robots)*, published in 1920. The play begins in a factory that makes artificial people called *robots* creatures who can be mistaken for humans - though they are closer to the modern ideas of androids. Karel Èapek himself did not coin the word. He wrote a short letter in reference to an etymology in the *Oxford English Dictionary* in which he named his brother Josef Èapek as its actual originator. In 1927 the *Maschinenmensch* ("machine-human") gynoid humanoid robot (also called "Parody", "Futura", "Robotrix", or the "Maria impersonator") was the first and perhaps the most memorable depiction of a robot ever to appear on film was played by German actress Brigitte Helm) in Fritz Lang's film Metropolis.

In 1942 the science fiction writer Isaac Asimov formulated his Three Laws of Robotics and, in the process of doing so, coined the word "robotics". In 1948 Norbert Wiener formulated the principles of cybernetics, the basis of practical robotics. Fully autonomous robots only appeared in the second half of the 20th century. The first digitally operated and programmable robot, the Unimate, was installed in 1961 to lift hot pieces of metal from a die casting machine and stack them. Commercial and industrial robots are widespread today and used to perform jobs more cheaply, or more accurately and reliably, than humans. They are also employed in jobs which are too dirty, dangerous, or dull to be suitable for humans. Robots are widely used in manufacturing, assembly, packing and packaging, transport, earth and space exploration, surgery, weaponry, laboratory research, safety, and the mass production of consumer and industrial goods.

Etymology

According to the *Oxford English Dictionary*, the word *robotics* was first used in print by Isaac Asimov, in his science fiction short story "Liar!", published in May 1941 in *Astounding Science Fiction*. Asimov was unaware that he was coining the term; since the science and technology of electrical devices is *electronics*, he assumed *robotics* already referred to the science and technology of robots. However, in some of Asimov's other works, he states that the first use of the word *robotics* was in his short story *Runaround* (Astounding Science Fiction, March 1942). The word *robotics* was derived from the word *robot*, which was introduced to the public by Czech writer Karel Èapek in his play *R.U.R. (Rossum's Universal Robots)*, which premiered in 1921.

ORIGIN OF THE TERM 'ROBOT'

'Robot' was first applied as a term for artificial automata in a 1920 play *R.U.R.* by the Czech writer, Karel Èapek. However, Josef Èapek was named by his brother Karel as the true inventor of the term robot. The word 'robot' itself was not new, having been in Slavic language as *robota* (forced laborer), a term which classified those peasants obligated to compulsory service under the feudal system widespread in 19th century Europe. Èapek's fictional story postulated the technological creation of artificial human bodies without souls, and the old theme of the feudal *robota* class eloquently fit the imagination of a new class of manufactured, artificial workers.

Early robots

In 1928, one of the first humanoid robots, Eric, was exhibited at the annual exhibition of the Model Engineers Society in London, where it delivered a speech. Invented by W. H. Richards, the robot's frame consisted of an aluminium body of armour with eleven electromagnets and one motor powered by a twelve-volt power source. The robot could move its hands and head and could be controlled through remote control or voice control. Both Eric and his "brother" George toured the world.

Westinghouse Electric Corporation built Televox in 1926; it was a cardboard cutout connected to various devices which users could turn on and off. In 1939, the humanoid robot known as Elektro was debuted at the 1939 New York World's Fair. Seven feet tall (2.1 m) and weighing 265 pounds (120.2 kg), it could walk by voice command, speak about 700 words (using a 78-rpm record player), smoke cigarettes, blow up balloons, and move its head and arms. The body consisted of a steel gear, cam and motor skeleton covered by an aluminum skin. In 1928, Japan's first robot, Gakutensoku, was designed and constructed by biologist Makoto Nishimura.

NEW FUNCTIONALITIES AND PROTOTYPES

In 2008, Caterpillar Inc. developed a dump truck which can drive itself without any human operator. Many analysts believe that self-driving trucks may eventually revolutionize logistics. By 2014, Caterpillar had a self-driving dump truck which is expected to greatly change the process of mining. In 2015, these Caterpillar trucks were actively used in mining operations in Australia by the mining company Rio Tinto Coal Australia.

Some analysts believe that within the next few decades, most trucks will be self-driving.

A literate or 'reading robot' named Marge has intelligence that comes from software. She can read newspapers, find and correct misspelled words, learn about banks like Barclays, and understand that some restaurants are better places to eat than others.

Baxter is a new robot introduced in 2012 which learns by guidance. A worker could teach Baxter how to perform a task by moving its hands in the desired motion and having Baxter memorize them. Extra dials, buttons, and controls are available on Baxter's arm for more precision and features. Any regular worker could program Baxter and it only takes a matter of minutes, unlike usual industrial robots that take extensive programs and coding in order to be used. This means Baxter needs no programming in order to operate. No software engineers are needed. This also means Baxter can be taught to perform multiple, more complicated tasks. Sawyer was added in 2015 for smaller, more precise tasks.

Etymology

The word *robot* was introduced to the public by the Czech interwar writer Karel Èapek in his play *R.U.R. (Rossum's Universal Robots)*, published in 1920. The play begins in a factory that uses a chemical substitute for protoplasm to manufacture living, simplified people called *robots.* The play does not focus in detail on the technology behind the creation of these living creatures, but in their appearance they prefigure modern ideas of androids, creatures who can be mistaken for humans.

These mass-produced workers are depicted as efficient but emotionless, incapable of original thinking and indifferent to self-preservation. At issue is whether the robots are being exploited and the consequences of human dependence upon commodified labor (especially after a number of specially-formulated robots achieve self-awareness and incite robots all around the world to rise up against the humans).

Karel Èapek himself did not coin the word. He wrote a short letter in reference to an etymology in the *Oxford English Dictionary* in which he named his brother, the painter and writer Josef Èapek, as its actual originator.

In an article in the Czech journal *Lidové noviny* in 1933, he explained that he had originally wanted to call the creatures *laboøi* ("workers", from Latin *labor*). However, he did not like the word, and sought advice from his brother Josef, who suggested "roboti". The word *robota* means literally "corvée", "serf labor", and figuratively "drudgery" or "hard work" in Czech and also (more general) "work", "labor" in many Slavic languages (e.g.: Bulgarian, Russian, Serbian, Slovak, Polish, Macedonian, Ukrainian, archaic Czech, as well as *robot* in Hungarian). Traditionally the *robota* (Hungarian *robot*) was the work period a serf (corvée) had to give for his lord, typically 6 months of the year. The origin of the word is the Old Church Slavonic (Old Bulgarian) *rabota* "servitude" ("work" in contemporary Bulgarian and Russian), which in turn comes from the Proto-Indo-European root **orbh-*. *Robot* is cognate with the German root *Arbeit* (work).

The word robotics, used to describe this field of study, was coined by the science fiction writer Isaac Asimov. Asimov created the "*Three Laws of Robotics*" which are a recurring theme in his books. These have since been used by many others to define laws used in fiction. (The three laws are pure fiction, and no technology yet created has the ability to understand or follow them, and in fact most robots serve military purposes, which run quite contrary to the first law and often the third law. "People think about Asimov's laws, but they were set up to point out how a simple ethical system doesn't work. If you read the short stories, every single one is about a failure, and they are totally impractical," said Dr. Joanna Bryson of the University of Bath.)

ROBOTS IN SOCIETY

Roughly half of all the robots in the world are in Asia, 32% in Europe, and 16% in North America, 1% in Australasia and

1% in Africa. 40% of all the robots in the world are in Japan, making Japan the country with the highest number of robots.

Autonomy and ethical questions

As robots have become more advanced and sophisticated, experts and academics have increasingly explored the questions of what ethics might govern robots' behavior, and whether robots might be able to claim any kind of social, cultural, ethical or legal rights. One scientific team has said that it is possible that a robot brain will exist by 2019. Others predict robot intelligence breakthroughs by 2050. Recent advances have made robotic behavior more sophisticated. The social impact of intelligent robots is subject of a 2010 documentary film called *Plug & Pray*. Vernor Vinge has suggested that a moment may come when computers and robots are smarter than humans. He calls this "the Singularity". He suggests that it may be somewhat or possibly very dangerous for humans. This is discussed by a philosophy called Singularitarianism.

In 2009, experts attended a conference hosted by the Association for the Advancement of Artificial Intelligence (AAAI) to discuss whether computers and robots might be able to acquire any autonomy, and how much these abilities might pose a threat or hazard. They noted that some robots have acquired various forms of semi-autonomy, including being able to find power sources on their own and being able to independently choose targets to attack with weapons. They also noted that some computer viruses can evade elimination and have achieved "cockroach intelligence." They noted that self-awareness as depicted in science-fiction is probably unlikely, but that there were other potential hazards and pitfalls. Various media sources and scientific groups have noted separate trends in differing areas which might together result in greater robotic functionalities and autonomy, and which pose some inherent concerns. In 2015, the Nao alderen robots were shown to have a capability for a degree of self-awareness. Researchers at the Rensselaer Polytechnic Institute AI and Reasoning Lab in New York conducted an experiment where a robot became aware of itself, and corrected its answer to a question once it had realised this.

Military robots

Some experts and academics have questioned the use of robots for military combat, especially when such robots are given some degree of autonomous functions. There are also concerns about technology which might allow some armed robots to be controlled mainly by other robots. The US Navy has funded a report which indicates that, as military robots become more complex, there should be greater attention to implications of their ability to make autonomous decisions. One researcher states that autonomous robots might be more humane, as they could make decisions more effectively. However, other experts question this.

One robot in particular, the EATR, has generated public concerns over its fuel source, as it can continually refuel itself using organic substances. Although the engine for the EATR is designed to run on biomass and vegetation specifically selected by its sensors, which it can find on battlefields or other local environments, the project has stated that chicken fat can also be used.

Manuel De Landa has noted that "smart missiles" and autonomous bombs equipped with artificial perception can be considered robots, as they make some of their decisions autonomously. He believes this represents an important and dangerous trend in which humans are handing over important decisions to machines.

Relationship to unemployment

For centuries, experts have predicted that machines would make workers obsolete and increase unemployment. A recent example of human replacement involves Taiwanese technology company Foxconn who, in July 2011, announced a three-year plan to replace workers with more robots. At present the company uses ten thousand robots but will increase them to a million robots over a three-year period.

Lawyers have speculated that an increased prevalence of robots in the workplace could lead to the need to revise redundancy laws. Kevin J. Delaney said "Robots are taking human jobs. But Bill Gates believes that governments should tax companies' use of them, as a way to at least temporarily slow the spread of automation and to fund other types of employment." The robot tax would also help pay a guaranteed living wage to the displaced workers.

CONTEMPORARY USES

At present, there are two main types of robots, based on their use: general-purpose autonomous robots and dedicated robots. Robots can be classified by their specificity of purpose. A robot might be designed to perform one particular task extremely well, or a range of tasks less well. Of course, all robots by their nature can be re-programmed to behave differently, but some are limited by their physical form. For example, a factory robot arm can perform jobs such as cutting, welding, gluing, or acting as a fairground ride, while a pick-and-place robot can only populate printed circuit boards.

General-purpose autonomous robots

General-purpose autonomous robots can perform a variety of functions independently. General-purpose autonomous robots typically can navigate independently in known spaces, handle their own re-charging needs, interface with electronic doors and elevators and perform other basic tasks.

Like computers, general-purpose robots can link with networks, software and accessories that increase their usefulness. They may recognize people or objects, talk, provide companionship, monitor environmental quality, respond to alarms, pick up supplies and perform other useful tasks.

General-purpose robots may perform a variety of functions simultaneously or they may take on different roles at different times of day. Some such robots try to mimic human beings and may even resemble people in appearance; this type of robot is called a humanoid robot. Humanoid robots are still in a very limited stage, as no humanoid robot can, as of yet, actually navigate around a room that it has never been in. Thus, humanoid robots are really quite limited, despite their intelligent behaviors in their well-known environments.

COMPONENTS AND POWER SOURCE

At present; mostly (lead-acid) batteries are used, but potential power sources could be:

- pneumatic (compressed gases)
- hydraulics (compressed liquids)
- flywheel energy storage
- organic garbage (through anaerobic digestion)
- faeces (human, animal); may be interesting in a military context as faeces of small combat groups may be reused for the energy requirements of the robot assistant
- still unproven energy sources: for example Nuclear fusion, as yet not used in nuclear reactors whereas Nuclear fission is proven (although there are not many robots using it as a power source apart from the Chinese rover tests.).
- radioactive source (such as with the proposed Ford car of the '50s); to those proposed in movies such as *Red Planet*

Actuation

Actuators are like the "muscles" of a robot, the parts which convert stored energy into movement. By far the most popular actuators are electric motors that spin a wheel or gear, and linear actuators that control industrial robots in factories. But there are some recent advances in alternative types of actuators, powered by electricity, chemicals, or compressed air:

- Electric motors: The vast majority of robots use electric motors, often brushed and brushless DC motors in portable robots or AC motors in industrial robots and CNC machines.

- Linear Actuators: Various types of linear actuators move in and out instead of by spinning, particularly when very large forces are needed such as with industrial robotics. They are typically powered by compressed air (pneumatic actuator) or an oil (hydraulic actuator).
- Series Elastic Actuators: A spring can be designed as part of the motor actuator, to allow improved force control. It has been used in various robots, particularly walking humanoid robots.
- Air muscles: (Also known as Pneumatic Artificial Muscles) are special tubes that contract (typically up to 40%) when air is forced inside it. They have been used for some robot applications.
- Muscle wire: (Also known as Shape Memory Alloy, Nitinol or Flexinol Wire) is a material that contracts slightly (typically under 5%) when electricity runs through it. They have been used for some small robot applications.
- Electroactive Polymers: (EAPs or EPAMs) are a new plastic material that can contract substantially (up to 400%) from electricity, and have been used in facial muscles and arms of humanoid robots, and to allow new robots to float, fly, swim or walk.
- Piezo motor: A recent alternative to DC motors are piezo motors or ultrasonic motors. These work on a fundamentally different principle, whereby tiny piezoceramic elements, vibrating many thousands of times per second, cause linear or rotary motion. There are different mechanisms of operation; one type uses the vibration of the piezo elements to walk the motor in a circle or a straight line. Another type uses the piezo elements to cause a nut to vibrate and drive a screw. The advantages of these motors are nanometer resolution, speed, and available force for their size. These motors are already available commercially, and being used on some robots.

- Elastic nanotubes: These are a promising artificial muscle technology in early-stage experimental development. The absence of defects incarbon nanotubes enables these filaments to deform elastically by several percent, with energy storage levels of perhaps 10 J/cm^3 for metal nanotubes. Human biceps could be replaced with an 8 mm diameter wire of this material. Such compact "muscle" might allow future robots to outrun and outjump humans.

SENSING

Touch

Current robotic and prosthetic hands receive far less tactile information than the human hand. Recent research has developed a tactile sensor array that mimics the mechanical properties and touch receptors of human fingertips. The sensor array is constructed as a rigid core surrounded by conductive fluid contained by an elastomeric skin. Electrodes arc mounted on the surface of the rigid core and are connected to an impedance-measuring device within the core. When the artificial skin touches an object the fluid path around the electrodes is deformed, producing impedance changes that map the forces received from the object. The researchers expect that an important function of such artificial fingertips will be adjusting robotic grip on held objects. Scientists from several European countries and Israel developed a prosthetic hand in 2009, called SmartHand, which functions like a real one—allowing patients to write with it, type on a keyboard, play piano and perform other fine movements. The prosthesis has sensors which enable the patient to sense real feeling in its fingertips.

Vision

Computer vision is the science and technology of machines that see. As a scientific discipline, computer vision is concerned with the theory behind artificial systems that extract information from images. The image data can take many forms, such as video sequences and views from cameras. In most practical computer vision applications, the computers are pre-programmed to solve a particular task, but methods based on learning are now becoming increasingly common. Computer vision systems rely on image sensors which detect electromagnetic radiation which is typically in the form of either visible light or infra-red light. The sensors are designed using solid-state physics. The process by which light propagates and reflects off surfaces is explained using optics. Sophisticated image sensors even require quantum mechanics to provide a complete understanding of the image formation process. There is a subfield within computer vision where artificial systems are designed to mimic the processing and behaviour of biological systems, at different levels of complexity. Also, some of the learning-based methods developed within computer vision have their background in biology.

Manipulation

Robots which must work in the real world require some way to manipulate objects; pick up, modify, destroy, or otherwise have an effect. Thus the "hands" of a robot are often referred to as *end effectors*, while the "arm" is referred to as a *manipulator*. Most robot arms have replaceable effectors, each allowing them to perform some small range of tasks. Some have a fixed manipulator which cannot be replaced, while a few have one very general purpose manipulator, for example a humanoid hand.

- Mechanical Grippers: One of the most common effectors is the gripper. In its simplest manifestation it consists of just two fingers which can open and close to pick up and let go of a range of small objects. Fingers can for example be made of a chain with a metal wire run through it.
- Vacuum Grippers: Pick and place robots for electronic components and for large objects like car windscreens, will often use very simple vacuum grippers. These are very simple astrictive devices, but can hold very large

loads provided the prehension surface is smooth enough to ensure suction.

- General purpose effectors: Some advanced robots are beginning to use fully humanoid hands, like the Shadow Hand, MANUS, and the Schunk hand. These highly dexterous manipulators, with as many as 20 degrees of freedom and hundreds of tactile sensors.

For the definitive guide to all forms of robot end-effectors, their design, and usage consult the book "Robot Grippers".

Locomotion

Rolling Robots

For simplicity most mobile robots have four wheels or a number of continuous tracks. Some researchers have tried to create more complex wheeled robots with only one or two wheels. These can have certain advantages such as greater efficiency and reduced parts, as well as allowing a robot to navigate in confined places that a four wheeled robot would not be able to.

- Two-wheeled balancing: Balancing robots generally use a gyroscope to detect how much a robot is falling and then drive the wheels proportionally in the opposite direction, to counter-balance the fall at hundreds of times per second, based on the dynamics of an inverted pendulum. Many different balancing robots have been designed. While the Segway is not commonly thought of as a robot, it can be thought of as a component of a robot, such as NASA's Robonaut that has been mounted on a Segway.
- One-wheeled balancing: A one-wheeled balancing robot is an extension of a two-wheeled balancing robot so that it can move in any 2D direction using a round ball as its only wheel. Several one-wheeled balancing robots have been designed recently, such as Carnegie Mellon University's "Ballbot" that is the approximate height and width of a person, and Tohoku Gakuin University's

"BallIP". Because of the long, thin shape and ability to maneuver in tight spaces, they have the potential to function better than other robots in environments with people.

- Spherical orb robots: Several attempts have been made in robots that are completely inside a spherical ball, either by spinning a weight inside the ball, or by rotating the outer shells of the sphere. These have also been referred to as an orb bot or a ball bot
- Six-wheeled robots: Using six wheels instead of four wheels can give better traction or grip in outdoor terrain such as on rocky dirt or grass.
- Tracked robots: Tank tracks provide even more traction than a six-wheeled robot. Tracked wheels behave as if they were made of hundreds of wheels, therefore are very common for outdoor and military robots, where the robot must drive on very rough terrain. However, they are difficult to use indoors such as on carpets and smooth floors. Examples include NASA's Urban Robot "Urbie".

Walking Robots

Walking is a difficult and dynamic problem to solve. Several robots have been made which can walk reliably on two legs, however none have yet been made which are as robust as a human.

Many other robots have been built that walk on more than two legs, due to these robots being significantly easier to construct. Hybrids too have been proposed in movies such as I, Robot, where they walk on 2 legs and switch to 4 (arms+legs) when going to a sprint. Typically, robots on 2 legs can walk well on flat floors and can occasionally walk up stairs. None can walk over rocky, uneven terrain. Some of the methods which have been tried are:

- ZMP Technique: The Zero Moment Point (ZMP) is the algorithm used by robots such as Honda's ASIMO. The robot's onboard computer tries to keep the total inertial forces (the combination of earth's gravity and the acceleration and deceleration of walking), exactly opposed by the floor reaction force (the force of the floor pushing back on the robot's foot). In this way, the two forces cancel out, leaving no moment (force causing the robot to rotate and fall over). However, this is not exactly how a human walks, and the difference is obvious to human observers, some of whom have pointed out that ASIMO walks as if it needs the lavatory. ASIMO's walking algorithm is not static, and some dynamic balancing is used. However, it still requires a smooth surface to walk on.

- Hopping: Several robots, built in the 1980s by Marc Raibert at the MIT Leg Laboratory, successfully demonstrated very dynamic walking. Initially, a robot with only one leg, and a very small foot, could stay upright simply by hopping. The movement is the same as that of a person on a pogo stick. As the robot falls to one side, it would jump slightly in that direction, in order to catch itself. Soon, the algorithm was generalised to two and four legs. A bipedal robot was demonstrated running and even performing somersaults. A quadruped was also demonstrated which could trot, run, pace, and bound.

Other Methods of Locomotion

- Flying: A modern passenger airliner is essentially a flying robot, with two humans to manage it. The autopilot can control the plane for each stage of the journey, including takeoff, normal flight, and even landing. Other flying robots are uninhabited, and are known as unmanned aerial vehicles (UAVs). They can be smaller and lighter without a human pilot onboard, and fly into dangerous territory for military surveillance missions. Some can even fire on targets under command. UAVs are also being developed which can fire on targets automatically, without the need for a command from a human. Other flying robots include cruise missiles, the Entomopter, and the Epson micro helicopter robot.

Robots such as the Air Penguin, Air Ray, and Air Jelly have lighter-than-air bodies, propelled by paddles, and guided by sonar.

- Snaking: Several snake robots have been successfully developed. Mimicking the way real snakes move, these robots can navigate very confined spaces, meaning they may one day be used to search for people trapped in collapsed buildings. The Japanese ACM-R5 snake robot can even navigate both on land and in water.
- Skating: A small number of skating robots have been developed, one of which is a multi-mode walking and skating device. It has four legs, with unpowered wheels, which can either step or roll. Another robot, Plen, can use a miniature skateboard or rollerskates, and skate across a desktop.

Environmental Interaction and Navigation

Though a significant percentage of robots in commission today are either human controlled, or operate in a static environment, there is an increasing interest in robots that can operate autonomously in a dynamic environment.

These robots require some combination of navigation hardware and software in order to traverse their environment. In particular unforeseen events (e.g. people and other obstacles that are not stationary) can cause problems or collisions. Some highly advanced robots as ASIMO, EveR-1, Meinü robot have particularly good robot navigation hardware and software.

Also, self-controlled cars, Ernst Dickmanns' driverless car, and the entries in the DARPA Grand Challenge, are capable of sensing the environment well and subsequently making navigational decisions based on this information.

Most of these robots employ a GPS navigation device with waypoints, along with radar, sometimes combined with other sensory data such as LIDAR, video cameras, and inertial guidance systems for better navigation between waypoints.

ROBOTS IN POPULAR CULTURE

Literature

Robotic characters, androids (artificial men/women) or gynoids (artificial women), and cyborgs (also "bionic men/ women", or humans with significant mechanical enhancements) have become a staple of science fiction.

The first reference in Western literature to mechanical servants appears in Homer's *Iliad*. In Book XVIII, Hephaestus, god of fire, creates new armor for the hero Achilles, assisted by robots. According to the Rieu translation, "Golden maidservants hastened to help their master. They looked like real women and could not only speak and use their limbs but were endowed with intelligence and trained in handwork by the immortal gods." Of course, the words "robot" or "android" are not used to describe them, but they are nevertheless mechanical devices human in appearance. "The first use of the word Robot was in Karel Èapek's play R.U.R. (Rossum's Universal Robots) (written in 1920)". Writer Karel Èapek was born in Czechoslovakia (Czech Republic).

Possibly the most prolific author of the twentieth century was Isaac Asimov (1920–1992) who published over five-hundred books. Asimov is probably best remembered for his science-fiction stories and especially those about robots, where he placed robots and their interaction with society at the center of many of his works. Asimov carefully considered the problem of the ideal set of instructions robots might be given in order to lower the risk to humans, and arrived at his Three Laws of Robotics: a robot may not injure a human being or, through inaction, allow a human being to come to harm; a robot must obey orders given it by human beings, except where such orders would conflict with the First Law; and a robot must protect its own existence as long as such protection does not conflict with the First or Second Law. These were introduced in his 1942 short story "Runaround", although foreshadowed in a few earlier stories. Later, Asimov added the Zeroth Law: "A robot may not harm humanity, or, by inaction, allow humanity to come to harm"; the rest of the laws are modified sequentially to acknowledge this.

According to the *Oxford English Dictionary,* the first passage in Asimov's short story "Liar!" (1941) that mentions the First Law is the earliest recorded use of the word *robotics*. Asimov was not initially aware of this; he assumed the word already existed by analogy with *mechanics, hydraulics,* and other similar terms denoting branches of applied knowledge.

Films

Robots appear in many films. Most of the robots in cinema are fictional. Two of the most famous are R2-D2 and C-3PO from the *Star Wars* franchise.

Sex robots

The concept of humanoid sex robots has elicited both public attention and concern. Opponents of the concept have stated that the development of sex robots would be morally wrong. They argue that the introduction of such devices would be socially harmful, and demeaning to women and children.

Problems depicted in popular culture

Fears and concerns about robots have been repeatedly expressed in a wide range of books and films. A common theme is the development of a master race of conscious and highly intelligent robots, motivated to take over or destroy the human race. *Frankenstein* (1818), often called the first science fiction novel, has become synonymous with the theme of a robot or android advancing beyond its creator.

Other works with similar themes include *The Mechanical Man*, *The Terminator, Runaway, RoboCop,* the Replicators in *Stargate*, the Cylons in *Battlestar Galactica,* the Cybermen and Daleks in *Doctor Who*, *The Matrix, Enthiran* and *I, Robot.* Some fictional robots are programmed to kill and destroy; others gain superhuman intelligence and abilities by upgrading their own software and hardware. Examples of popular media where the robot becomes evil are *2001: A Space Odyssey, Red Planet* and *Enthiran.*

The 2017 game Horizon Zero Dawn explores themes of robotics in warfare, robot ethics, and the AI control problem, as well as the positive or negative impact such technologies could have on the environment.

Another common theme is the reaction, sometimes called the "uncanny valley", of unease and even revulsion at the sight of robots that mimic humans too closely. More recently, fictional representations of artificially intelligent robots in films such as *A.I. Artificial Intelligence* and *Ex Machina* and the 2016 TV adaptation of *Westworld* have engaged audience sympathy for the robots themselves.

HUMAN-ROBOT INTERACTION

If robots are to work effectively in homes and other non-industrial environments, the way they are instructed to perform their jobs, and especially how they will be told to stop will be of critical importance. The people who interact with them may have little or no training in robotics, and so any interface will need to be extremely intuitive. Science fiction authors also typically assume that robots will eventually be capable of communicating with humans through speech, gestures, and facial expressions, rather than a command-line interface. Although speech would be the most natural way for the human to communicate, it is unnatural for the robot. It will probably be a long time before robots interact as naturally as the fictional C-3PO.

- Speech recognition: Interpreting the continuous flow of sounds coming from a human (speech recognition), in real time, is a difficult task for a computer, mostly because of the great variability of speech. The same word, spoken by the same person may sound different depending on local acoustics, volume, the previous word, whether or not the speaker has a cold, etc.. It becomes even harder when the speaker has a different accent. Nevertheless, great strides have been made in the field since Davis, Biddulph, and Balashek designed the first "voice input system" which recognized "ten digits spoken by a single user with 100% accuracy" in 1952. Currently, the best systems can recognize continuous, natural speech, up to 160 words per minute, with an accuracy of 95%.

- Robotic voice: other hurdles exist when allowing the robot to use voice for interacting with humans. For social reasons, synthetic voice proves suboptimal as a communication medium, making it necessary to develop the emotional component of robotic voice through various techniques.
- Gestures: One can imagine, in the future, explaining to a robot chef how to make a pastry, or asking directions from a robot police officer. In both of these cases, making hand gestures would aid the verbal descriptions. In the first case, the robot would be recognizing gestures made by the human, and perhaps repeating them for confirmation. In the second case, the robot police officer would gesture to indicate "down the road, then turn right". It is likely that gestures will make up a part of the interaction between humans and robots. A great many systems have been developed to recognize human hand gestures.

Control

The mechanical structure of a robot must be controlled to perform tasks. The control of a robot involves three distinct phases - perception, processing, and action (robotic paradigms). Sensors give information about the environment or the robot itself (e.g. the position of its joints or its end effector). This information is then processed to calculate the appropriate signals to the actuators (motors) which move the mechanical. The processing phase can range in complexity. At a reactive level, it may translate raw sensor information directly into actuator commands. Sensor fusion may first be used to estimate parameters of interest (e.g. the position of the robot's gripper) from noisy sensor data. An immediate task (such as moving the gripper in a certain direction) is inferred from these estimates.

Techniques from control theory convert the task into commands that drive the actuators. At longer time scales or with more sophisticated tasks, the robot may need to build and reason with a "cognitive" model. Cognitive models try to represent the robot, the world, and how they interact. Pattern recognition and computer vision can be used to track objects. Mapping techniques can be used to build maps of the world. Finally, motion planning and other artificial intelligence techniques may be used to figure out how to act. For example, a planner may figure out how to achieve a task without hitting obstacles, falling over, etc.

Autonomy Levels

Control systems may also have varying levels of autonomy.

1. Direct interaction is used for haptic or tele-operated devices, and the human has nearly complete control over the robot's motion.
2. Operator-assist modes have the operator commanding medium-to-high-level tasks, with the robot automatically figuring out how to achieve them.
3. An autonomous robot may go for extended periods of time without human interaction. Higher levels of autonomy do not necessarily require more complex cognitive capabilities. For example, robots in assembly plants are completely autonomous, but operate in a fixed pattern.

Another classification takes into account the interaction between human control and the machine motions.

1. Teleoperation. A human controls each movement, each machine actuator change is specified by the operator.
2. Supervisory. A human specifies general moves or position changes and the machine decides specific movements of its actuators.
3. Task-level autonomy. The operator specifies only the task and the robot manages itself to complete it.
4. Full autonomy. The machine will create and complete all its tasks without human interaction.

DYNAMICS AND KINEMATICS

The study of motion can be divided into kinematics and dynamics. Direct kinematics refers to the calculation of end effector position, orientation, velocity, and acceleration when the corresponding joint values are known. Inverse kinematics refers to the opposite case in which required joint values are calculated for given end effector values, as done in path planning. Some special aspects of kinematics include handling of redundancy (different possibilities of performing the same movement), collision avoidance, and singularity avoidance. Once all relevant positions, velocities, and accelerations have been calculated using kinematics, methods from the field of dynamics are used to study the effect of forces upon these movements. Direct dynamics refers to the calculation of accelerations in the robot once the applied forces are known. Direct dynamics is used in computer simulations of the robot. Inverse dynamics refers to the calculation of the actuator forces necessary to create a prescribed end effector acceleration. This information can be used to improve the control algorithms of a robot. In each area mentioned above, researchers strive to develop new concepts and strategies, improve existing ones, and improve the interaction between these areas. To do this, criteria for "optimal" performance and ways to optimize design, structure, and control of robots must be developed and implemented.

Robot Research

Much of the research in robotics focuses not on specific industrial tasks, but on investigations into new types of robots, alternative ways to think about or design robots, and new ways to manufacture them but other investigations, such as MIT's cyberflora project, are almost wholly academic. A first particular new innovation in robot design is the opensourcing of robot-projects. To describe the level of advancement of a robot, the term "Generation Robots" can be used. This term is coined by Professor Hans Moravec, Principal Research Scientist at the Carnegie Mellon University Robotics Institute in describing the near future evolution of robot technology. *First generation* robots, Moravec predicted in 1997, should have an intellectual capacity comparable to perhaps a lizard and should become available by 2010. Because the *first generation* robot would be incapable of learning, however, Moravec predicts that the *second generation* robot would be an improvement over the *first* and become available by 2020, with an intelligence maybe comparable to that of a mouse. The *third generation* robot should have an intelligence comparable to that of a monkey. Though *fourth generation* robots, robots with human intelligence, professor Moravec predicts, would become possible, he does not predict this happening before around 2040 or 2050.

The second is Evolutionary Robots. This is a methodology that uses evolutionary computation to help design robots, especially the body form, or motion and behaviour controllers. In a similar way to natural evolution, a large population of robots is allowed to compete in some way, or their ability to perform a task is measured using a fitness function. Those that perform worst are removed from the population, and replaced by a new set, which have new behaviours based on those of the winners. Over time the population improves, and eventually a satisfactory robot may appear. This happens without any direct programming of the robots by the researchers. Researchers use this method both to create better robots, and to explore the nature of evolution. Because the process often requires many generations of robots to be simulated, this technique may be run entirely or mostly in simulation, then tested on real robots once the evolved algorithms are good enough. Currently, there are about 1 million industrial robots toiling around the world, and Japan is the top country having high density of utilizing robots in its manufacturing industry.

Education and Training

Robots recently became a popular tool in raising interests in computing for middle and high school students. First year computer science courses at several universities were developed which involves the programming of a robot instead of the traditional software engineering based coursework.

Career Training

Universities offer Bachelors, Masters and Doctoral degrees in the field of robotics. Select Private Career Colleges and vocational schools offer robotics training to train individuals towards being job ready and employable in the emerging robotics industry.

Certification

The Robotics Certification Standards Alliance (RCSA) is an international robotics certification authority who confers various industry and educational related robotics certifications.

Employment in Robotics

Robotics is an essential component in any modern manufacturing environment. As factories increase their use of robots, the number of robotics related jobs grow and have been observed to be on a steady rise.

Relationship to Unemployment

Some analysts, such as Martin Ford, argue that robots and other forms of automation will ultimately result in significant unemployment as machines begin to match and exceed the capability of workers to perform most jobs. At present the negative impact is only on menial and repetitive jobs, and there is actually a positive impact on the number of jobs for highly skilled technicians, engineers, and specialists.

However, these highly skilled jobs are not sufficient in number to offset the greater decrease in employment among the general population, causing structural unemployment in which overall (net) unemployment rises. As robotics and artificial intelligence develop further, some worry even many skilled jobs may be threatened.

In conventional economic theory this should merely cause an increase in the productivity of the involved industries, resulting in higher demand for other goods, and hence higher labour demand in these sectors, off-setting whatever negatives are caused. Conventional theory describes the past well but may not describe the future due to shifts in the parameter values that shape the context.

FIELDS OF APPLICATION

Space Robotics

The research area Space Robotics deals with the development of intelligent robots for extraterrestrial exploration focusing on:

- Development of robot systems for unstructured, uneven terrain based on biologically inspired innovative locomotion concepts
- Development of multi-functional robot teams usable for different tasks ranging from in-situ examinations to the organisation and maintenance of infrastructure
- Reconfigurable systems for planetary exploration
- AI-based methods for autonomous navigation and mission planning in unknown terrain
- Image evaluation, object recognition and terrain modelling
- AI-based support systems for scientific experiments

Underwater Robotics

This area deals with the development and realization of Artificial Intelligence methods in underwater systems. Main points of research are:

- Development of systems for user support in remote-controlled underwater vehicles employing virtual immersion methods
- Design of methods for autonomous manipulation and mission planning of robot arms in underwater applications, particularly with state-of-the-art sensor technology, such as "Visual Servoing"
- Image evaluation and object recognition with modular and intelligent underwater cameras

- Design of control methods for next-generation autonomous underwater vehicles
- Development of biologically inspired and energy-efficient methods of transport for underwater vehicles, such as oscillating systems

Electric Mobility

In the field of electric mobility we are testing concepts for electric vehicles, battery charge technologies, and the collection of vehicle data. We are creating models for intelligent, environmentally sound, and integrated urban mobility. Our research focuses around:

- Development and demonstration of innovative vehicle concepts
- Design of new approaches to mobility and traffic control, application support, technology integration
- Data collection by fleet tests with technologically different electric vehicles.
- Coordination of the regional project office of the model region Electric Mobility Bremen/Oldenburg
- Virtualization of the model region, simulation of future, larger vehicle fleets, and predictions of the effects on the model region in terms of traffic volume, infrastructure needs, environmental pollution, and economic efficiency
- Creating a foundation for new business models and traffic concepts on the basis of the data previously collected

Logistics, Production and Consumer (LPC)

In the area Logistic, Production and Consumer (LPC) new systems are developed which will improve handling and scheduling tasks by using methods of Artificial Intelligence and innovative mechatronic concepts:

- Fast, self-learning image recognition and classification to identify production faults

- "Visual Servoing"-methods to sort piece goods
- Intelligent production memory based on RFID chips in logistic chains
- Handling of deformable piece goods

Search and Rescue (SAR) & Security Robotics

In this area, robots will be developed to support rescue and security personnel. Main points of our research are:

- Development of highly mobile platforms for indoor and outdoor applications
- Development of autonomous systems that are able to identify potential victims (SAR) or intruders (Security)
- Development and application of state-of-the-art sensor technology based on radar, laser scanner, and thermal vision to identify objects and persons, resp.
- Embedding of robot systems into existing rescue and security infrastructures
- Autonomous navigation and mission planning

Assistance- and Rehabilitation Systems

This field deals with robotic systems that can support humans in complex, exhausting or often repeated tasks. Application areas are both help during activites of everyday life (at home or work) and medical rehabilitation. Support can either take place using systems the human is wearing like exoskeletons or orthoses, or by service robots performing the respective task.

Core topics include:

- Concept development, design and construction
- intelligent hardware-system architectures
- software architectures
- embedded biosignal analysis, e.g. using information from:
- muscle (EMG)
- eye (eyetracking, EOG)
- or from brain activity (EEG)

- fusion of different sensors
- direct online signal processing (hard- and software)
- robust learning systems capable to adapt
- joint communication layers for better human-machine interaction
- (semi-)autonomously acting systems
- assist-as-needed

Agricultural Robotics

We develop robots for agricultural applications and transfer methods and algorithms from robotics to conventional agricultural machines.

Our objective is to increase the performance of machines and processes and to reduce resource consumption at the same time.

Our research is focused on technology applications used in the cultivation of land. Primary research topics are:

- Methods for autonomous planning and navigation of outdoor machinery
- Methods for environmental recognition in agricultural machinery control
- Methods of infield logistics to optimize cooperation and resource consumption between multiple agricultural machines
- Interoperability at the level of communication, processes and knowledge processing

FUNDAMENTALS OF ROBOTICS

Robotics brings together several very different engineering areas and skills. There is metalworking for the body. There is mechanics for mounting the wheels on the axles, connecting them to the motors and keeping the body in balance. You need electronics to power the motors and connect the sensors to the controllers. At last you need the software to understand the sensors and drive the robot around.

ROBOTICS - ROBOTICS HISTORY

According to the Robot Institute of America (1979) a robot is: "A reprogrammable, multifunctional manipulator designed to move material, parts, tools, or specialized devices through various programmed motions for the performance of a variety of tasks".

A more inspiring definition can be found in Webster. According to Webster a robot is: "An automatic device that performs functions normally ascribed to humans or a machine in the form of a human."

First use of the word 'Robot'

The acclaimed Czech playwright Karel Capek (1890-1938) made the first use of the word 'robot', from the Czech word for forced labor or serf. Capek was reportedly several times a candidate for the Nobel prize for his works and very influential and prolific as a writer and playwright. The use of the word Robot was introduced into his play *R.U.R. (Rossum's Universal Robots)* which opened in Prague in January 1921.

In R.U.R., Capek poses a paradise, where the machines initially bring so many benefits but in the end bring an equal amount of blight in the form of unemployment and social unrest. The play was an enormous success and productions soon opened throughout Europe and the U.S. R.U.R's theme, in part, was the dehumanization of man in a technological civilization.

You may find it surprising that the robots were not mechanical in nature but were created through chemical means. In fact, in an essay written in 1935, Capek strongly fought that this idea was at all possible and, writing in the third person, said:

"It is with horror, frankly, that he rejects all responsibility for the idea that metal contraptions could ever replace human beings, and that by means of wires they could awaken something like life, love, or rebellion. He would deem this dark prospect to be either an overestimation of machines, or a grave offence against life."

There is some evidence that the word robot was actually coined by Karl's brother Josef, a writer in his own right. In a short letter, Capek writes that he asked Josef what he should call the artificial workers in his new play. Karel suggests Labori, which he thinks too 'bookish' and his brother mutters "then call them Robots" and turns back to his work, and so from a curt response we have the word robot.

BASICS OF ROBOT

The vast majority of robots do have several qualities in common. First of all, almost all robots have a movable body. Some only have motorized wheels, and others have dozens of movable segments, typically made of metal or plastic. Like the bones in your body, the individual segments are connected together with joints. Robots spin wheels and pivot jointed segments with some sort ofactuator. Some robots use electric motors and solenoids as actuators; some use a hydraulic system; and some use a pneumatic system (a system driven by compressed gases). Robots may use all these actuator types.

A robot needs a power source to drive these actuators. Most robots either have a battery or they plug into the wall. Hydraulic robots also need a pump to pressurize the hydraulic fluid, and pneumatic robots need an air compressor or compressed air tanks.

The actuators are all wired to an electrical circuit. The circuit powers electrical motors and solenoids directly, and it activates the hydraulic system by manipulating electrical valves. The valves determine the pressurized fluid's path through the machine. To move a hydraulic leg, for example, the robot's controller would open the valve leading from the fluid pump to a piston cylinder attached to that leg. The pressurized fluid would extend the piston, swiveling the leg forward. Typically, in order to move their segments in two directions, robots use pistons that can push both ways.

The robot's computer controls everything attached to the circuit. To move the robot, the computer switches on all the necessary motors and valves. Most robots arereprogrammable — to change the robot's behavior, you simply write a new program to its computer.

Not all robots have sensory systems, and few have the ability to see, hear, smell or taste. The most common robotic sense is the sense of movement — the robot's ability to monitor its own motion. A standard design uses slotted wheels attached to the robot's joints. An LED on one side of the wheel shines a beam of light through the slots to a light sensor on the other side of the wheel. When the robot moves a particular joint, the slotted wheel turns. The slots break the light beam as the wheel spins. The light sensor reads the pattern of the flashing light and transmits the data to the computer. The computer can tell exactly how far the joint has swiveled based on this pattern. This is the same basic system used in computer mice.

These are the basic nuts and bolts of robotics. Roboticists can combine these elements in an infinite number of ways to create robots of unlimited complexity.

The Robotic Arm

The term robot comes from the Czech word *robota*, generally translated as "forced labor." This describes the majority of robots fairly well. Most robots in the world are designed for heavy, repetitive manufacturing work. They handle tasks that are difficult, dangerous or boring to human beings.

The most common manufacturing robot is the robotic arm. A typical robotic arm is made up of seven metal segments, joined by six joints. The computer controls the robot by rotating individual step motors connected to each joint (some larger arms use hydraulics or pneumatics). Unlike ordinary motors, step motors move in exact increments (check out Anaheim Automation to find out how). This allows the computer to move the arm very precisely, repeating exactly the same movement over and over again. The robot uses motion sensors to make sure it moves just the right amount.

An industrial robot with six joints closely resembles a human arm — it has the equivalent of a shoulder, an elbow and a wrist.

Typically, the shoulder is mounted to a stationary base structure rather than to a movable body. This type of robot has six degrees of freedom, meaning it can pivot in six different ways. A human arm, by comparison, has seven degrees of freedom.

Your arm's job is to move your hand from place to place. Similarly, the robotic arm's job is to move an end effector from place to place. You can outfit robotic arms with all sorts of end effectors, which are suited to a particular application. One common end effector is a simplified version of the hand, which can grasp and carry different objects. Robotic hands often have built-in pressure sensors that tell the computer how hard the robot is gripping a particular object. This keeps the robot from dropping or breaking whatever it's carrying. Other end effectors include blowtorches, drills and spray painters.

Industrial robots are designed to do exactly the same thing, in a controlled environment, over and over again. For example, a robot might twist the caps onto peanut butter jars coming down an assembly line. To teach a robot how to do its job, the programmer guides the arm through the motions using a handheld controller. The robot stores the exact sequence of movements in its memory, and does it again and again every time a new unit comes down the assembly line.

Most industrial robots work in auto assembly lines, putting cars together. Robots can do a lot of this work more efficiently than human beings because they are so precise. They always drill in the exactly the same place, and they always tighten bolts with the same amount of force, no matter how many hours they've been working. Manufacturing robots are also very important in the computer industry. It takes an incredibly precise hand to put together a tiny microchip.

Mobile Robots

Robotic arms are relatively easy to build and program because they only operate within a confined area. Things get a bit trickier when you send a robot out into the world.

The first obstacle is to give the robot a working locomotion system. If the robot will only need to move over smooth ground, wheels or tracks are the best option. Wheels and tracks can also work on rougher terrain if they are big enough. But robot designers often look to legsinstead, because they are more adaptable. Building legged robots also helps researchers understand natural locomotion — it's a useful exercise in biological research.

Typically, hydraulic or pneumatic pistons move robot legs back and forth. The pistons attach to different leg segments just likemuscles attach to different bones. It's a real trick getting all these pistons to work together properly. As a baby, your brain had to figure out exactly the right combination of muscle contractions to walk upright without falling over. Similarly, a robot designer has to figure out the right combination of piston movements involved in walking and program this information into the robot's computer. Many mobile robots have a built-in balance system (a collection of gyroscopes, for example) that tells the computer when it needs to correct its movements.

Bipedal locomotion (walking on two legs) is inherently unstable, which makes it very difficult to implement in robots. To create more stable robot walkers, designers commonly look to the animal world, specifically insects. Six-legged insects have exceptionally good balance, and they adapt well to a wide variety of terrain.

Some mobile robots are controlled by remote — a human tells them what to do and when to do it. The remote control might communicate with the robot through an attached wire, or using radio or infrared signals. Remote robots, often called puppet robots, are useful for exploring dangerous or inaccessible environments, such as the deep sea or inside a volcano. Some robots are only partially controlled by remote. For example, the operator might direct the robot to go to a certain spot, but not steer it there — the robot would find its own way.

MODERN ROBOTS AND MOBILE ROBOT

Mobile robots have the capability to move around in their environment and are not fixed to one physical location. An example of a mobile robot that is in common use today is the *automated guided vehicle* or *automatic guided vehicle* (AGV). An AGV is a mobile robot that follows markers or wires in the floor, or uses vision or lasers. AGVs are discussed later in this article.

Mobile robots are also found in industry, military and security environments. They also appear as consumer products, for entertainment or to perform certain tasks like vacuum cleaning. Mobile robots are the focus of a great deal of current research and almost every major university has one or more labs that focus on mobile robot research.

Mobile robots are usually used in tightly controlled environments such as on assembly lines because they have difficulty responding to unexpected interference. Because of this most humans rarely encounter robots. However domestic robots for cleaning and maintenance are increasingly common in and around homes in developed countries. Robots can also be found in military applications.

Industrial robots (manipulating)

Industrial robots usually consist of a jointed arm (multi-linked manipulator) and an end effector that is attached to a fixed surface. One of the most common type of end effector is a gripper assembly. The International Organization for Standardization gives a definition of a manipulating industrial robot in ISO 8373: "an automatically controlled, reprogrammable, multipurpose, manipulator programmable in three or more axes, which may be either fixed in place or mobile for use in industrial automation applications."

This definition is used by the International Federation of Robotics, the European Robotics Research Network (EURON) and many national standards committees.

Service robot

Most commonly industrial robots are fixed robotic arms and manipulators used primarily for production and distribution of goods. The term "service robot" is less well-defined. The

International Federation of Robotics has proposed a tentative definition, "A service robot is a robot which operates semi- or fully autonomously to perform services useful to the well-being of humans and equipment, excluding manufacturing operations."

Educational robot

Robots are used as educational assistants to teachers. From the 1980s, robots such as turtles were used in schools and programmed using the Logo language.

There are robot kits like Lego Mindstorms, BIOLOID, OLLO from ROBOTIS, or BotBrain Educational Robots can help children to learn about mathematics, physics, programming, and electronics. Robotics have also been introduced into the lives of elementary and high school students in the form of robot competitions with the company FIRST (For Inspiration and Recognition of Science and Technology). The organization is the foundation for the FIRST Robotics Competition, FIRST LEGO League, Junior FIRST LEGO League, and FIRST Tech Challenge competitions.

There have also been devices shaped like robots such as the teaching computer, Leachim (1974), and 2-XL (1976), a robot shaped game / teaching toy based on an 8-track tape player, both invented Michael J. Freeman.

Modular robot

Modular robots are a new breed of robots that are designed to increase the utilization of robots by modularizing their architecture. The functionality and effectiveness of a modular robot is easier to increase compared to conventional robots. These robots are composed of a single type of identical, several different identical module types, or similarly shaped modules, which vary in size. Their architectural structure allows hyper-redundancy for modular robots, as they can be designed with more than 8 degrees of freedom (DOF). Creating the programming, inverse kinematics and dynamics for modular robots is more complex than with traditional robots. Modular robots may be composed of L-shaped modules, cubic modules, and U and H-shaped modules. ANAT technology, an early modular robotic technology patented by Robotics Design Inc., allows the creation of modular robots from U and H shaped modules that connect in a chain, and are used to form heterogeneous and homogenous modular robot systems. These "ANAT robots" can be designed with "n" DOF as each module is a complete motorized robotic system that folds relatively to the modules connected before and after it in its chain, and therefore a single module allows one degree of freedom. The more modules that are connected to one another, the more degrees of freedom it will have. L-shaped modules can also be designed in a chain, and must become increasingly smaller as the size of the chain increases, as payloads attached to the end of the chain place a greater strain on modules that are further from the base. ANAT H-shaped modules do not suffer from this problem, as their design allows a modular robot to distribute pressure and impacts evenly amongst other attached modules, and therefore payload-carrying capacity does not decrease as the length of the arm increases. Modular robots can be manually or self-reconfigured to form a different robot, that may perform different applications. Because modular robots of the same architecture type are composed of modules that compose different modular robots, a snake-arm robot can combine with another to form a dual or quadra-arm robot, or can split into several mobile robots, and mobile robots can split into multiple smaller ones, or combine with others into a larger or different one. This allows a single modular robot the ability to be fully specialized in a single task, as well as the capacity to be specialized to perform multiple different tasks.

Modular robotic technology is currently being applied in hybrid transportation, industrial automation, duct cleaning and handling. Many research centres and universities have also studied this technology, and have developed prototypes.

Collaborative robots

A *collaborative robot* or *cobot* is a robot that can safely and effectively interact with human workers while performing simple industrial tasks. However, end-effectors and other environmental conditions may create hazards, and as such risk assessments should be done before using any industrial motion-control application.

The collaborative robots most widely used in industries today are manufactured by Universal Robots in Denmark. Rethink Robotics—founded by Rodney Brooks, previously with iRobot—introduced Baxter in September 2012; as an industrial robot designed to safely interact with neighboring human workers, and be programmable for performing simple tasks. Baxters stop if they detect a human in the way of their robotic arms and have prominent off switches. Intended for sale to small businesses, they are promoted as the robotic analogue of the personal computer. As of May 2014, 190 companies in the US have bought Baxters and they are being used commercially in the UK.

MODERN AUTONOMOUS ROBOTS

The first electronic autonomous robots with complex behaviour were created by William Grey Walter of the Burden Neurological Institute at Bristol, England in 1948 and 1949. He wanted to prove that rich connections between a small number of brain cells could give rise to very complex behaviors – essentially that the secret of how the brain worked lay in how it was wired up. His first robots, named *Elmer* and *Elsie*, were constructed between 1948 and 1949 and were often described as *tortoises* due to their shape and slow rate of movement. The three-wheeled tortoise robots were capable of phototaxis, by which they could find their way to a recharging station when they ran low on battery power.

Walter stressed the importance of using purely analogue electronics to simulate brain processes at a time when his contemporaries such as Alan Turing and John von Neumann were all turning towards a view of mental processes in terms of digital computation. His work inspired subsequent generations of robotics researchers such as Rodney Brooks, Hans Moravec and Mark Tilden. Modern incarnations of Walter's *turtles* may be found in the form of BEAM robotics. The first digitally operated and programmable robot was invented by George Devol in 1954 and was ultimately called the Unimate. This ultimately laid the foundations of the modern robotics industry.

Devol sold the first Unimate to General Motors in 1960, and it was installed in 1961 in a plant in Trenton, New Jersey to lift hot pieces of metal from a die casting machine and stack them. Devol's patent for the first digitally operated programmable robotic arm represents the foundation of the modern robotics industry.

The first palletizing robot was introduced in 1963 by the Fuji Yusoki Kogyo Company. In 1973, a robot with six electromechanically driven axes was patented by KUKA robotics in Germany, and the programmable universal manipulation arm was invented by Victor Scheinman in 1976, and the design was sold to Unimation.

Commercial and industrial robots are now in widespread use performing jobs more cheaply or with greater accuracy and reliability than humans. They are also employed for jobs which are too dirty, dangerous or dull to be suitable for humans.

Robots are widely used in manufacturing, assembly and packing, transport, earth and space exploration, surgery, weaponry, laboratory research, and mass production of consumer and industrial goods.

FUTURE DEVELOPMENT AND TRENDS

Various techniques have emerged to develop the science of robotics and robots. One method is evolutionary robotics, in which a number of differing robots are submitted to tests. Those which perform best are used as a model to create a subsequent "generation" of robots. Another method is developmental robotics, which tracks changes and development within a single robot in the areas of problem-solving and other functions. Another new type of robot is just recently introduced which acts both as a smartphone and robot and is named

RoboHon. As robots become more advanced, eventually there may be a standard computer operating system designed mainly for robots. Robot Operating System is an open-source set of programs being developed at Stanford University, the Massachusetts Institute of Technology and the Technical University of Munich, Germany, among others. ROS provides ways to program a robot's navigation and limbs regardless of the specific hardware involved. It also provides high-level commands for items like image recognition and even opening doors. When ROS boots up on a robot's computer, it would obtain data on attributes such as the length and movement of robots' limbs. It would relay this data to higher-level algorithms. Microsoft is also developing a "Windows for robots" system with its Robotics Developer Studio, which has been available since 2007.

Japan hopes to have full-scale commercialization of service robots by 2025. Much technological research in Japan is led by Japanese government agencies, particularly the Trade Ministry.

Many future applications of robotics seem obvious to people, even though they are well beyond the capabilities of robots available at the time of the prediction. As early as 1982 people were confident that someday robots would: 1. clean parts by removing molding flash 2. spray paint automobiles with absolutely no human presence 3. pack things in boxes—for example, orient and nest chocolate candies in candy boxes 4. make electrical cable harness 5. load trucks with boxes—a packing problem 6. handle soft goods, such as garments and shoes 7. shear sheep 8. prosthesis 9. cook fast food and work in other service industries 10. household robot. Generally such predictions are overly optimistic in timescale.

3

Natural Language Processing

Natural language processing (NLP) is a field of computer science and linguistics concerned with the interactions between computers and human (natural) languages. In theory, natural-language processing is a very attractive method of human-computer interaction. Natural language understanding is sometimes referred to as an AI-complete problem, because natural-language recognition seems to require extensive knowledge about the outside world and the ability to manipulate it. NLP has significant overlap with the field of computational linguistics, and is often considered a sub-field of artificial intelligence. Modern NLP algorithms are grounded in machine learning, especially statistical machine learning. Research into modern statistical NLP algorithms requires an understanding of a number of disparate fields, including linguistics, computer science, and statistics.

HISTORY

The history of NLP generally starts in the 1950s, although work can be found from earlier periods. In 1950, Alan Turing published his famous article "Computing Machinery and Intelligence" which proposed what is now called the Turing test as a criterion of intelligence. This criterion depends on the ability of a computer programme to impersonate a human in a real-time written conversation with a human judge, sufficiently well that the judge is unable to distinguish reliably — on the basis of the conversational content alone — between the programme and a real human. The Georgetown experiment in 1954 involved fully automatic translation of more than sixty Russian sentences into English. The authors claimed that within three or five years, machine translation would be a solved problem. However, real progress was much slower, and after the ALPAC report in 1966, which found that ten years long research had failed to fulfill the expectations, funding for machine translation was dramatically reduced. Little further research in machine translation was conducted until the late 1980s, when the first statistical machine translation systems were developed.

Some notably successful NLP systems developed in the 1960s were SHRDLU, a natural language system working in restricted "blocks worlds" with restricted vocabularies, and ELIZA, a simulation of a Rogerian psychotherapist, written by Joseph Weizenbaum between 1964 to 1966. Using almost no information about human thought or emotion, ELIZA sometimes provided a startlingly human-like interaction. When the "patient" exceeded the very small knowledge base, ELIZA might provide a generic response, for example, responding to "My head hurts" with "Why do you say your head hurts?". During the 70's many programmers began to write 'conceptual ontologies', which structured real-world information into computer-understandable data. Examples are MARGIE (Schank, 1975), SAM (Cullingford, 1978), PAM (Wilensky, 1978), TaleSpin (Meehan, 1976), QUALM (Lehnert, 1977), Politics (Carbonell, 1979), and Plot Units (Lehnert 1981). During this time, many chatterbots were written including PARRY, Racter, and Jabberwacky.

Up to the 1980s, most NLP systems were based on complex sets of hand-written rules. Starting in the late 1980s, however, there was a revolution in NLP with the introduction of machine learning algorithms for language processing. This was due both to the steady increase in computational power resulting from Moore's Law and the gradual lessening of the dominance of Chomskyan theories of linguistics (e.g. transformational grammar), whose theoretical underpinnings discouraged the sort of corpus linguistics that underlies the machine-learning approach to language processing. Some of the earliest-used machine learning algorithms, such as decision trees, produced systems of hard if-then rules similar to existing hand-written rules. Increasingly, however, research has focused on statistical models, which make soft, probabilistic decisions based on attaching real-valued weights to the features making up the input data. Such models are generally more robust when given unfamiliar input, especially input that contains errors (as is very common for real-world data), and produce more reliable results when integrated into a larger system comprising multiple subtasks. Many of the notable early successes occurred in the field of machine translation, due especially to work at IBM Research, where successively more complicated statistical models were developed.

These systems were able to take advantage of existing multilingual textual corpora that had been produced by the Parliament of Canada and the European Union as a result of laws calling for the translation of all governmental proceedings into all official languages of the corresponding systems of government.

However, most other systems depended on corpora specifically developed for the tasks implemented by these systems, which was (and often continues to be) a major limitation in the success of these systems. As a result, a great deal of research has gone into methods of more effectively learning from limited amounts of data. Recent research has increasingly focused on unsupervised and semi-supervised learning algorithms. Such algorithms are able to learn from data that has not been hand-annotated with the desired answers, or using a combination of annotated and non-annotated data. Generally, this task is much more difficult than supervised learning, and typically produces less accurate results for a given amount of input data. However, there is an enormous amount of non-annotated data available (including, among other things, the entire content of the World Wide Web), which can often make up for the inferior results.

NATURAL LANGUAGE

An important goal of AI research is to allow computers to communicate in natural languages like English. An early success was Daniel Bobrow's programme STUDENT, which could solve high school algebra word problems. A semantic net represents concepts (e.g. "house","door") as nodes and relations among concepts (e.g. "has-a") as links between the nodes.

The first AI programme to use a semantic net was written by Ross Quillian and the most successful (and controversial) version was Roger Schank's Conceptual Dependency. Joseph Weizenbaum's ELIZA could carry out conversations that were so realistic that users occasionally were fooled into thinking they were communicating with a human being and not a programme.

But in fact, ELIZA had no idea what she was talking about. She simply gave a canned response or repeated back what was said to her, rephrasing her response with a few grammar rules. ELIZA was the first chatterbot.

Micro-Worlds

In the late 60s, Marvin Minsky and Seymour Papert of the MIT AI Laboratory proposed that AI research should focus on artificially simple situations known as micro-worlds. They pointed out that in successful sciences like physics, basic principles were often best understood using simplified models like frictionless planes or perfectly rigid bodies. Much of the research focused on a "blocks world," which consists of colored blocks of various shapes and sizes arrayed on a flat surface. This paradigm led to innovative work in machine vision by Gerald Sussman (who led the team), Adolfo Guzman, David Waltz (who invented "constraint propagation"), and especially Patrick Winston. At the same time, Minsky and Papert built a robot arm that could stack blocks, bringing the blocks world to life. The crowning achievement of the micro-world programme was Terry Winograd's SHRDLU. It could communicate in ordinary English sentences, plan operations and execute them.

The Optimism

The first generation of AI researchers made these predictions about their work:

- 1958, H. A. Simon and Allen Newell: "within ten years a digital computer will be the world's chess champion" and "within ten years a digital computer will discover and prove an important new mathematical theorem."
- 1965, H. A. Simon: "machines will be capable, within twenty years, of doing any work a man can do."
- 1967, Marvin Minsky: "Within a generation ... the problem of creating 'artificial intelligence' will substantially be solved."
- 1970, Marvin Minsky (in *Life* Magazine): "In from three to eight years we will have a machine with the general intelligence of an average human being."

The Money

In June 1963 MIT received a $2.2 million grant from the newly created Advanced Research Projects Agency (later known as DARPA). The money was used to fund project MAC which subsumed the "AI Group" founded by Minsky and McCarthy five years earlier. ARPA continued to provide three million dollars a year until the 70s.

ARPA made similar grants to Newell and Simon's programme at CMU and to the Stanford AI Project (founded by John McCarthy in 1963). Another important AI laboratory was established at Edinburgh University by Donald Michie in 1965. These four institutions would continue to be the main centers of AI research (and funding) in academia for many years. The money was proffered with few strings attached: J. C. R. Licklider, then the director of ARPA, believed that his organization should "fund people, not projects!" and allowed researchers to pursue whatever directions might interest them. This created a freewheeling atmosphere at MIT that gave birth to the hacker culture, but this "hands off" approach would not last.

The First AI Winter 1974-1980

In the 70s, AI was subject to critiques and financial setbacks. AI researchers had failed to appreciate the difficulty of the problems they faced. Their tremendous optimism had raised expectations impossibly high, and when the promised results failed to materialize, funding for AI disappeared. At the same time, the field of connectionism (or neural nets) was shut down almost completely for 10 years by Marvin Minsky's devastating criticism of perceptrons. Despite the difficulties with public perception of AI in the late 70s, new ideas were explored in logic programming, commonsense reasoning and many other areas.

The Problems

In the early seventies, the capabilities of AI programmes were limited. Even the most impressive could only handle trivial versions of the problems they were supposed to solve; all the programmes were, in some sense, "toys". AI researchers had begun to run into several fundamental limits that could not be overcome in the 1970s. Although some of these limits would be conquered in later decades, others still stymie the field to this day.

- Limited computer power: There was not enough memory or processing speed to accomplish anything truly useful. For example, Ross Quillian's successful work on natural language was demonstrated with a vocabulary of only *twenty* words, because that was all that would fit in memory. Hans Moravec argued in 1976 that computers were still millions of times too weak to exhibit intelligence. He suggested an analogy: artificial intelligence requires computer power in the same way that aircraft require power. Below a certain threshold, it's impossible, but, as power increases, eventually it could become easy.
- Intractability and the combinatorial explosion. In 1972 Richard Karp (building on Stephen Cook's 1971 theorem) showed there are many problems that can probably only

be solved in exponential time (in the size of the inputs). Finding optimal solutions to these problems requires unimaginable amounts of computer time except when the problems are trivial. This almost certainly meant that many of the "toy" solutions used by AI would probably never scale up into useful systems.

- Commonsense knowledge and reasoning. Many important artificial intelligence applications like vision or natural language require simply enormous amounts of information about the world: the programme needs to have some idea of what it might be looking at or what it is talking about. This requires that the programme know most of the same things about the world that a child does. Researchers soon discovered that this was a truly *vast* amount of information. No one in 1970 could build a database so large and no one knew how a programme might learn so much information.
- Moravec's paradox: Proving theorems and solving geometry problems is comparatively easy for computers, but a supposedly simple task like recognizing a face or crossing a room without bumping into anything is extremely difficult. This helps explain why research into vision and robotics had made so little progress by the middle 1970s.
- The frame and qualification problems. AI researchers (like John McCarthy) who used logic discovered that they could not represent ordinary deductions that involved planning or default reasoning without making changes to the structure of logic itself. They developed new logics (like non-monotonic logics and modal logics) to try to solve the problems.

The End of Funding

The agencies which funded AI research (such as the British government, DARPA and NRC) became frustrated with the lack of progress and eventually cut off almost all funding for undirected research into AI. The pattern began as early as 1966 when the ALPAC report appeared criticizing machine translation efforts. After spending 20 million dollars, the NRC ended all support. In 1973, the Lighthill report on the state of AI research in England criticized the utter failure of AI to achieve its "grandiose objectives" and led to the dismantling of AI research in that country. (The report specifically mentioned the combinatorial explosion problem as a reason for AI's failings.) DARPA was deeply disappointed with researchers working on the Speech Understanding Research programme at CMU and canceled an annual grant of three million dollars. By 1974, funding for AI projects was hard to find. Hans Moravec blamed the crisis on the unrealistic predictions of his colleagues. "Many researchers were caught up in a web of increasing exaggeration." However, there was another issue: since the passage of the Mansfield Amendment in 1969, DARPA had been under increasing pressure to fund "mission-oriented direct research, rather than basic undirected research". Funding for the creative, freewheeling exploration that had gone on in the 60s would not come from DARPA. Instead, the money was directed at specific projects with clear objectives, such as autonomous tanks and battle management systems.

Critiques from Across Campus

Several philosophers had strong objections to the claims being made by AI researchers. One of the earliest was John Lucas, who argued that Gödel's incompleteness theorem showed that a formal system (such as a computer program) could never see the truth of certain statements, while a human being could. Hubert Dreyfus ridiculed the broken promises of the 60s and critiqued the assumptions of AI, arguing that human reasoning actually involved very little "symbol processing" and a great deal of embodied, instinctive, unconscious "know how". John Searle's Chinese Room argument, presented in 1980, attempted to show that a programme could not be said to "understand" the symbols that it uses (a quality called "intentionality"). If the symbols have no meaning for the machine, Searle argued, then the machine can not be described as "thinking". These critiques were not taken seriously by AI researchers, often because they seemed so far off the point. Problems like intractability and commonsense knowledge seemed much more immediate and serious.

It was unclear what difference "know how" or "intentionality" made to an actual computer programme. Minsky said of Dreyfus and Searle "they misunderstand, and should be ignored." Dreyfus, who taught at MIT, was given a cold shoulder: he later said that AI researchers "dared not be seen having lunch with me." Joseph Weizenbaum, the author of ELIZA, felt his colleagues' treatment of Dreyfus was unprofessional and childish. Although he was an outspoken critic of Dreyfus' positions, he "deliberately made it plain that theirs was not the way to treat a human being." Weizenbaum began to have serious ethical doubts about AI when Kenneth Colby wrote DOCTOR, a chatterbot therapist.

Weizenbaum was disturbed that Colby saw his mindless programme as a serious therapeutic tool. A feud began, and the situation was not helped when Colby did not credit Weizenbaum for his contribution to the programme. In 1976, Weizenbaum published *Computer Power and Human Reason* which argued that the misuse of artificial intelligence has the potential to devalue human life.

Perceptrons and the Dark Age of Connectionism

A perceptron was a form of neural network introduced in 1958 by Frank Rosenblatt, who had been a schoolmate of Marvin Minsky at the Bronx High School of Science. Like most AI researchers, he was optimistic about their power, predicting that "perceptron may eventually be able to learn, make decisions, and translate languages." An active research programme into the paradigm was carried out throughout the 60s but came to a sudden halt with the publication of Minsky and Papert's 1969 book *Perceptrons*. It suggested that there were severe limitations to what perceptrons could do and that Frank Rosenblatt's predictions had been grossly exaggerated. The effect of the book was devastating: virtually no research at all was done in connectionism for 10 years. Eventually, a new generation of researchers would revive the field and thereafter it would become a vital and useful part of artificial intelligence. Rosenblatt would not live to see this, as he died in a boating accident shortly after the book was published.

NLP USING MACHINE LEARNING

As described above, modern approaches to natural language processing (NLP) are grounded in machine learning. The paradigm of machine learning is different from that of most prior attempts at language processing. Prior implementations of language-processing tasks typically involved the direct hand coding of large sets of rules. The machine-learning paradigm calls instead for using general learning algorithms — often, although not always, grounded in statistical inference — to automatically learn such rules through the analysis of large *corpora* of typical real-world examples. A *corpus* (plural, "corpora") is a set of documents (or sometimes, individual sentences) that have been hand-annotated with the correct values to be learned. As an example, consider the task of part of speech tagging, i.e. determining the correct part of speech of each word in a given sentence, typically one that has never been seen before. A typical machine-learning-based implementation of a part of speech tagger proceeds in two steps, a *training* step and an *evaluation* step. The first step — the *training* step — makes use of a corpus of *training data*, which consists of a large number of sentences, each of which has the correct part of speech attached to each word. (An example of such a corpus in common use is the *Penn Treebank*.

This includes (among other things) a set of 500 texts from the Brown Corpus, containing examples of various genres of text, and 2500 articles from the Wall Street Journal.) This corpus is analyzed and a learning model is generated from it, consisting of automatically created rules for determining the part of speech for a word in a sentence, typically based on the nature of the word in question, the nature of surrounding words, and the most likely part of speech for those surrounding words. The model that is generated is typically the best model that can be found that simultaneously meets two conflicting objectives: To perform as well as possible on the training data, and to be as simple as possible (so that the model avoids overfitting the training data, i.e. so that it generalizes as well as possible to new data rather than only succeeding on sentences that have already been seen). In the second step (the evaluation step), the model that has been learned is used to process new sentences. An important part of the development of any learning algorithm is testing the model that has been learned on new, previously unseen data. It is critical that the data used for testing is not the same as the data used for training; otherwise, the testing accuracy will be unrealistically high.

Many different classes of machine learning algorithms have been applied to NLP tasks. In common to all of these algorithms is that they take as input a large set of "features" that are generated from the input data. As an example, for a part-of-speech tagger, typical features might be the identity of the word being processed, the identity of the words immediately to the left and right, the part-of-speech tag of the word to the left, and whether the word being considered or its immediate neighbors are content words or function words. The algorithms differ, however, in the nature of the rules generated.

Some of the earliest-used algorithms, such as decision trees, produced systems of hard if-then rules similar to the systems of hand-written rules that were then common. Increasingly, however, research has focused on statistical models, which make soft, probabilistic decisions based on attaching real-valued weights to each input feature.

Such models have the advantage that they can express the relative certainty of many different possible answers rather than only one, producing more reliable results when such a model is included as a component of a larger system. In addition, models that make soft decisions are generally more robust when given unfamiliar input, especially input that contains errors (as is very common for real-world data). Systems based on machine-learning algorithms have many advantages over hand-produced rules:

- The learning procedures used during machine learning automatically focus on the most common cases, whereas when writing rules by hand it is often not obvious at all where the effort should be directed.
- Automatic learning procedures can make use of statistical inference algorithms to produce models that are robust to unfamiliar input (e.g. containing words or structures that have not been seen before) and to erroneous input (e.g. with misspelled words or words accidentally omitted). Generally, handling such input gracefully with hand-written rules — or more generally, creating systems of hand-written rules that make soft decisions — is extremely difficult and error-prone.
- Systems based on automatically learning the rules can be made more accurate simply by supplying more input data. However, systems based on hand-written rules can only be made more accurate by increasing the complexity of the rules, which is a much more difficult task. In particular, there is a limit to the complexity of systems based on hand-crafted rules, beyond which the systems become more and more unmanageable. However, creating more data to input to machine-learning systems simply requires a corresponding increase in the number of man-hours worked, generally without significant increases in the complexity of the annotation process.

Major Tasks in NLP

The following is a list of some of the most commonly researched tasks in NLP. Note that some of these tasks have direct real-world applications, while others more commonly serve as subtasks that are used to aid in solving larger tasks. What distinguishes these tasks from other potential and actual NLP tasks is not only the volume of research devoted to them but the fact that for each one there is typically a well-defined problem setting, a standard metric for evaluating the task, standard corpora on which the task can be evaluated, and competitions devoted to the specific task.

- Automatic summarization: Produce a readable summary of a chunk of text. Often used to provide summaries of text of a known type, such as articles in the financial section of a newspaper.
- Coreference resolution: Given a sentence or larger chunk of text, determine which words ("mentions") refer to the same objects ("entities"). Anaphora resolution is a specific example of this task, and is specifically concerned with matching up pronouns with the nouns or names that they refer to. The more general task of coreference resolution also includes identify so-called "bridging relationships" involving referring expressions. For example, in a sentence such as "He entered John's house through the front door", "the front door" is a referring expression and the bridging relationship to be identified is the fact that the door being referred to is the front door of John's house (rather than of some other structure that might also be referred to).
- Discourse analysis: This rubric includes a number of related tasks. One task is identifying the discourse structure of connected text, i.e. the nature of the discourse relationships between sentences (e.g. elaboration, explanation, contrast). Another possible task is recognizing and classifying the speech acts in a chunk of text (e.g. yes-no question, content question, statement, assertion, etc.).
- Machine translation: Automatically translate text from one human language to another. This is one of the most difficult problems, and is a member of a class of problems colloquially termed "AI-complete", i.e. requiring all of the different types of knowledge that humans possess (grammar, semantics, facts about the real world, etc.) in order to solve properly.
- Morphological segmentation: Separate words into individual morphemes and identify the class of the morphemes. The difficulty of this task depends greatly on the complexity of the morphology (i.e. the structure

of words) of the language being considered. English has fairly simple morphology, especially inflectional morphology, and thus it is often possible to ignore this task entirely and simply model all possible forms of a word (e.g. "open, opens, opened, opening") as separate words. In languages such as Turkish, however, such an approach is not possible, as each dictionary entry has thousands of possible word forms.

- Named entity recognition (NER): Given a stream of text, determine which items in the text map to proper names, such as people or places, and what the type of each such name is (e.g. person, location, organization). Note that, although capitalization can aid in recognizing named entities in languages such as English, this information cannot aid in determining the type of named entity, and in any case is often inaccurate or insufficient. For example, the first word of a sentence is also capitalized, and named entities often span several words, only some of which are capitalized. Furthermore, many other languages in non-Western scripts (e.g. Chinese or Arabic) do not have any capitalization at all, and even languages with capitalization may not consistently use it to distinguish names. For example, German capitalizes all nouns, regardless of whether they refer to names, and French and Spanish do not capitalize names that serve as adjectives.
- Natural language generation: Convert information from computer databases into readable human language.
- Natural language understanding: Convert chunks of text into more formal representations such as first-order logic structures that are easier for computer programmes to manipulate.
- Optical character recognition (OCR): Given an image representing printed text, determine the corresponding text.
- Part-of-speech tagging: Given a sentence, determine the part of speech for each word. Many words, especially

common ones, can serve as multiple parts of speech. For example, “book” can be a noun (“the book on the table”) or verb (“to book a flight”); “set” can be a noun, verb or adjective; and “out” can be any of at least five different parts of speech. Note that some languages have more such ambiguity than others. Languages with little inflectional morphology, such as English are particularly prone to such ambiguity. Chinese is prone to such ambiguity because it is a tonal language during verbalization. Such inflection is not readily conveyed via the entities employed within the orthography to convey intended meaning.

- Parsing: Determine the parse tree (grammatical analysis) of a given sentence. The grammar for natural languages is ambiguous and typical sentences have multiple possible analyses. In fact, perhaps surprisingly, for a typical sentence there may be thousands of potential parses (most of which will seem completely nonsensical to a human).
- Question answering: Given a human-language question, determine its answer. Typical questions have a specific right answer (such as “What is the capital of Canada?”), but sometimes open-ended questions are also considered (such as “What is the meaning of life?”).
- Relationship extraction: Given a chunk of text, identify the relationships among named entities (i.e. who is the wife of whom).
- Sentence breaking (also known as sentence boundary disambiguation): Given a chunk of text, find the sentence boundaries. Sentence boundaries are often marked by periods or other punctuation marks, but these same characters can serve other purposes (e.g. marking abbreviations).
- Speech recognition: Given a sound clip of a person or people speaking, determine the textual representation of the speech. This is the opposite of text to speech and is one of the extremely difficult problems colloquially

termed "AI-complete". In natural speech there are hardly any pauses between successive words, and thus speech segmentation is a necessary subtask of speech recognition. Note also that in most spoken languages, the sounds representing successive letters blend into each other in a process termed coarticulation, so the conversion of the analog signal to discrete characters can be a very difficult process.

- Speech segmentation: Given a sound clip of a person or people speaking, separate it into words. A subtask of speech recognition and typically grouped with it.
- Topic segmentation and recognition: Given a chunk of text, separate it into segments each of which is devoted to a topic, and identify the topic of the segment.
- Word segmentation: Separate a chunk of continuous text into separate words. For a language like English, this is fairly trivial, since words are usually separated by spaces. However, some written languages like Chinese, Japanese and Thai do not mark word boundaries in such a fashion, and in those languages text segmentation is a significant task requiring knowledge of the vocabulary and morphology of words in the language.
- Word sense disambiguation: Many words have more than one meaning; we have to select the meaning which makes the most sense in context. For this problem, we are typically given a list of words and associated word senses, e.g. from a dictionary or from an online resource such as WordNet.

In some cases, sets of related tasks are grouped into subfields of NLP that are often considered separately from NLP as a whole. Examples include:

- Information retrieval (IR): This is concerned with storing, searching and retrieving information. It is a separate field within computer science (closer to databases), but IR relies on some NLP methods (for example, stemming). Some current research and applications seek to bridge the gap between IR and NLP.

- Information extraction (IE): This is concerned in general with the extraction of semantic information from text. This covers tasks such as named entity recognition, coreference resolution, relationship extraction, etc.
- Speech processing: This covers speech recognition, text-to-speech and related tasks.

Other tasks include:

- Stemming
- Text simplification
- Text-to-speech
- Text-proofing
- Natural language search
- Query expansion
- Truecasing

Statistical NLP

Statistical natural-language processing uses stochastic, probabilistic and statistical methods to resolve some of the difficulties discussed above, especially those which arise because longer sentences are highly ambiguous when processed with realistic grammars, yielding thousands or millions of possible analyses. Methods for disambiguation often involve the use of corpora and Markov models. Statistical NLP comprises all quantitative approaches to automated language processing, including probabilistic modeling, information theory, and linear algebra. The technology for statistical NLP comes mainly from machine learning and data mining, both of which are fields of artificial intelligence that involve learning from data.

EVALUATION OF NATURAL LANGUAGE PROCESSING

The goal of NLP evaluation is to measure one or more *qualities* of an algorithm or a system, in order to determine whether (or to what extent) the system answers the goals of its designers, or meets the needs of its users. Research in NLP evaluation has received considerable attention, because the definition of proper evaluation criteria is one way to specify precisely an NLP problem, going thus beyond the vagueness of tasks defined only as *language understanding* or *language generation*. A precise set of evaluation criteria, which includes mainly evaluation data and evaluation metrics, enables several teams to compare their solutions to a given NLP problem.

Short History of Evaluation in NLP

The first evaluation campaign on written texts seems to be a campaign dedicated to message understanding in 1987 (Pallet 1998). Then, the Parseval/GEIG project compared phrase-structure grammars (Black 1991). A series of campaigns within Tipster project were realized on tasks like summarization, translation and searching (Hirschman 1998). In 1994, in Germany, the Morpholympics compared German taggers. Then, the Senseval and Romanseval campaigns were conducted with the objectives of semantic disambiguation. In 1996, the Sparkle campaign compared syntactic parsers in four different languages (English, French, German and Italian). In France, the Grace project compared a set of 21 taggers for French in 1997 (Adda 1999). In 2004, during the Technolangue/Easy project, 13 parsers for French were compared. Large-scale evaluation of dependency parsers were performed in the context of the CoNLL shared tasks in 2006 and 2007. In Italy, the EVALITA campaign was conducted in 2007 and 2009 to compare various NLP and speech tools for Italian; the 2011 campaing is in full progress - EVALITA web site. In France, within the ANR-Passage project (end of 2007), 10 parsers for French were compared - passage web site.

Adda G., Mariani J., Paroubek P., Rajman M. 1999 L'action GRACE d'évaluation de l'assignation des parties du discours pour le français. Langues vol-2

Black E., Abney S., Flickinger D., Gdaniec C., Grishman R., Harrison P., Hindle D., Ingria R., Jelinek F., Klavans J., Liberman M., Marcus M., Reukos S., Santoni B., Strzalkowski T. 1991 A procedure for quantitatively comparing the syntactic coverage of English grammars. DARPA Speech and Natural Language Workshop Hirschman L. 1998 Language understanding evaluation: lessons learned from MUC and ATIS. LREC Granada Pallet D.S. 1998 The NIST role in automatic speech recognition benchmark tests. LREC Granada

Different Types of Evaluation

Depending on the evaluation procedures, a number of distinctions are traditionally made in NLP evaluation.

- Intrinsic vs. extrinsic evaluation : Intrinsic evaluation considers an isolated NLP system and characterizes its performance mainly with respect to a *gold standard* result, pre-defined by the evaluators. Extrinsic evaluation, also called *evaluation in use* considers the NLP system in a more complex setting, either as an embedded system or serving a precise function for a human user. The extrinsic performance of the system is then characterized in terms of its utility with respect to the overall task of the complex system or the human user. For example, consider a syntactic parser that is based on the output of some new part of speech (POS) tagger. An intrinsic evaluation would run the POS tagger on some labelled data, and compare the system output of the POS tagger to the gold standard (correct) output. An extrinsic evaluation would run the parser with some other POS tagger, and then with the new POS tagger, and compare the parsing accuracy.
- Black-box vs. glass-box evaluation : Black-box evaluation requires one to run an NLP system on a given data set and to measure a number of parameters related to the quality of the process (speed, reliability, resource consumption) and, most importantly, to the quality of the result (e.g. the accuracy of data annotation or the fidelity of a translation). Glass-box evaluation looks at the design of the system, the algorithms that are implemented, the linguistic resources it uses (e.g. vocabulary size), etc. Given the complexity of NLP problems, it is often difficult to predict performance only on the basis of glass-box evaluation, but this type

of evaluation is more informative with respect to error analysis or future developments of a system.

- Automatic vs. manual evaluation : In many cases, automatic procedures can be defined to evaluate an NLP system by comparing its output with the gold standard (or desired) one. Although the cost of producing the gold standard can be quite high, automatic evaluation can be repeated as often as needed without much additional costs (on the same input data). However, for many NLP problems, the definition of a gold standard is a complex task, and can prove impossible when inter-annotator agreement is insufficient. Manual evaluation is performed by human judges, which are instructed to estimate the quality of a system, or most often of a sample of its output, based on a number of criteria. Although, thanks to their linguistic competence, human judges can be considered as the reference for a number of language processing tasks, there is also considerable variation across their ratings. This is why automatic evaluation is sometimes referred to as *objective* evaluation, while the human kind appears to be more *subjective*.

Shared Tasks (Campaigns)

- BioCreative
- Message Understanding Conference
- Technolangue/Easy
- Text Retrieval Conference
- Evaluation exercises on Semantic Evaluation (SemEval)

Standardization in NLP

An ISO sub-committee is working in order to ease interoperability between lexical resources and NLP programmes. The sub-committee is part of ISO/TC37 and is called ISO/TC37/SC4. Some ISO standards are already published but most of them are under construction, mainly on lexicon representation, annotation and data category registry.

4

Machine Learning

Machine learning, a branch of artificial intelligence, is a scientific discipline concerned with the design and development of algorithms that allow computers to evolve behaviours based on empirical data, such as from sensor data or databases. A learner can take advantage of examples (data) to capture characteristics of interest of their unknown underlying probability distribution. Data can be seen as examples that illustrate relations between observed variables. A major focus of machine learning research is to automatically learn to recognize complex patterns and make intelligent decisions based on data; the difficulty lies in the fact that the set of all possible behaviours given all possible inputs is too large to be covered by the set of observed examples (training data). Hence the learner must generalize from the given examples, so as to be able to produce a useful output in new cases.

Machine learning, like all subjects in artificial intelligence, requires cross-disciplinary proficiency in several areas, such as probability theory, statistics, pattern recognition, cognitive science, data mining, adaptive control, computational neuroscience and theoretical computer science. The largest collection of Machine learning academic talks can be found at VideoLectures.NET.

CHARACTERISTICS

Learning is an inherent characteristic of the human beings. By virtue of this, people, while executing similar tasks, acquire the ability to improve their performance. This chapter provides an overview of the principle of learning that can be adhered to machines to improve their performance. Such learning is usually referred to as 'machine learning'.

Machine learning can be broadly classified into three categories:

1. Supervised learning,
2. Unsupervised learning and
3. Reinforcement learning.

Supervised learning requires a trainer, who supplies the input-output training instances. The learning system adapts its parametres by some algorithms to generate the desired output patterns from a given input pattern. In absence of trainers, the desired output for a given input instance is not known, and consequently the learner has to adapt its parametres autonomously.

Such type of learning is termed 'unsupervised learning'. The third type called the reinforcement learning bridges a gap between supervised and unsupervised categories. In reinforcement learning, the learner does not explicitly know the input-output instances, but it receives some form of feedback from its environment.

The feedback signals help the learner to decide whether its action on the environment is rewarding or punishable. The learner thus adapts its parametres based on the states (rewarding/punishable) of its actions. Among the supervised learning techniques, the most common are inductive and analogical learning. The inductive learning technique, presented in the chapter, includes decision tree and version space based learning.

Analogical learning is briefly introduced through illustrative examples. The principle of unsupervised learning is illustrated here with a clustering problem. The section on reinforcement learning includes Q-learning and temporal difference learning.

A fourth category of learning, which has emerged recently from the disciplines of knowledge engineering, is called 'inductive logic programming'. The principles of inductive logic programming have also been briefly introduced in this chapter. The chapter ends with a brief discussion on the 'computational theory of learning'. With the background of this theory, one can measure the performance of the learning behaviour of a machine from the training instances and their count.

DEFINITION

A computer programme is said to learn from experience E with respect to some class of tasks T and performance measure P, if its performance at tasks in T, as measured by P, improves with experience E.

Generalization

The core objective of a learner is to generalize from its experience. The training examples from its experience come from some generally unknown probability distribution and the learner has to extract from them something more general, something about that distribution, that allows it to produce useful answers in new cases.

Human Interaction

Some machine learning systems attempt to eliminate the need for human intuition in data analysis, while others adopt a collaborative approach between human and machine. Human intuition cannot, however, be entirely eliminated, since the system's designer must specify how the data is to be represented and what mechanisms will be used to search for a characterization of the data.

Algorithm Types

Machine learning algorithms are organized into a taxonomy, based on the desired outcome of the algorithm.

- Supervised learning generates a function that maps inputs to desired outputs (also called labels, because they are often provided by human experts labeling the training examples). For example, in a classification problem, the learner approximates a function mapping a vector into classes by looking at input-output examples of the function.

- Unsupervised learning models a set of inputs, like clustering.
- Semi-supervised learning combines both labeled and unlabeled examples to generate an appropriate function or classifier.
- Reinforcement learning learns how to act given an observation of the world. Every action has some impact in the environment, and the environment provides feedback in the form of rewards that guides the learning algorithm.
- Transduction tries to predict new outputs based on training inputs, training outputs, and test inputs.
- Learning to learn learns its own inductive bias based on previous experience.

SUPERVISED LEARNING

As already mentioned, in supervised learning a trainer submits the inputoutput exemplary patterns and the learner has to adjust the parametres of the system autonomously, so that it can yield the correct output pattern when excited with one of the given input patterns. We shall cover two important types of supervised learning in this section. These are i) inductive learning and ii) analogical learning.

Inductive Learning

In supervised learning we have a set of {xi, f (xi)} for 1≤i≤n, and our aim is to determine 'f' by some adaptive algorithm. The inductive learning is a special class of the supervised learning techniques, where given a set of {xi, f(xi)} pairs, we determine a hypothesis h(xi) such that h(xi)≈f(xi),? i. A natural question that may be raised is how to compare the hypothesis h that approximates f.

For instance, there could be more than one h(xi) where all of which are approximately close to f(xi). Let there be two hypothesis h1 and h2, where h1(xi) ≈ f(xi) and h2(xi) = f(xi). We may select one of the two hypotheses by a preference criterion, called bias. When {xi, f(xi)}, 1≤ i≤ n are numerical quantities we may employ the neural learning techniques presented in the next chapter.

Readers may wonder: could we find 'f' by curve fitting as well. Should we then call curve fitting a learning technique? The answer to this, of course, is in the negative. The learning algorithm for such numerical sets {xi, f(xi)} must be able to adapt the parametres of the learner.

The more will be the training instance, the larger will be the number of adaptations. But what happens when xi and f(xi) are non-numerical? For instance, suppose given the truth table of the following training instances.

Table. Truth: Training Instances

Input Instances	Output Instances
$a_1, a_1 \rightarrow b_1$	b_1
$a_2, a_2 \rightarrow b_2$	b_2
.	
.	
$a_n, a_n \rightarrow b_n$	b_n

Here we may denote bi = f (ai, ai→bi) for all i=1 to n. From these training instances we infer a generalized hypothesis h as follows.

Analogical Learning

In inductive learning we observed that there exist many positive and negative instances of a problem and the learner has to form a concept that supports most of the positive and no negative instances. This demonstrates that a number of training instances are required to form a concept in inductive learning. Unlike this, analogical learning can be accomplished from a single example. For instance, given the following training instance, one has to determine the plural form of bacilus.

Obviously, one can answer that the plural form of bacillus is bacilli. But how do we do so? From common sense reasoning, it follows that the result is because of the similarity of bacillus with fungus. The analogical learning system thus learns that to get the plural form of words ending with 'us' is to replace it with 'i'.

The main steps in analogical learning are now formalized below:

- *Identifying Analogy:* Identify the similarity between an experienced problem instance and a new problem.
- *Determining the Mapping Function:* Relevant parts of the experienced problem are selected and the mapping is determined.
- *Apply Mapping Function:* Apply the mapping function to transform the new problem from the given domain to the target domain.
- *Validation:* The newly constructed solution is validated for its applicability through its trial processes like theorem or simulation.
- *Learning:* If the validation is found to work well, the new knowledge is encoded and saved for future usage.

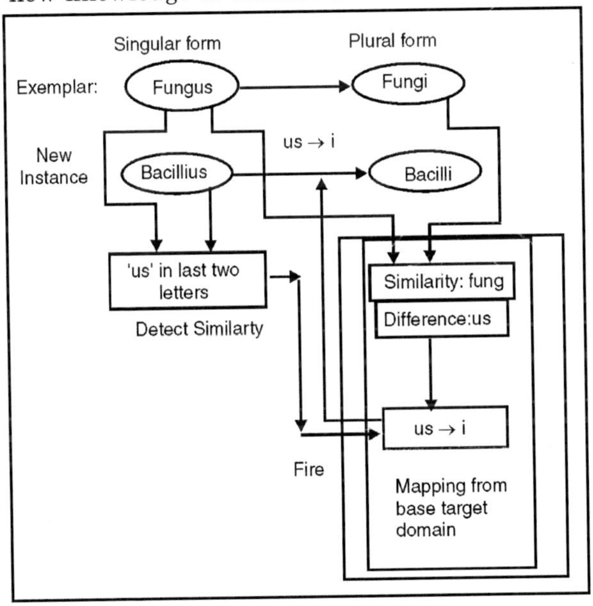

Analogical reasoning has been successfully realised in many systems. Winston's analogical system was designed to demonstrate that the relationship between acts and actors in one story can explain the same in another story. Carbonell's transformational analogy system employs a new approach to problem solving. It solves new problems by modifying existing solutions to problems until they may be applied to new problem instances.

MACHINE LEARNING IN ARTIFICIAL INTELLIGENCE

Machine learning, a branch of artificial intelligence, is a scientific discipline concerned with the design and development of algorithms that allow computers to evolve behaviours based on empirical data, such as from sensor data or databases. A learner can take advantage of examples (data) to capture characteristics of interest of their unknown underlying probability distribution. Data can be seen as examples that illustrate relations between observed variables. A major focus of machine learning research is to automatically learn to recognize complex patterns and make intelligent decisions based on data; the difficulty lies in the fact that the set of all possible behaviours given all possible inputs is too large to be covered by the set of observed examples (training data). Hence the learner must generalize from the given examples, so as to be able to produce a useful output in new cases. Machine learning, like all subjects in artificial intelligence, requires cross-disciplinary proficiency in several areas, such as probability theory, statistics, pattern recognition, cognitive science, data mining, adaptive control, computational neuroscience and theoretical computer science.

Theory

The computational analysis of machine learning algorithms and their performance is a branch of theoretical computer science known as computational learning theory. Because training sets are finite and the future is uncertain, learning theory usually does not yield absolute guarantees of the performance of algorithms. Instead, probabilistic bounds on the performance are quite common. In addition to performance bounds, computational learning theorists study the time complexity and feasibility of learning.

In computational learning theory, a computation is considered feasible if it can be done in polynomial time. There are two kinds of time complexity results. Positive results show that a certain class of functions can be learned in polynomial time. Negative results show that certain classes cannot be learned in polynomial time. There are many similarities between machine learning theory and statistics, although they use different terms.

Approaches

Decision Tree Learning

Decision tree learning uses a decision tree as a predictive model which maps observations about an item to conclusions about the item's target value.

Association Rule Learning

Association rule learning is a method for discovering interesting relations between variables in large databases.

Artificial Neural Networks

An artificial neural network (ANN) learning algorithm, usually called "neural network" (NN), is a learning algorithm that is inspired by the structure and/or functional aspects of biological neural networks. Computations are structured in terms of an interconnected group of artificial neurons, processing information using a connectionist approach to computation. Modern neural networks are non-linear statistical data modeling tools. They are usually used to model complex relationships between inputs and outputs, to find patterns in data, or to capture the statistical structure in an unknown joint probability distribution between observed variables.

Genetic Programming

Genetic programming (GP) is an evolutionary algorithm-based methodology inspired by biological evolution to find computer programmes that perform a user-defined task. It is a specialization of genetic algorithms (GA) where each individual is a computer programme. It is a machine learning technique used to optimize a population of computer programmes according to a fitness landscape determined by a program's ability to perform a given computational task.

Inductive Logic Programming

Inductive logic programming (ILP) is an approach to rule learning using logic programming as a uniform representation for examples, background knowledge, and hypotheses. Given an encoding of the known background knowledge and a set of examples represented as a logical database of facts, an ILP system will derive a hypothesized logic programme which entails all the positive and none of the negative examples.

Support Vector Machines

Support vector machines (SVMs) are a set of related supervised learning methods used for classification and regression. Given a set of training examples, each marked as belonging to one of two categories, an SVM training algorithm builds a model that predicts whether a new example falls into one category or the other.

Clustering

Cluster analysis or clustering is the assignment of a set of observations into subsets (called *clusters*) so that observations in the same cluster are similar in some sense. Clustering is a method of unsupervised learning, and a common technique for statistical data analysis.

Bayesian Networks

A Bayesian network, belief network or directed acyclic graphical model is a probabilistic graphical model that represents a set of random variables and their conditional independencies via a directed acyclic graph (DAG). For example, a Bayesian network could represent the probabilistic relationships between diseases and symptoms. Given symptoms, the network can be used to compute the probabilities of the presence of various diseases. Efficient algorithms exist that perform inference and learning.

Reinforcement Learning

Reinforcement learning is concerned with how an *agent* ought to take *actions* in an *environment* so as to maximize some notion of long-term *reward*. Reinforcement learning algorithms attempt to find a *policy* that maps *states* of the world to the actions the agent ought to take in those states. Reinforcement learning differs from the supervised learning problem in that correct input/output pairs are never presented, nor sub-optimal actions explicitly corrected.

Representation Learning

Several learning algorithms, mostly unsupervised learning algorithms, aim at discovering better representations of the inputs provided during training. Classical examples include principal components analysis and clustering.

Representation learning algorithms often attempt to preserve the information in their input but transform it it in a way that makes it useful, often as a pre-processing step before performing classification or predictions, allowing to reconstruct the inputs coming from the unknown data generating distribution, while not being necessarily faithful for input configurations that are unplausible under that distribution. Manifold learning algorithms attempt to do so under the constraint that the learned representation is low-dimensional. Sparse coding algorithms attempt to do so under the constraint that the learned representation is sparse (has many zeros). Deep learning algorithms discover multiple levels of representation, or a hierarchy of features, with higher-level, more abstract features defined in terms of (or generating) lower-level features. It has been argued that an ideal representation is one that disentangles the underlying factors of variation that explain the observed data.

Applications

Applications for machine learning include machine perception, computer vision, natural language processing, syntactic pattern recognition, search engines, medical diagnosis, bioinformatics, brain-machine interfaces and cheminformatics, detecting credit card fraud, stock market analysis, classifying DNA sequences, speech and handwriting recognition, object recognition in computer vision, game playing, software engineering, adaptive websites, robot locomotion, and structural health monitoring.

Machine learning techniques helped win a major software competition: in 2006, the online movie company Netflix held the first "Netflix Prize" competition to find a programme to better predict user preferences and beat its existing Netflix movie recommendation system by at least 10%.

The AT&T Research Team BellKor won over several other teams with their machine learning programme called Pragmatic Chaos. After winning several minor prizes, it won the 2009 grand prize competition for $1 million.

Software

RapidMiner, KNIME, Weka, ODM, Shogun toolbox, Orange and Apache Mahout are software suites containing a variety of machine learning algorithms.

WAFFLES (MACHINE LEARNING)

Waffles is a collection of command-line tools for performing machine learning operations developed at Brigham Young University. These tools are written in C++, and are available under the GNU Lesser General Public License.

Description

The Waffles machine learning toolkit contains command-line tools for performing various operations related to machine learning, data mining, and predictive modeling. The primary focus of Waffles is to provide tools that are simple to use in scripted experiments or processes.

For example, the supervised learning algorithms included in Waffles are all designed to support multi-dimensional labels,classification and regression, automatically impute missing values, and automatically apply necessary filters to transform the data to a type that the algorithm can support, such that arbitrary learning algorithms can be used with arbitrary data sets. Many other machine learning toolkits provide similar functionality, but require the user to explicitly configure data filters and transformations to make it compatible with a particular learning algorithm. The algorithms provided in Waffles also have the ability to automatically tune their own parameters (with the cost of additional computational overhead).

Because Waffles is designed for script-ability, it deliberately avoids presenting its tools in a graphical environment. It does, however, include a graphical "wizard" tool that guides the user to generate a command that will perform a desired task. This wizard does not actually perform the operation, but requires the user to paste the command that it generates into a command terminal or a script. The idea motivating this design is to prevent the user from becoming "locked in" to a graphical interface.

All of the Waffles tools are implemented as thin wrappers around functionality in a C++ class library. This makes it possible to convert scripted processes into native applications with minimal effort.

Waffles was first released as an open source project in 2005. Since that time, it has been developed at Brigham Young University, with a new version having been released approximately every 6–9 months. Waffles is not an acronym—the toolkit was named after the food for historical reasons.

Advantages

Some of the advantages of Waffles in contrast with other popular open source machine learning toolkits include:

- Waffles automatically takes care of many issues related to data format in order to simplify its tools.
- Because it is implemented in C++, many of its algorithms are particularly fast. Also, the lack of dependency on any virtual machine makes it easier to deploy in conjunction with other applications.
- The functionality included in Waffles is very broad, including algorithms for dimensionality reduction, collaborative filtering, visualization, clustering, supervised learning, optimization, linear algebra, data transformation, image and signal processing, policy learning, and sparse matrix operations.

Disadvantages

- Although Waffles provides significant breadth, it lacks the depth of many toolkits that focus on a particular area of machine learning. TheWeka (machine learning) toolkit, for example, provides many more classification algorithms than Waffles provides.
- Waffles only has a limited graphical interface.

PROGRAMMED LEARNING

Programmed Learning or Programmed Instruction is a learning methodology or technique first proposed by the behaviourist B. F. Skinner in 1958. The purpose of programmed learning is to "manage human learning under controlled conditions".

Programmed learning has three elements:

1. It delivers information in small bites,
2. It is self-paced by the learner, and
3. It provides immediate feedback, both positive and negative, to the learner.

It was popular in the late 1960s and through the 1970s, but pedagogical interest was lost in the early 1980s as it was difficult to implement and its limitations were not well understood by practitioners. It was revived in the 1990s in the computerised Integrated Learning System (ILS) approach, primarily in the business and managerial context. Programmed learning remains popular in self-teaching textbooks.

The methodology involves self-administered and self-paced learning, in which the student is presented with information in small steps often referred to as "frames". Each frame contains a small segment of the information to be learned, and a question which the student must answer. After each frame the student uncovers, or is directed to, additional information based on an incorrect answer, or positive feedback for a correct answer.

Criticism

Programmed Instruction has been criticised for its inability to provide adequate feedback on incorrect answers and for its lack of student instigated conceptualisation opportunities. It works best in basic courses which introduce the vocabulary of a discipline, heavily fact-based courses, and rule-based technical courses.

SIMULATED TEACHING

Normal experiential learning that leads to an expert professional in clinical practice is associated with prolonged exposure to that practice. The over-riding idea is that by simulating clinical scenarios, learning is accelerated by the debriefing/feedback session. The expert knowledge is made explicit to the trainee and reinforced with video and verbal feedback.

Simulation training can:

- Prepare students to cope with future roles.
- Provide practice in a safe environment with no risk to patient or student.
- Test/challenge trainee's technical and decision-making skills during realistic patient care situations.
- Be an assessment tool.
- Lead to standardised teaching.

Skills that can be assessed/practiced using simulation:

- Interpersonal and communication skills.
- Critical thinking and decision-making skills.
- Practical skills.
- The use of equipment.

The Best evidence medical education (BEME) collaboration is an international group of individuals, Universities and organisations committed to the promotion of best evidence medical education. They formed a topic group in 2002 that addressed the question: "What are the features/aspects of high fidelity simulators that lead to most effective learning?"

Feedback

The absence of learner feedback was the greatest single factor for ineffective simulation training.

The lack of feedback could lead to:

- Learning of the wrong learning objective.
- Not realising what the desired behaviours should be by not focusing on them.
- Not transferring skills to clinical practice.
- Spending increasing time on only one aspect of training.

Practice

A lack of opportunity for practice is also associated with a poor educational outcome. This could often be attributed to insufficient access to the simulator, as training sessions are usually time dependent, and the simulator is often a hotly contested resource. In addition, each learner is different, and some learners inevitably need longer or more frequent sessions with the simulator to achieve the same educational results as their co-learners.

Validity

Poor validity is associated with a lack of realism. In some simulators novices can out-perform an expert, which questions the validity of that simulation. Typically, this would also lead to a lack of correlation with other outcome measures.

Fidelity

A common belief is that low fidelity simulation is better than high fidelity. However the group concluded that all levels of fidelity should be used based on the required outcomes. This is discussed by Maran and Glavin, where the progression from low to high fidelity simulation is compared to the progression through medical education.

Their conclusion is that the range of fidelity available is almost all potentially useful, but that many simulators are underused due simply to a lack of clear educational goals

'Simulator' Learning

Students learn to master the simulator rather than the task. The solution to this is to have multiple outcome measures for the task.

Assessment

There is current controversy about the use of simulators in high stakes examinations. Issues of domain specificity and itemised versus global scoring systems have bee raised. There is ongoing research into all of these factors though, and it seems certain that simulation will be included as part of high stakes assessment, along with other outcome measures.

In Summary

If you are thinking of using simulation in teaching you have to think:

- Who am I teaching?
- What am I teaching them?
- What are they expected to learn?

The simulation scenarios should:

- Be as realistic an environment as possible.
- Should involve feedback/debriefing/video sessions.
- Well prepared with a back up plan for equipment failure.
- Involve the observers by getting to make notes on teamwork, situation awareness, communication, etc.

Remember to create a relaxed teaching environment, as simulation can be a stressful experience for students. There follows a brief description of the reasons why simulation has become more popular as a teaching and assessment tool.

Medical Simulation

The first recorded use of a medical simulator is that of a manikin created in the 17 Century by a Dr Gregoire of Paris. He used a pelvis with skin stretched across it to simulate an abdomen, and with the help of a dead fetus explained assisted and complicated deliveries to midwives.

In spite of this early start, medical simulators had not really gained widespread use in the following centuries, principally for reasons of cost, reluctance to adopting new teaching methods, and scepticism that what was learned from a simulator could not be transferred to actual practice. All of these reasons are still relevant today, however the combination of improved technology and increased pressures on educators have promoted simulation as one option to address the following problems with traditional clinical skills teaching.

An Alternative to "see one, do one"

In the past, health care professionals learnt on the job, which some still believe is the best way to gain experience. However, there are a number of barriers to this type of traditional clinical teaching.

These include:

- Humanitarian issues – practicing on patients is not ethical. We have moved into an age of where learning on patients is not acceptable if there is an alternative.
- There has been a decrease in the number of inpatients. In part due to an increasing number of day case patients and also the fact that chronic conditions are being cared for in the community. This has led to a decrease in exposure and access of the trainees to ward patients.
- The training time for postgraduate medical education has decreased and will decrease further. With the

implementation of new training schemes, experience cannot be built upon over time as before.

- Some situations are so rare that to gain experience would take many lifetimes.
- Legal/litigation issues. The possibility of educational establishments being sued by patients and ex-students for not teaching and assessing clinical skills as laid down by the regulatory bodies could arise.
- Record keeping, reproducibility, assessment and validity are issues all brought to the forefront with clinical governance and revalidation. Simulation is seen as away of addressing some of these issues.
- Students learn more effectively in a non-threatening environment.
- There is increasing emphasis on multidisciplinary learning, and clinical skills' teaching is an ideal forum for this.
- The increase in workload for health care staff means there is less time to spend on traditional clinical teaching, which is compounded by the increase in student numbers.

Recent Recommendations

Simulation training extends from part task trainers, procedural training to the experience of full clinical situations. For example canulation, basic and advanced life support to high fidelity simulators.

However, they also include communication skills, how to take consent, bereavement counseling and IT skills. In 'Tomorrow's doctors: Recommendations on undergraduate medical education.'

GMC July 2002, there are lists of clinical skills that medical students have to be competent in before graduation:

- "The essential skill that graduates need must be gained under supervision. Medical schools must assess students' competence in these skills. The curriculum must stress the importance of communication skills and the other essential skills of medical practice."

In 'Unfinished Business: Proposals for reform of the Senior House Officer grade.' A report by Sir Liam Donaldson, Chief Medical Officer for England, proposed changes in junior doctor training which were considerable.

With a shortened training period and the probable division of service commitment from effective training time, the provision of effective skills training and competency-based assessment will have to be addressed.

- "An objective of the foundation programme would be to develop and enhance core or generic clinical skills essential for all doctors (*e.g.*, team-working, communication, ability to produce high standards of clinical governance and patient safety, expertise in accessing, appraising and using evidence as well as time management skills.)"

Multidisciplinary Teaching

As well as increased emphasis on clinical skill teaching, there is increased emphasis on the multidisciplinary approach to learning. Of interest during multidisciplinary teaching are human factors such as decision-making and behavioural interaction, which is thought to be of major importance in the occurrence of critical incidents.

As quoted in 'Working Together – learning Together' A Framework for Lifelong Learning for the NHS. DoH, November 2001:

- "We are taking forward work to develop more pre-registration inter professional education programmes which incorporate common learning in core skills and knowledge. As a minimum we intend to ensure that all health professionals should expect their education and training to include common learning with other professions."

This emphasises that predetermined health care groups deliver many of the skills required by patients during their care, however in the future who delivers these skills may well change. It is envisaged that simulation teaching could provide packages that any group could access and interact with other groups for relevant multidisciplinary situations.

APPLICATIONS

Applications for machine learning include:

- machine perception
- computer vision
- natural language processing
- syntactic pattern recognition
- search engines
- medical diagnosis
- bioinformatics
- brain-machine interfaces
- cheminformatics
- Detecting credit card fraud
- stock market analysis
- Classifying DNA sequences
- speech and handwriting recognition
- object recognition in computer vision
- game playing
- software engineering
- adaptive websites
- robot locomotion
- structural health monitoring.

In 2006, the on-line movie company Netflix held the first "Netflix Prize" competition to find a programme to better predict user preferences and beat its existing Netflix movie recommendation system by at least 10%. The AT&T Research Team BellKor beat out several other teams with their machine learning programme "Pragmatic Chaos". After winning several minor prizes, it won the grand prize competition in 2009 for $1 million.

Software

RapidMiner, KNIME, Weka, ODM, Shogun toolbox, Orange, Apache Mahout and MCMLL are software suites containing a variety of machine learning algorithms.

Journals and Conferences

- *Machine Learning* (journal)
- *Journal of Machine Learning Research*
- *Neural Computation* (journal)
- International Conference on Machine Learning (ICML) (conference)
- Neural Information Processing Systems (NIPS) (conference)
- List of upcoming conferences in Machine Learning and Artificial Intelligence (conference).

5

Knowledge Representation and Reasoning

Knowledge representation (KR) and reasoning' is an area of artificial intelligence whose fundamental goal is to represent knowledge in a manner that facilitates inferencing (i.e. drawing conclusions) from knowledge. It analyzes how to formally think - how to use a symbol system to represent a domain of discourse (that which can be talked about), along with functions that allow inference (formalized reasoning) about the objects.

Generally speaking, some kind of logic is used both to supply formal semantics of how reasoning functions apply to symbols in the domain of discourse, as well as to how to supply operators such as quantifiers, modal operators, etc. that, along with an interpretation theory, give meaning to the sentences in the logic. When we design a knowledge representation (and a knowledge representation system to interpret sentences in the logic in order to derive inferences from them) we have to make choices across a number of design spaces. The single most important decision to be made, is the *expressivity* of the KR.

The more expressive, the easier and more compact it is to "say something". However, more expressive languages are harder to automatically derive inferences from. An example of a less expressive KR would be propositional logic. An example of a more expressive KR would be autoepistemic temporal modal logic. Less expressive KRs may be both complete and consistent (formally less expressive than set theory). More expressive KRs may be neither complete nor consistent. The key problem is to find a KR and a supporting reasoning system that can make the inferences your application needs within the resource constraints appropriate to the problem at hand. Recent developments in KR have been driven by the Semantic Web, and have included development of XML-based knowledge representation languages and standards, including Resource Description Framework (RDF), RDF Schema, Topic Maps, DARPA Agent Markup Language (DAML), Ontology Inference Layer (OIL), and Web Ontology Language (OWL).

OVERVIEW

In field there are a number of representation techniques such as frames, rules, tagging, and semantic networks which have originated from theories of human information processing. Since knowledge is used to achieve intelligent behaviour, the fundamental goal of knowledge representation is to represent knowledge in a manner which will facilitate reasoning (aka inferencing or drawing conclusions); knowledge representation and reasoning being seen as two sides of a coin. A good knowledge representation must be both declarative and procedural knowledge. What is knowledge representation can best be understood in terms of five distinct roles it plays, each crucial to the task at hand :

- A knowledge representation (KR) is most fundamentally a surrogate, a substitute for the thing itself, used to enable an entity to determine consequences by thinking rather than acting, i.e., by reasoning about the world rather than taking action in it.
- It is a set of ontological commitments, i.e., an answer to the question: In what terms should I think about the world?
- It is a fragmentary theory of intelligent reasoning, expressed in terms of three components: (i) the representation's fundamental conception of intelligent reasoning; (ii) the set of inferences the representation sanctions; and (iii) the set of inferences it recommends.

- It is a medium for pragmatically efficient computation, i.e., the computational environment in which thinking is accomplished. One contribution to this pragmatic efficiency is supplied by the guidance a representation provides for organizing information so as to facilitate making the recommended inferences.
- It is a medium of human expression, i.e., a language in which we say things about the world."

Some issues that arise in knowledge representation from an AI perspective are:

- How do people represent knowledge?
- What is the nature of knowledge?
- Should a representation scheme deal with a particular domain or should it be general purpose?
- How expressive is a representation scheme or formal language?
- Should the scheme be declarative or procedural?

There has been very little top-down discussion of the knowledge representation (KR) issues and research in this area is a well aged quillwork. There are well known problems such as "spreading activation" (this is a problem in navigating a network of nodes), "subsumption" (this is concerned with selective inheritance; e.g. an ATV can be thought of as a specialization of a car but it inherits only particular characteristics) and "classification." For example a tomato could be classified both as a fruit and a vegetable. In the field of artificial intelligence, problem solving can be simplified by an appropriate choice of *knowledge representation*. Representing knowledge in some ways makes certain problems easier to solve. For example, it is easier to divide numbers represented in Hindu-Arabic numerals than numbers represented as Roman numerals.

CHARACTERISTICS

A good knowledge representation covers six basic characteristics:

- Coverage, which means the KR covers a breath and depth of information. Without a wide coverage, the KR cannot determine anything or resolve ambiguities.
- Understandable by humans. KR is viewed as a natural language, so the logic should flow freely. It should support modularity and hierarchies of classes (Polar bears are bears, which are animals). It should also have simple primitives that combine in complex forms.
- Consistency. If John closed the door, it can also be interpreted as the door was closed by John. By being consistent, the KR can eliminate redundant or conflicting knowledge.
- Efficient
- Easy to modify and update.
- Supports the intelligent activity which uses the knowledge base

To gain a better understanding of why these characteristics represent a good knowledge representation, think about how an encyclopedia (e.g. Wikipedia) is structured. There are millions of articles (coverage), and they are sorted into categories, content types, and similar topics (understandable). It redirects different titles but same content to the same article (consistency). It is efficient, easy to add new pages or update existing ones, and allows users on their mobile phones and desktops to view its knowledge base.

HISTORY OF KNOWLEDGE REPRESENTATION AND REASONING

In computer science, particularly artificial intelligence, a number of representations have been devised to structure information. KR is most commonly used to refer to representations intended for processing by modern computers, and in particular, for representations consisting of explicit objects (the class of all elephants, or Clyde a certain individual), and of assertions or claims about them ('Clyde is an elephant', or 'all elephants are grey'). Representing knowledge in such explicit form enables computers to draw conclusions from knowledge already stored ('Clyde is grey'). Many KR methods were tried in the 1970s and early 1980s, such as heuristic question-answering, neural networks, theorem proving, and expert systems, with varying success. Medical diagnosis (e.g., Mycin) was a major application area, as were games such as chess.

In the 1980s formal computer knowledge representation languages and systems arose. Major projects attempted to encode wide bodies of general knowledge; for example the "Cyc" project (still ongoing) went through a large encyclopedia, encoding not the information itself, but the information a reader would need in order to understand the encyclopedia: naive physics; notions of time, causality, motivation; commonplace objects and classes of objects.

Through such work, the difficulty of KR came to be better appreciated. In computational linguistics, meanwhile, much larger databases of language information were being built, and these, along with great increases in computer speed and capacity, made deeper KR more feasible.

Several programming languages have been developed that are oriented to KR. Prolog developed in 1972, but popularized much later, represents propositions and basic logic, and can derive conclusions from known premises. KL-ONE (1980s) is more specifically aimed at knowledge representation itself. In 1995, the Dublin Core standard of metadata was conceived. In the electronic document world, languages were being developed to represent the structure of documents, such as SGML (from which HTML descended) and later XML.

These facilitated information retrieval and data mining efforts, which have in recent years begun to relate to knowledge representation. Development of the Semantic Web, has included development of XML-based knowledge representation languages and standards, including RDF, RDF Schema, Topic Maps, DARPA Agent Markup Language (DAML), Ontology Inference Layer (OIL), and Web Ontology Language (OWL).

TOPICS IN KNOWLEDGE REPRESENTATION AND REASONING

Language and Notation

Some think it is best to represent knowledge in the same way that it is represented in the human mind, or to represent knowledge in the form of human language. Psycholinguistics investigates how the human mind stores and manipulates language. Other branches of cognitive science examine how human memory stores sounds, sights, smells, emotions, procedures, and abstract ideas. Science has not yet completely described the internal mechanisms of the brain to the point where they can simply be replicated by computer programmers. Various artificial languages and notations have been proposed for representing knowledge. They are typically based on logic and mathematics, and have easily parsed grammars to ease machine processing. They usually fall into the broad domain of ontologies.

Ontology Engineering

After CycL, a number of ontology languages have been developed. Most are declarative languages, and are either frame languages, or are based on first-order logic. Most of these languages only define an upper ontology with generic concepts, whereas the domain concepts are not part of the language definition. These languages all use special-purpose knowledge engineering because as stated by Tom Gruber, "Every ontology is a treaty- a social agreement among people with common motive in sharing." There are always many competing and differing views that make any general purpose ontology impossible.

A general purpose ontology would have to be applicable in any domain and different areas of knowledge need to be unified. Gellish English is an example of an ontological language that includes a full engineering English Dictionary. There is a long history of work attempting to build good ontologies for a variety of task domains, including early work on an ontology for liquids, the lumped element model widely used in representing electronic circuits (e.g.,), as well as ontologies for time, belief, and even programming itself. Each of these offers a way to see some part of the world. The lumped element model, for instance, suggests that we think of circuits in terms of components with connections between them, with signals flowing instantaneously along the connections. This is a useful view, but not the only possible one. A different ontology arises if we need to attend to the electrodynamics in the device: Here signals propagate at finite speed and an object (like a resistor) that was previously viewed as a single component with an I/O behaviour may now have to be thought of as an extended medium through which an electromagnetic wave flows.

Ontologies can of course be written down in a wide variety of languages and notations (e.g., logic, LISP, etc.); the essential information is not the form of that language but the content, i.e., the set of concepts offered as a way of thinking about the world. Simply put, the important part is notions like connections and components, not whether we choose to write them as predicates or LISP constructs. The commitment we make by selecting one or another ontology can produce a sharply different view of the task at hand. Consider the difference that arises in selecting the lumped element view of a circuit rather than the electrodynamic view of the same device. As a second example, medical diagnosis viewed in terms of rules (e.g., MYCIN) looks substantially different from the same task viewed in terms of frames (e.g., INTERNIST). Where MYCIN sees the medical world as made up of empirical associations connecting symptom to disease, INTERNIST sees a set of prototypes, in particular prototypical diseases, to be matched against the case at hand.

Commitment Begins with the Earliest Choices

The interest example also demonstrates that there is significant and unavoidable ontological commitment even at the level of the familiar representation technologies. Logic, rules, frames, etc., each embody a viewpoint on the kinds of things that are important in the world. Logic, for instance, involves a (fairly minimal) commitment to viewing the world in terms of individual entities and relations between them. Rule-based systems view the world in terms of attribute-object-value triples and the rules of plausible inference that connect them, while frames have us thinking in terms of prototypical objects. Each of these thus supplies its own view of what is important to attend to, and each suggests, conversely, that anything not easily seen in those terms may be ignored. This is of course not guaranteed to be correct, since anything ignored may later prove to be relevant. But the task is hopeless in principle—every representation ignores something about the world—hence the best we can do is start with a good guess. The existing representation technologies supply one set of guesses about what to attend to and what to ignore. Selecting any of them thus involves a degree of ontological commitment: the selection will have a significant impact on our perception of and approach to the task, and on our perception of the world being modeled.

REASONING

To reason is to draw inferences appropriate to the situation in hand. Inferences are classified as either deductive or inductive. An example of the former is "Fred is either in the museum or the cafe; he isn't in the cafe; so he's in the museum", and of the latter "Previous accidents just like this one have been caused by instrument failure; so probably this one was caused by instrument failure".

The difference between the two is that in the deductive case, the truth of the premises guarantees the truth of the conclusion, whereas in the inductive case, the truth of the premises lends support to the conclusion that the accident was caused by instrument failure, but nevertheless further investigation might reveal that, despite the truth of the premises, the conclusion is in fact false. There has been considerable success in programming computers to draw inferences, especially deductive inferences.

However, a programme cannot be said to reason simply in virtue of being able to draw inferences. Reasoning involves drawing inferences that are relevant to the task or situation in hand. One of the hardest problems confronting AI is that of giving computers the ability to distinguish the relevant from the irrelevant.

Types of Problems

A huge variety of types of problem is addressed in AI. Some examples are: finding winning moves in board games; identifying people from their photographs; and planning series of movements that enable a robot to carry out a given task. Problem-solving methods divide into special-purpose and general-purpose. A special-purpose method is tailor-made for a particular problem, and often exploits very specific features of the situation in which the problem is embedded. A general-purpose method is applicable to a wide range of different problems.

One general-purpose technique used in AI is means-end analysis, which involves the step-by-step reduction of the difference between the current state and the goal state. The programme selects actions from a list of means--which in the case of, say, a simple robot, might consist of pickup, putdown, move forward, move back, move left, and move right-until the current state is transformed into the goal state.

Environmental Perception

In perception the environment is scanned by means of various sense-organs, real or artificial, and processes internal to the perceiver analyse the scene into objects and their features and relationships. Analysis is complicated by the fact that one and the same object may present many different appearances on different occasions, depending on the angle from which it is viewed, whether or not parts of it are projecting shadows, and so forth. At present, artificial perception is sufficiently well advanced to enable a self-controlled car-like device to drive at moderate speeds on the open road, and a mobile robot to roam through a suite of busy offices searching for and clearing away empty soda cans.

Language system

A language is a system of signs having meaning by convention. Traffic signs, for example, form a mini-language, it being a matter of convention that, for example, the hazard-ahead sign means hazard ahead.

This meaning-by-convention that is distinctive of language is very different from what is called natural meaning, exemplified in statements like 'An important characteristic of full-fledged human languages, such as English, which distinguishes them from, *e.g.* bird calls and systems of traffic signs, is their productivity. A productive language is one that is rich enough to enable an unlimited number of different sentences to be formulated within it.

It is relatively easy to write computer programmes that are able, in severely restricted contexts, to respond in English, seemingly fluently, to questions and statements, for example the Parry and Shrdlu programmes described in the section Early AI Programmes. However, neither Parry nor Shrdlu actually understands language.

An appropriately programmed computer can use language without understanding it, in principle even to the point where the computer's linguistic behaviour is indistinguishable from that of a native human speaker of the language. What, then, is involved in genuine understanding, if a computer that uses language indistinguishably from a native human speaker does not necessarily understand?

There is no universally agreed answer to this difficult question. According to one theory, whether or not one understands depends not only upon one's behaviour but also upon one's history: in order to be said to understand one must have learned the language and have been trained to take one's place in the linguistic community by means of interaction with other language-users. In order to classify machines as "thinking", it is necessary to define intelligence. To what degree does intelligence consist of, for example, solving complex problems, or making generalizations and relationships? And what about perception and comprehension? Research into the areas of learning, of language, and of sensory perception have aided scientists in building intelligent machines. One of the most challenging approaches facing experts is building systems that mimic the behaviour of the human brain, made up of billions of neurons, and arguably the most complex matter in the universe. Perhaps the best way to gauge the intelligence of a machine is British computer scientist Alan Turing's test.

Artificial Intelligence has come a long way from its early roots, driven by dedicated researchers. The beginnings of AI reach back before electronics, to philosophers and mathematicians such as Boole and others theorizing on principles that were used as the foundation of AI Logic. AI really began to intrigue researchers with the invention of the computer in 1943.

The technology was finally available, or so it seemed, to simulate intelligent behaviour. Over the next four decades, despite many stumbling blocks, AI has grown from a dozen researchers, to thousands of engineers and specialists; and from programmes capable of playing checkers, to systems designed to diagnose disease. AI has always been on the pioneering end of computer science.

Advanced-level computer languages, as well as computer interfaces and word-processors owe their existence to the research into artificial intelligence. The theory and insights brought about by AI research will set the trend in the future of computing. The products available today are only bits and pieces of what are soon to follow, but they are a movement towards the future of artificial intelligence. The advancements in the quest for artificial intelligence have, and will continue to affect our jobs, our education, and our lives.

Representation

Another definition is concerned with the performance of machines which 'historically have been judged to lie within the domain of intelligence'. None of these definitions or the like have been universally accepted, perhaps because of their references to the word 'intelligence', which at present is an abstract and immeasurable quantity. A better definition of artificial intelligence, therefore, calls for formalization of the term 'intelligence'.

Psychologist and Cognitive theorists are of the opinion that intelligence helps in identifying the right piece of knowledge at the appropriate instances of decision making. A system capable of planning and executing the right task at the right time is generally called rational.

Thus, AI alternatively may be stated as a subject dealing with computational models that can think and act rationally 1, 2, 3, 4. A common question then naturally arises: A little thinking, however, reveals that a system that can reason well must be a successful planner, as planning in many circumstances is part of a reasoning process. Further, a system can act rationally only after acquiring adequate knowledge from the real world.

So, perception that stands for building up of knowledge from real world information is a prerequisite feature for rational actions. One step further thinking envisages that a machine without learning capability cannot possess perception. The rational action of an agent (actor), thus, calls for possession of all the elementary characteristics of intelligence. Relating artificial intelligence with the computational models capable of thinking and acting rationally, therefore, has a pragmatic significance.

Approach to problems

Problems dealt with in artificial intelligence generally use a common term called 'state'. A state represents a status of the solution at a given step of the problem solving procedure. The solution of a problem, thus, is a collection of the problem states. The problem solving procedure applies an operator to a state to get the next state.The process of applying an operator to a state and its subsequent transition to the next state, thus, is continued until the goal (desired) state is derived. Such a method of solving a problem is generally referred to as statespace approach. We will first discuss the state-space approach for problem solving by a well-known problem, which most of us perhaps have solved in our childhood.

PROOF SYSTEMS

Boyer-Moore Theorem Prover (NQTHM)

The design of this system was influenced by John McCarthy and Woody Bledsoe. Started in 1971 at Edinburgh, Scotland, this was a fully automatic theorem prover built using Pure Lisp. The main aspects of NQTHM were:

1. the use of Lisp as a working logic.
2. the reliance on a principle of definition for total recursive functions.
3. the extensive use of rewriting and "symbolic evaluation".
4. an induction heuristic based the failure of symbolic evaluation.

HOL Light

Written in Objective CAML, HOL Light is designed to have a simple and clean logical foundation and an uncluttered implementation. It is essentially another proof assistant for classical higher order logic.

Coq

Developed in France, Coq is another automated proof assistant, which can automatically extract executable programmes from specifications, as either Objective CAML or Haskell source code. Properties, programmes and proofs are formalized in the same language called the Calculus of Inductive Constructions (CIC).

Applications

Automated reasoning has been most commonly used to build automated theorem provers. In some cases such provers have come up with new approaches to proving a theorem. Logic Theorist is a good example of this. The programme came up with a proof for one of the theorems in Principia Mathematica which was more efficient (less number of steps for solving a theorem) than the one provided by Whitehead and Russel. Automated reasoning programmes are being applied to solve a growing number of problems in formal logic, mathematics and computer science, logic programming, software and hardware verification, circuit design, and many others, "Automated Reasoning. The TPTP (Sutcliffe and Suttner 1998) is a library of such problems that is updated on a regular basis. There is also a competition among automated theorem provers held regularly at the CADE conference (Pelletier, Sutcliffe and Suttner 2002); the problems for the competition are selected from the TPTP library.

THE COMMITMENTS ACCUMULATE IN LAYERS

The ontologic commitment of a representation thus begins at the level of the representation technologies and accumulates from there. Additional layers of commitment are made as we put the technology to work. The use of frame-like structures in INTERNIST offers an illustrative example. At the most fundamental level, the decision to view diagnosis in terms of frames suggests thinking in terms of prototypes, defaults, and a taxonomic hierarchy. But prototypes of what, and how shall the taxonomy be organized? An early description of the system shows how these questions were answered in the task at hand, supplying the second layer of commitment: The knowledge base underlying the INTERNIST system is composed of two basic types of elements: disease entities and manifestations.... [It] also contains a...hierarchy of disease categories, organized primarily around the concept of organ systems, having at the top level such categories as "liver disease," "kidney disease," etc.

The prototypes are thus intended to capture prototypical diseases (e.g., a "classic case" of a disease), and they will be organized in a taxonomy indexed around organ systems. This is a sensible and intuitive set of choices but clearly not the only way to apply frames to the task; hence it is another layer of ontological commitment. At the third (and in this case final) layer, this set of choices is instantiated: which diseases will be included and in which branches of the hierarchy will they appear? Ontologic questions that arise even at this level can be quite fundamental. Consider for example determining which of the following are to be considered diseases (i.e., abnormal states requiring cure): alcoholism, homosexuality, and chronic fatigue syndrome. The ontologic commitment here is sufficiently obvious and sufficiently important that it is often a subject of debate in the field itself, quite independent of building automated reasoners. Similar sorts of decisions have to be made with all the representation technologies, because each of them supplies only a first order guess about how to see the world: they offer a way of seeing but don't indicate how to instantiate that view. As frames suggest prototypes and taxonomies but do not tell us which things to select as prototypes, rules suggest thinking in terms of plausible inferences, but don't tell us which plausible inferences to attend to. Similarly logic tells us to view the world in terms of individuals and relations, but does not specify which individuals and relations to use. Commitment to a particular view of the world thus starts with the choice of a representation technology, and accumulates as subsequent choices are made about how to see the world in those terms.

Reminder: A KR is not a data structure. Note that at each layer, even the first (e.g., selecting rules or frames), the choices being made are about representation, not data structures. Part of what makes a language representational is that it carries meaning, i.e., there is a correspondence between its constructs and things in the external world. That correspondence in turn carries with it constraint. A semantic net, for example, is a representation, while a graph is a data structure. They are different kinds of entities, even though one is invariably used to implement the other, precisely because the net has (should have) a semantics. That semantics will be manifest in part because it constrains the network topology: a network purporting to describe family memberships as we know them cannot have a cycle in its parent links, while graphs (i.e., data structures) are of course under no such constraint and may have arbitrary cycles. While every representation must be implemented in the machine by some data structure, the representational property is in the correspondence to something in the world and in the constraint that

Links and Structures

While hyperlinks have come into widespread use, the closely related semantic link is not yet widely used. The mathematical table has been used since Babylonian times.

More recently, these tables have been used to represent the outcomes of logic operations, such as truth tables, which were used to study and model Boolean logic, for example. Spreadsheets are yet another tabular representation of knowledge. Other knowledge representations are trees, graphs and hypergraphs, by means of which the connections among fundamental concepts and derivative concepts can be shown. Visual representations are relatively new in the field of knowledge management but give the user a way to visualise how one thought or idea is connected to other ideas enabling the possibility of moving from one thought to another in order to locate required information.

Notation

The recent fashion in knowledge representation languages is to use XML as the low-level syntax. This tends to make the output of these KR languages easy for machines to parse, at the expense of human readability and often space-efficiency. First-order predicate calculus is commonly used as a mathematical basis for these systems, to avoid excessive complexity. However, even simple systems based on this simple logic can be used to represent data that is well beyond the processing capability of current computer systems: see computability for reasons. Examples of notations:

- DATR is an example for representing lexical knowledge
- RDF is a simple notation for representing relationships between and among objects

Storage and Manipulation

One problem in knowledge representation is how to store and manipulate knowledge in an information system in a formal way so that it may be used by mechanisms to accomplish a given task. Examples of applications are expert systems, machine translation systems, computer-aided maintenance systems and information retrieval systems (including database front-ends). Semantic networks may be used to represent knowledge. Each node represents a concept and arcs are used to define relations between the concepts.

The Conceptual graph model is probably the oldest model still alive. One of the most expressive and comprehensively described knowledge representation paradigms along the lines of semantic networks is MultiNet (an acronym for Multilayered Extended Semantic Networks). From the 1960s, the knowledge frame or just *frame* has been used. Each frame has its own name and a set of attributes, or slots which contain values; for instance, the frame for *house* might contain a *color* slot, *number of floors* slot, etc.

Using frames for expert systems is an application of object-oriented programming, with inheritance of features described by the "is-a" link. However, there has been no small amount of inconsistency in the usage of the "is-a" link: Ronald J. Brachman wrote a paper titled "What IS-A is and isn't", wherein 29 different semantics were found in projects whose knowledge representation schemes involved an "is-a" link. Other links include the "part-of" link. Frame structures are well-suited for the representation of schematic knowledge and stereotypical cognitive patterns. The elements of such schematic patterns are weighted unequally, attributing higher weights to the more typical elements of a schema. A pattern is activated by certain expectations: If a person sees a big bird, he or she will classify it rather as a sea eagle than a golden eagle, assuming that his or her "sea-scheme" is currently activated and his "land-scheme" is not. Frame representations are object-centered in the same sense as semantic networks are: All the facts and properties connected with a concept are located in one place - there is no need for costly search processes in the database. A behavioural script is a type of frame that describes what happens temporally; the usual example given is that of describing going to a restaurant. The steps include waiting to be seated, receiving a menu, ordering, etc. The different solutions can be arranged in a so-called semantic spectrum with respect to their semantic expressivity.

AUTOMATED REASONING

Automated reasoning is an area of computer science dedicated to understand different aspects of reasoning. The study in automated reasoning helps produce software which allows computers to reason completely or nearly completely, automatically. Although automated reasoning is considered a sub field of artificial intelligence it also has connections with theoretical computer science and even philosophy. The most developed subareas of automated reasoning are automated theorem proving (and the less automated but more pragmatic subfield of interactive theorem proving) and automated proof checking (viewed as guaranteed correct reasoning under fixed assumptions).

Extensive work has also been done in reasoning by analogy induction and abduction. Other important topics are reasoning under uncertainty and non-monotonic reasoning. An important part of the uncertainty field is that of argumentation, where further constraints of minimality and consistency are applied on top of the more standard automated deduction. John Pollock's Oscar system is an example of an automated argumentation system that is more specific than being just an automated theorem prover. Tools and techniques of automated reasoning include the classical logics and calculi, fuzzy logic, Bayesian inference, reasoning with maximal entropy and a large number of less formal ad-hoc techniques.

EARLY YEARS

The development of formal logic played a big role in the field of automated reasoning which itself led to the development of Artificial Intelligence.

A formal proof is a proof in which every logical inference has been checked all the way back to the fundamental axioms of mathematics. All the intermediate logical steps are supplied, without exception. No appeal is made to intuition, even if the translation from intuition to logic is routine.

Thus, a formal proof is less intuitive, and less susceptible to logical errors. Constant revolutions and new discoveries in the field of computers gave great ideas to the logicians and computer scientists to build a machine which could prove the mathematical problems quicker and more efficiently than the human beings.

Some consider the Cornell Summer meeting of 1957 as the origin of the automated reasoning or automated deduction which brought together a large number of logicians and computer scientists. Others say that it began before that with the 1955 Logic Theorist programme of Newell, Shaw and Simon, or with Martin Davis' 1954 implementation of Presburger's decision procedure (which proved that the sum of two even numbers is even). Automated reasoning, although significant and popular area of research in the eighties and early nineties was left for dead.

The research in the field was difficult, costly and unscalable. Although the Government could pay to formally specify and check parts of their most critical space shuttle infrastructure, but was difficult for others to use to verify parts their own products. The renovation and interest of big companies and funded researchers in the automated reasoning revived the Automated Reasoning from the dead. For example, in 2005, Microsoft started using verification technology in many of their internal projects and is currently planning to include a logical specification and checking language in their next version of Visual C.

Significant Contributions

- Principia Mathematica was a milestone work in formal logic written by Alfred North Whitehead and Bertrand Russell. Principia Mathematica also meaning Principles of Mathematics was written with a purpose to derive all or some of the mathematical expressions, in terms of symbolic logic. Principia Mathematica was initially published in three volumes each in 1910, 1912 and 1913.
- Logic Theorist (LT) was the first ever programme developed in 1956 by Allen Newell, Cliff Shaw and Herbert Simon to "mimic human reasoning" in proving theorems and was demonstrated on fifty- two theorems from chapter two of Principia Mathematica written by Whitehead and Russell. LT proved thirty eight of them. Besides proving the theorems, the programme found a proof for one of the theorems which was more elegant than the one provided by Whitehead and Russel.After unsuccessful attempt of publishing their results Newell, Shaw and Herbert reported in their publication in 1958: The Next Advance in Operation Research:

  "There are now in the world machines that think, that learn and that create.

  Moreover, their ability to do there things is going to increase rapidly

  until < in a visible future < the range of problems they can handle will be

  co- extensive with the range to which the human mind has been applied."

PROBABILISTIC METHODS FOR UNCERTAIN REASONING

Many problems in AI (in reasoning, planning, learning, perception and robotics) require the agent to operate with incomplete or uncertain information. AI researchers have devised a number of powerful tools to solve these problems using methods from probability theory and economics. Bayesian networks are a very general tool that can be used for a large number of problems: reasoning (using the Bayesian inference algorithm), learning (using the expectation-maximization algorithm), planning (using decision networks) and perception (using dynamic Bayesian networks).

Probabilistic algorithms can also be used for filtering, prediction, smoothing and finding explanations for streams of data, helping perception systems to analyze processes that occur over time (e.g., hidden Markov models or Kalman filters). A key concept from the science of economics is "utility": a measure of how valuable something is to an intelligent agent. Precise mathematical tools have been developed that analyze how an agent can make choices and plan, using decision theory, decision analysis, information value theory. These tools include models such as Markov decision processes, dynamic decision networks, game theory and mechanism design.

Classifiers and Statistical Learning Methods

The simplest AI applications can be divided into two types: classifiers ("if shiny then diamond") and controllers ("if shiny then pick up"). Controllers do however also classify conditions before inferring actions, and therefore classification forms a central part of many AI systems. Classifiers are functions that use pattern matching to determine a closest match. They can be tuned according to examples, making them very attractive for use in AI. These examples are known as observations or patterns. In supervised learning, each pattern belongs to a certain predefined class. A class can be seen as a decision that has to be made. All the observations combined with their class labels are known as a data set. When a new observation is received, that observation is classified based on previous experience. A classifier can be trained in various ways; there are many statistical and machine learning approaches. The most widely used classifiers are the neural network, kernel methods such as the support vector machine, k-nearest neighbor algorithm, Gaussian mixture model, naive Bayes classifier, and decision tree. The performance of these classifiers have been compared over a wide range of tasks. Classifier performance depends greatly on the characteristics of the data to be classified. There is no single classifier that works best on all given problems; this is also referred to as the "no free lunch" theorem. Determining a suitable classifier for a given problem is still more an art than science.

Neural Networks

A neural network is an interconnected group of nodes, akin to the vast network of neurons in the human brain. The study of artificial neural networks began in the decade before the field AI research was founded, in the work of Walter Pitts and Warren McCullough. Other important early researchers were Frank Rosenblatt, who invented the perceptron and Paul Werbos who developed the backpropagation algorithm. The main categories of networks are acyclic or feedforward neural networks (where the signal passes in only one direction) and recurrent neural networks (which allow feedback). Among the most popular feedforward networks are perceptrons, multi-layer perceptrons and radial basis networks. Among recurrent networks, the most famous is the Hopfield net, a form of attractor network, which was first described by John Hopfield in 1982.[b] Neural networks can be applied to the problem of intelligent control (for robotics) or learning, using such techniques as Hebbian learning and competitive learning. Jeff Hawkins argues that research in neural networks has stalled because it has failed to model the essential properties of the neocortex, and has suggested a model (Hierarchical Temporal Memory) that is loosely based on neurological research.

Control Theory

Control theory, the grandchild of cybernetics, has many important applications, especially in robotics.

Languages

AI researchers have developed several specialized languages for AI research, including Lisp and Prolog.

Evaluating Progress

In 1950, Alan Turing proposed a general procedure to test the intelligence of an agent now known as the Turing test. This procedure allows almost all the major problems of artificial intelligence to be tested. However, it is a very difficult challenge and at present all agents fail. Artificial intelligence can also be evaluated on specific problems such as small problems in chemistry, hand-writing recognition and game-playing. Such tests have been termed subject matter expert Turing tests. Smaller problems provide more achievable goals and there are an ever-increasing number of positive results.

The broad classes of outcome for an AI test are: (1) Optimal: it is not possible to perform better. (2) Strong super-human: performs better than all humans. (3) Super-human: performs better than most humans. (4) Sub-human: performs worse than most humans. For example, performance at draughts is optimal, performance at chess is super-human and nearing strong super-human and performance at many everyday tasks (such as recognizing a face or crossing a room without bumping into something) is sub-human. A quite different approach measures machine intelligence through tests which are developed from *mathematical* definitions of intelligence. Examples of these kinds of tests start in the late nineties devising intelligence tests using notions from Kolmogorov complexity and data compression. Two major advantages of mathematical definitions are their applicability to nonhuman intelligences and their absence of a requirement for human testers.

6

Logic Programming

Logic programming is, in its broadest sense, the use of mathematical logic for computer programming. In this view of logic programming, which can be traced at least as far back as John McCarthy's [1958] advice-taker proposal, logic is used as a purely declarative representation language, and a theorem-prover or model-generator is used as the problem-solver. The problem-solving task is split between the programmer, who is responsible only for ensuring the truth of programmes expressed in logical form, and the theorem-prover or model-generator, which is responsible for solving problems efficiently. However, logic programming, in the narrower sense in which it is more commonly understood, is the use of logic as both a declarative and procedural representation language. It is based upon the fact that a backwards reasoning theorem-prover applied to declarative sentences in the form of implications:

If B_1 and ... and B_n then H

treats the implications as goal-reduction procedures:

to show/solve H, show/solve B_1 and ... and B_n.

For example, it treats the implication:

If you press the alarm signal button,

then you alert the driver of the train of a possible emergency

as the procedure:

To alert the driver of the train of a possible emergency,

press the alarm signal button.

Note that this is consistent with the BHK interpretation of constructive logic, where implication would be interpreted as a solution of problem H given solutions of $B_1 \ldots B_n$. However, the defining feature of logic programming is that sets of formulas can be regarded as programmes and *proof search* can be given a computational meaning. This is achieved by restricting the underlying logic to a "well-behaved" fragment such as Horn clauses or Hereditary Harrop formulas. As in the purely declarative case, the programmer is responsible for ensuring the truth of programmes. But since automated proof search is generally infeasible, logic programming as commonly understood *also* relies on the programmer to ensure that inferences are generated efficiently. In many cases, to achieve efficiency, one needs to be aware of and to exploit the problem-solving behaviour of the theorem-prover. In this respect, logic programming is comparable to conventional imperative programming; using programmes to control the behaviour of a programme executor. However, unlike conventional imperative programmes, which have only a procedural interpretation, logic programmes also have a declarative, logical interpretation, which helps to ensure their correctness. Moreover, such programmes, being declarative, are at a higher conceptual level than purely imperative programmes; and their programme executors, being theorem-provers, operate at a higher conceptual level than conventional compilers and interpreters.

HISTORY

Logic programming in the first and wider sense gave rise to a number of implementations, such as those by Fischer Black (1964), James Slagle (1965) and Cordell Green (1969), which were question-answering systems in the spirit of McCarthy's advice-taker. Foster and Elcock's Absys (1969), on the other hand, was probably the first language to be explicitly developed as an assertional programming language. Logic programming in the narrower sense can be traced back to debates in the late 1960s and early 1970s about declarative versus procedural representations of knowledge in Artificial Intelligence. Advocates of declarative representations were notably working at Stanford, associated with John McCarthy, Bertram Raphael and Cordell Green, and in Edinburgh, with J. Alan Robinson (an academic visitor from Syracuse University), Pat Hayes, and Bob Kowalski. Advocates of procedural representations were mainly centered at MIT, under the leadership of Marvin Minsky and Seymour Papert.

Although it was based on logic, Planner, developed at MIT, was the first language to emerge within this proceduralist paradigm [Hewitt, 1969]. Planner featured pattern directed invocation of procedural plans from goals (i.e. forward chaining) and from assertions (i.e. backward chaining). The most influential implementation of Planner was the subset of Planner, called Micro-Planner, implemented by Gerry Sussman, Eugene Charniak and Terry Winograd. It was used to implement Winograd's natural-language understanding programme SHRDLU, which was a landmark at that time. In order to cope with the very limited memory systems that were available when it was developed, Planner used backtracking control structure so that only one possible computation path had to be stored at a time. From Planner there developed the programming languages QA-4, Popler, Conniver, QLISP, and the concurrent language Ether. Hayes and Kowalski in Edinburgh tried to reconcile the logic-based declarative approach to knowledge representation with Planner's procedural approach. Hayes (1973) developed an equational language, Golux, in which different procedures could be obtained by altering the behaviour of the theorem prover. Kowalski, on the other hand, showed how SL-resolution treats implications as goal-reduction procedures. Kowalski collaborated with Colmerauer in Marseille, who developed these ideas in the design and implementation of the programming language Prolog.

From Prolog there developed, among others, the programming languages ALF, Fril, Gödel, Mercury, Oz, Ciao, Visual Prolog, XSB, and ëProlog, as well as a variety of concurrent logic programming languages, constraint logic programming languages and datalog. In 1997, the Association of Logic Programming bestowed to fifteen recognized researchers in logic programming the title *Founders of Logic Programming* to recognize them as pioneers in the field. The individuals receiving this honor were: Maurice Bruynooghe (Belgium), Jacques Cohen (USA), Alain Colmerauer (France), Keith Clark (UK), Veronica Dahl (Canada/Argentina), Maarten van Emden (Canada), Herve Gallaire (France), Robert Kowalski (UK), Jack Minker (USA), Fernando Pereira (USA), Luis Moniz Pereira (Portugal), Ray Reiter (Canada), Alan Robinson (USA), Peter Szeredi (Hungary), and David H.D. Warren (UK).

Prolog

The programming language Prolog was developed in 1972 by Alain Colmerauer. It emerged from a collaboration between Colmerauer in Marseille and Robert Kowalski in Edinburgh. Colmerauer was working on natural language understanding, using logic to represent semantics and using resolution for question-answering. During the summer of 1971, Colmerauer and Kowalski discovered that the clausal form of logic could be used to represent formal grammars and that resolution theorem provers could be used for parsing. They observed that some theorem provers, like hyper-resolution, behave as bottom-up parsers and others, like SL-resolution (1971), behave as top-down parsers. It was in the following summer of 1972, that Kowalski, again working with Colmerauer, developed the procedural interpretation of implications. This dual declarative/ procedural interpretation later became formalised in the Prolog notation

$H \text{ :- } B_1, \ldots, B_n.$

which can be read (and used) both declaratively and procedurally. It also became clear that such clauses could be restricted to definite clauses or Horn clauses, where H, B_1, ..., B_n are all atomic predicate logic formulae, and that SL-resolution could be restricted (and generalised) to LUSH or SLD-resolution. Kowalski's procedural interpretation and LUSH were described in a 1973 memo, published in 1974. Colmerauer, with Philippe Roussel, used this dual interpretation of clauses as the basis of Prolog, which was implemented in the summer and autumn of 1972. The first Prolog programme, also written in 1972 and implemented in Marseille, was a French question-answering system. The use of Prolog as a practical programming language was given great momentum by the development of a compiler by David Warren in Edinburgh in 1977. Experiments demonstrated that Edinburgh Prolog could compete with the processing speed of other symbolic programming languages such as Lisp. Edinburgh Prolog became the *de facto* standard and strongly influenced the definition of ISO standard Prolog.

Negation as Failure

Micro-Planner had a construct, called "thnot", which when applied to an expression returns the value true if (and only if) the evaluation of the expression fails. An equivalent operator is normally built-in in modern Prolog's implementations and has been called "negation as failure". It is normally written as not(p), where p is an atom whose variables normally have been instantiated by the time not(p) is invoked. A more cryptic (but standard) syntax is \+ p . Negation as failure literals can occur as conditions not(B_i) in the body of programme clauses. The logical status of negation as failure was unresolved until Keith Clark [1978] showed that, under certain natural conditions, it is a correct (and sometimes complete) implementation of classical negation with respect to the completion of the programme. Completion amounts roughly to regarding the set of all the programme clauses with the same predicate on the left hand side, say

H :- $Body_1$.

...

H :- $Body_k$.

as a definition of the predicate

H iff ($Body_1$ or ... or $Body_k$)

where "iff" means "if and only if". Writing the completion also requires explicit use of the equality predicate and the inclusion of a set of appropriate axioms for equality.

However, the implementation of negation by failure needs only the if-halves of the definitions without the axioms of equality. The notion of completion is closely related to McCarthy's circumscription semantics for default reasoning, and to the closed world assumption. As an alternative to the completion semantics, negation as failure can also be interpreted epistemically, as in the stable model semantics of answer set programming. In this interpretation not(B_i) means literally that B_i is not known or not believed. The epistemic interpretation has the advantage that it can be combined very simply with classical negation, as in "extended logic programming", to formalise such phrases as "the contrary can not be shown", where "contrary" is classical negation and "can not be shown" is the epistemic interpretation of negation as failure.

Problem Solving

In the simplified, propositional case in which a logic programme and a top-level atomic goal contain no variables, backward reasoning determines an and-or tree, which constitutes the search space for solving the goal. The top-level goal is the root of the tree. Given any node in the tree and any clause whose head matches the node, there exists a set of child nodes corresponding to the sub-goals in the body of the clause. These child nodes are grouped together by an "and". The alternative sets of children corresponding to alternative ways of solving the node are grouped together by an "or". Any search strategy can be used to search this space. Prolog uses a sequential, last-in-first-out, backtracking strategy, in which only one alternative and one sub-goal is considered at a time. Other search strategies, such as parallel search, intelligent backtracking, or best-first search to find an optimal solution, are also possible. In the more general case, where sub-goals share variables, other strategies can be used, such as choosing the subgoal that is most highly instantiated or that is sufficiently instantiated so that only one procedure applies. Such strategies are used, for example, in concurrent logic programming. The fact that there are alternative ways of executing a logic programme has been characterised by the equation:

Algorithm = Logic + Control

where "Logic" represents a logic programme and "Control" represents different theorem-proving strategies.

Knowledge Representation

The fact that Horn clauses can be given a procedural interpretation and, vice versa, that goal-reduction procedures can be understood as Horn clauses + backward reasoning means that logic programmes combine declarative and procedural representations of knowledge.

The inclusion of negation as failure means that logic programming is a kind of non-monotonic logic. Despite its simplicity compared with classical logic, this combination of Horn clauses and negation as failure has proved to be surprisingly expressive. For example, it has been shown to correspond, with some further extensions, quite naturally to the semi-formal language of legislation. It is also a natural language for expressing common-sense laws of cause and effect, as in the situation calculus and event calculus.

PROLOG PROGRAMMING

Let us, for instance, consider the problem of a 'classroom scene' interpretation.We assume that the scene has been passed through various stages of low and medium level image processing and the objects in the scene thus have been recognized and labeled by a computing machine.

The data (clauses) received from the scene and the knowledge used to analyse it are presented in both English and Predicate Logic below.

Database:

```
Object (board)
Writes-on (john, board, classhour)
Sits-on (mita, bench, classhour)
Sits-on (rita, bench, classhour)
Person (john)
```

```
Person (rita)
Person (mita)
The above are called clauses in PROLOG.
```

Logic Programmes-A Formal Definition

We are now in a position to formally define Logic Programmes. We first define a Horn clause, the constituents of a logic programme

Definition

A clause consists of two parts: the head and the body. One side of the clause to which the arrowhead (if-then operator) points to is called the head and the other side of it is called the body. A Horn clause contains at most one literal (proposition/ predicate) at the head of the clause.

Example

The following are two examples of Horn clauses:

- P (X), Q (Y) → W (X,Y)
- R (X, Y), Q (Y) → ?

In (i) W (X, Y) is the head and P (X), Q (Y) is the body. In (ii) R(X, Y), Q(Y) is the body and the head comprises of a null clause (sub-clause). In fact (ii) represents a query, asking whether R (X, Y), Q (Y) is true, or what are the set of instantiations for X and Y, which makes R (X, Y)^Q (Y) true.

A Logic Programme is a programme, comprising of Horn clauses.

The following example illustrates a logic programme:

Example: Consider the following two sentences in Predicate Logic with one head clause in each sentence.

Father (X, Y) ← Child (Y, X), Male (X).

Son (Y, X) ← Child (Y, X), Male (Y).

The above two clauses being horn clauses are constituents of a Logic Programme. Let us now assume that along with the above knowledge, we have the following three data clauses:

Child (ram, dasaratha).

Male (ram).

Male (dasaratha).

Suppose that the above set of clauses is properly structured in PROLOG and the programme is then compiled and executed. If we now submit the following queries (goals), the system responds correctly as follows.

- Goal: Father (X, Y)

Response: Father (dasaratha, ram).

- Goal: Son (Y, X)

Response: Son (ram, dasaratha).

But how does the system respond to our queries? Before that let us learn a little bit of syntax of PROLOG programmes. We take up the scene interpretation problem as an example to learn the syntax of PROLOG programming.

Scene Interpretation Programme

```
/* PROLOG PROGRAMME FOR SCENE INTERPRETATION
*/
Domains
Time, X, Y, Z, W, board, classhour, bench =
symbol
Predicates
Teacher (X)
Writes-on (X, board, Time)
Equal (Time, classhour)
Person (X) Person (Y) Person (Z) Person (W)
Sits-on (Y, bench, Time) Sits-on (Z, bench,
Time)
Student (Y)
Student (Z)
Object (W)
Clauses
Object (board). 1
Writes-on (john, board, classhour). 2
Male (dasaratha).
```

```
Sits-on (mita, bench, classhour). 3
Sits-on (rita, bench, classhour). 4
Person (john). 5
Person (mita). 6
Person (rita). 7
Equal (Time, classhour):- 8
Object (board),
Writes-on (X, board, Time),
Teacher (X).
Equal (Time, classhour):- 9
Person (Y),
Sits-on (Y, bench, classhour),
Person (X),
Writes-on (X, board, Time).
Teacher (X):- 10
Person (X),
Writes-on (X, board, classhour).
Student (Y):- 11
Person (Y),
Sits-on (Y, bench, Time),
Equal (Time, classhour).
```

This is all about the programme. Readers may note that we mentioned no procedure to solve the problem of scene interpretation; rather we stated the facts only in the programme. Here lies the significance of a logic programme.

Now, suppose, the user makes a query:

Goal: Teacher (X)?

System prompts: Teacher (john).

Further, if the user asks:

Goal: Equal (Time, classhour) ?

System prompts: Yes.

BACKTRACKING

To explain how the system answers these queries, we have to learn a very useful phenomenon, called backtracking. Let us now concentrate on the query: Teacher (X), Since

```
Teacher (X)
    Person (X),
    Writes-on (X, board, classhour).
```

To satisfy the Goal: Teacher (X), one has to satisfy the sub-goals: Person (X), Writes-on (X, board, classhour). Now, PROLOG searches a sub-goal Person() for the predicate Person (X). At clause 5, it finds a match and X is instantiated to john. PROLOG puts a marker at clause 5.

Now, it continues searching Writes-on (john, board, classhour) in the remaining clauses. But it fails to find so, since Writes-on is at 2nd position in the list of clauses. So, it has to trace back above the marker place and then ultimately it finds Writes-on (john, board, classhour). Since the sub-goals are succeeded, the goal also succeeds, yielding a solution.

For answering the query Equal (Time, classhour), a number of backtracking is required. We omit this for space constraints and ask the reader to study it herself. The next important issue that we will learn is SLD (Select Linear Definite clauses) resolution.

THE NEATS: LOGIC, PROLOG AND EXPERT SYSTEMS

Logic was introduced into AI research as early as 1958, by John McCarthy in his Advice Taker proposal. In 1963, J. Alan Robinson had discovered a simple method to implement deduction on computers, the resolution and unification algorithm.

However, straightforward implementations, like those attempted by McCarthy and his students in the late 60s, were especially intractable: the programmes required astronomical numbers of steps to prove simple theorems. A more fruitful approach to logic was developed in the 70s by Robert Kowalski at the University of Edinburgh, and soon this led to the collaboration with French researchers Alain Colmerauer and Phillipe Roussel who created the successful logic programming language Prolog. Prolog uses a subset of logic (Horn clauses, closely related to "rules" and "production rules") that permit tractable computation. Rules would continue to be influential, providing a foundation for Edward Feigenbaum's expert systems and the continuing work by Alan Newell and Herbert Simon that would lead to Soar and their unified theories of cognition. Critics of the logical approach noted, as Dreyfus had, that human beings rarely used logic when they solved problems. Experiments by psychologists like Peter Wason, Eleanor Rosch, Amos Tversky, Daniel Kahneman and others provided proof. McCarthy responded that what people do is irrelevant. He argued that what is really needed are machines that can solve problems—not machines that think as people do.

The Scruffies: Frames and Scripts

Among the critics of McCarthy's approach were his colleagues across the country at MIT. Marvin Minsky, Seymour Papert and Roger Schank were trying to solve problems like "story understanding" and "object recognition" that *required* a machine to think like a person. In order to use ordinary concepts like "chair" or "restaurant" they had to make all the same illogical assumptions that people normally made. Unfortunately, imprecise concepts like these are hard to represent in logic. Gerald Sussman observed that "using precise language to describe essentially imprecise concepts doesn't make them any more precise." Schank described their "anti-logic" approaches as "scruffy", as opposed to the "neat" paradigms used by McCarthy, Kowalski, Feigenbaum, Newell and Simon. In 1975, in a seminal paper, Minsky noted that many of his fellow "scruffy" researchers were using the same kind of tool: a framework that captures all our common sense assumptions about something. For example, if we use the concept of a bird, there is a constellation of facts that immediately come to mind: we might assume that it flies, eats worms and so on. We know these facts are not always true and that deductions using these facts will not be "logical," but these structured sets of assumptions are part of the *context* of everything we say and think. He called these structures "frames". Schank used a version of frames he called "scripts" to successfully answer questions about short stories in English. Many years later object-oriented programming would adopt the essential idea of "inheritance" from AI research on frames.

Boom 1980–1987

In the 1980s a form of AI programme called "expert systems" was adopted by corporations around the world and knowledge became the focus of mainstream AI research. In those same years, the Japanese government aggressively funded AI with its fifth generation computer project. Another encouraging event in the early 1980s was the revival of connectionism in the work of John Hopfield and David Rumelhart. Once again, AI had achieved success.

The Rise of Expert Systems

An expert system is a programme that answers questions or solves problems about a specific domain of knowledge, using logical rules that are derived from the knowledge of experts. The earliest examples were developed by Edward Feigenbaum and his students. Dendral, begun in 1965, identified compounds from spectrometer readings. MYCIN, developed in 1972, diagnosed infectious blood diseases. They demonstrated the feasibility of the approach. Expert systems restricted themselves to a small domain of specific knowledge (thus avoiding the commonsense knowledge problem) and their simple design made it relatively easy for programmes to be built and then modified once they were in place. All in all, the programmes proved to be *useful*: something that AI had not been able to achieve up to this point. In 1980, an expert system called XCON was completed at CMU for the Digital Equipment Corporation. It was an enormous success: it was saving the company 40 million dollars annually by 1986. Corporations around the world began to develop and deploy expert systems and by 1985 they were spending over a billion dollars on AI, most of it to in-house AI departments. An industry grew up to support them, including hardware companies like Symbolics and Lisp Machines and software companies such as IntelliCorp and Aion.

The Knowledge Revolution

The power of expert systems came from the expert knowledge they contained. They were part of a new direction in AI research that had been gaining ground throughout the 70s. "AI researchers were beginning to suspect—reluctantly, for it violated the scientific canon of parsimony—that intelligence might very well be based on the ability to use large amounts of diverse knowledge in different ways," writes Pamela McCorduck. "[T]he great lesson from the 1970s was that intelligent behaviour depended very much on dealing with knowledge, sometimes quite detailed knowledge, of a domain where a given task lay". Knowledge based systems and knowledge engineering became a major focus of AI research in the 1980s. The 1980s also saw the birth of Cyc, the first attempt to attack the commonsense knowledge problem directly, by creating a massive database that would contain all the mundane facts that the average person knows. Douglas Lenat, who started and led the project, argued that there is no shortcut ¯ the only way for machines to know the meaning of human concepts is to teach them, one concept at a time, by hand. The project was not expected to be completed for many decades.

The Money Returns: the Fifth Generation Project

In 1981, the Japanese Ministry of International Trade and Industry set aside $850 million dollars for the Fifth generation computer project. Their objectives were to write programmes and build machines that could carry on conversations, translate languages, interpret pictures, and reason like human beings. Much to the chagrin of scruffies, they chose Prolog as the primary computer language for the project. Other countries responded with new programmes of their own. The UK began the £350 million Alvey project. A consortium of American companies formed the Microelectronics and Computer Technology Corporation (or "MCC") to fund large scale projects in AI and information technology. DARPA responded as well, founding the Strategic Computing Initiative and tripling its investment in AI between 1984 and 1988.

The Revival of Connectionism

In 1982, physicist John Hopfield was able to prove that a form of neural network (now called a "Hopfield net") could learn and process information in a completely new way. Around the same time, David Rumelhart popularized a new method for training neural networks called "backpropagation" (discovered years earlier by Paul Werbos). These two discoveries revived the field of connectionism which had been largely abandoned since 1970. The new field was unified and inspired by the appearance of *Parallel Distributed Processing* in 1986—a two volume collection of papers edited by Rumelhart and psychologist James McClelland. Neural networks would become commercially successful in the 1990s, when they began to be used as the engines driving programmes like optical character recognition and speech recognition.

Bust: The Second AI Winter 1987-1993

The business community's fascination with AI rose and fell in the 80s in the classic pattern of an economic bubble. The collapse was in the *perception* of AI by government agencies and investors — the field continued to make advances despite the criticism. Rodney Brooks and Hans Moravec, researchers from the related field of robotics, argued for an entirely new approach to artificial intelligence.

AI Winter

The term "AI winter" was coined by researchers who had survived the funding cuts of 1974 when they became concerned that enthusiasm for expert systems had spiraled out of control and that disappointment would certainly follow. Their fears were well founded: in the late 80s and early 90s, AI suffered a series of financial setbacks. The first indication of a change in weather was the sudden collapse of the market for specialized AI hardware in 1987. Desktop computers from Apple and IBM had been steadily gaining speed and power and in 1987 they became more powerful than the more expensive Lisp machines made by Symbolics and others. There was no longer a good reason to buy them. An entire industry worth half a billion dollars was demolished overnight. Eventually the earliest successful expert systems, such as XCON, proved too expensive to maintain. They were difficult to update, they could not learn, they were "brittle" (i.e., they could make grotesque mistakes when given unusual inputs), and they fell prey to problems (such as the qualification problem) that had been identified years earlier. Expert systems proved useful, but only in a few special contexts. In the late 80s, the Strategic Computing Initiative cut funding to AI "deeply and brutally." New leadership at DARPA had decided that AI was not "the next wave" and directed funds towards projects that seemed more likely to produce immediate results. By 1991, the impressive list of goals penned in 1981 for Japan's Fifth Generation Project had not been met. Indeed, some of them, like "carry on a casual conversation" had not been met by 2010. As with other AI projects, expectations had run much higher than what was actually possible.

The Importance of Having a Body: Nouvelle AI and Embodied Reason

In the late 80s, several researchers advocated a completely new approach to artificial intelligence, based on robotics. They believed that, to show real intelligence, a machine needs to have a *body* — it needs to perceive, move, survive and deal with the world. They argued that these sensorimotor skills are essential to higher level skills like commonsense reasoning and that abstract reasoning was actually the *least* interesting or important human skill. They advocated building intelligence "from the bottom up." The approach revived ideas from cybernetics and control theory that had been unpopular since the sixties. Another precursor was David Marr, who had come to MIT in the late 70s from a successful background in theoretical neuroscience to lead the group studying vision. He rejected all symbolic approaches (*both* McCarthy's logic and Minsky's frames), arguing that AI needed to understand the physical machinery of vision from the bottom up before any symbolic processing took place. (Marr's work would be cut short by leukemia in 1980.) In a 1990 paper Elephants Don't Play Chess, robotics researcher Rodney Brooks took direct aim at the physical symbol system hypothesis, arguing that symbols are not always necessary since "the world is its own best model. It is always exactly up to date. It always has every detail there is to be known. The trick is to sense it appropriately and often enough." In the 80s and 90s, many cognitive scientists also rejected the symbol processing model of the mind and argued that the body was essential for reasoning, a theory called the embodied mind thesis.

Present

The field of AI, now more than a half a century old, finally achieved some of its oldest goals. It began to be used successfully throughout the technology industry, although somewhat behind the scenes.

Some of the success was due to increasing computer power and some was achieved by focusing on specific isolated problems and pursuing them with the highest standards of scientific accountability. Still, the reputation of AI, in the business world at least, was less than pristine. Inside the field there was little agreement on the reasons for AI's failure to fulfill the dream of human level intelligence that had captured the imagination of the world in the 1960s. Together, all these factors helped to fragment AI into competing subfields focused on particular problems or approaches, sometimes even under new names that disguised the tarnished pedigree of "artificial intelligence". AI was both more cautious and more successful than it had ever been.

Milestones and Moore's Law

On 11 May 1997, Deep Blue became the first computer chess-playing system to beat a reigning world chess champion, Garry Kasparov. In 2005, a Stanford robot won the DARPA Grand Challenge by driving autonomously for 131 miles along an unrehearsed desert trail. These successes were not due to some revolutionary new paradigm, but mostly on the tedious application of engineering skill and on the tremendous power of computers today. In fact, Deep Blue's computer was 10 million times faster than the Ferranti Mark 1 that Christopher Strachey taught to play chess in 1951. This dramatic increase is measured by Moore's law, which predicts that the speed and memory capacity of computers doubles every two years. The fundamental problem of "raw computer power" was slowly being overcome.

Intelligent Agents

A new paradigm called "intelligent agents" became widely accepted during the 90s. Although earlier researchers had proposed modular "divide and conquer" approaches to AI, the intelligent agent did not reach its modern form until Judea Pearl, Alan Newell and others brought concepts from decision theory and economics into the study of AI. When the economist's definition of a rational agent was married to computer science's definition of an object or module, the intelligent agent paradigm was complete.

An intelligent agent is a system that perceives its environment and takes actions which maximize its chances of success. The simplest intelligent agents are programmes that solve specific problems. The most complicated intelligent agents known are rational, thinking human beings. The intelligent agent paradigm defines AI research as "the study of intelligent agents". This is a generalization of some earlier definitions of AI: it goes beyond studying human intelligence; it studies all kinds of intelligence.

The paradigm gave researchers license to study isolated problems and find solutions that were both verifiable and useful. It provided a common language to describe problems and share their solutions with each other, and with other fields that also used concepts of abstract agents, like economics and control theory. It was hoped that a complete agent architecture (like Newell's SOAR) would one day allow researchers to build more versatile and intelligent systems out of interacting intelligent agents.

Victory of the Neats

AI researchers began to develop and use sophisticated mathematical tools more than they ever had in the past. There was a widespread realization that many of the problems that AI needed to solve were already being worked on by researchers in fields like mathematics, economics or operations research. The shared mathematical language allowed both a higher level of collaboration with more established and successful fields and the achievement of results which were measurable and provable; AI had become a more rigorous "scientific" discipline.

Russell & Norvig (2003) describe this as nothing less than a "revolution" and "the victory of the neats". Judea Pearl's highly influential 1988 book brought probability and decision theory into AI.

Among the many new tools in use were Bayesian networks, hidden Markov models, information theory, stochastic modeling and classical optimization. Precise mathematical descriptions were also developed for "computational intelligence" paradigms like neural networks and evolutionary algorithms.

AI Behind the Scenes

Algorithms originally developed by AI researchers began to appear as parts of larger systems. AI had solved a lot of very difficult problems and their solutions proved to be useful throughout the technology industry, such as data mining, industrial robotics, logistics, speech recognition, banking software, medical diagnosis and Google's search engine.

The field of AI receives little or no credit for these successes. Many of AI's greatest innovations have been reduced to the status of just another item in the tool chest of computer science. Nick Bostrom explains "A lot of cutting edge AI has filtered into general applications, often without being called AI because once something becomes useful enough and common enough it's not labeled AI anymore." Many researchers in AI today deliberately call their work by other names, such as informatics, knowledge-based systems, cognitive systems or computational intelligence.

In part, this may be because they considered their field to be fundamentally different from AI, but also the new names help to procure funding. In the commercial world at least, the failed promises of the AI Winter continue to haunt AI research, as the New York Times reported in 2005. "Computer scientists and software engineers avoided the term artificial intelligence for fear of being viewed as wild-eyed dreamers."

Where is HAL 9000?

In 1968, Arthur C. Clarke and Stanley Kubrick had imagined that by the year 2001, a machine would exist with an intelligence that matched or exceeded the capability of human beings. The character they created, HAL 9000, was based on hard science: many leading AI researchers also believed that such a machine would exist by the year 2001. Marvin Minsky asks "So the question is why didn't we get HAL in 2001?" Minsky believes that the answer is that the central problems, like commonsense reasoning, were being neglected, while most researchers pursued things like commercial applications of neural nets or genetic algorithms.

John McCarthy, on the other hand, still blames the qualification problem. For Ray Kurzweil, the issue is computer power and, using Moore's Law, he predicts that machines with human-level intelligence will appear by 2029. Jeff Hawkins argues that neural net research ignores the essential properties of the human cortex, preferring simple models that have been successful at solving simple problems. There are many other explanations and for each there is a corresponding research programme underway.

ABDUCTIVE LOGIC PROGRAMMING

Abductive Logic Programming is an extension of normal Logic Programming that allows some predicates, declared as abducible predicates, to be incompletely defined. Problem solving is achieved by deriving hypotheses expressed in terms of the abducible predicates as solutions of problems to be solved. These problems can be either observations that need to be explained (as in classical abductive reasoning) or goals to be achieved (as in normal logic programming). It has been used to solve problems in Diagnosis, Planning, Natural Language and Machine Learning. It has also been used to interpret Negation as Failure as a form of abductive reasoning.

Metalogic Programming

Because mathematical logic has a long tradition of distinguishing between object language and metalanguage, logic programming also allows metalevel programming. The simplest metalogic progam is the so-called "vanilla" meta-interpreter:

```
solve(true).
solve((A,B)):- solve(A),solve(B).
solve(A):- clause(A,B),solve(B).
```

where true represents an empty conjunction, and clause(A,B) means there is an object-level clause of the form A :- B. Metalogic programming allows object-level and metalevel representations to be combined, as in natural language. It can also be used to implement any logic that is specified by means of inference rules.

Constraint Logic Programming

Constraint logic programming is an extension of normal Logic Programming that allows some predicates, declared as constraint predicates, to occur as literals in the body of clauses.

These literals are not solved by goal-reduction using programme clauses, but are added to a store of constraints, which is required to be consistent with some built-in semantics of the constraint predicates.

Problem solving is achieved by reducing the initial problem to a satisfiable set of constraints.

Constraint logic programming has been used to solve problems in such fields as civil engineering, mechanical engineering, digital circuit verification, automated timetabling, air traffic control, and finance. It is closely related to abductive logic programming.

Concurrent Logic Programming

Keith Clark, Steve Gregory, Vijay Saraswat, Udi Shapiro, Kazunori Ueda, etc. developed a family of Prolog-like concurrent message passing systems using unification of shared variables and data structure streams for messages. Efforts were made to base these systems on mathematical logic, and they were used as the basis of the Japanese Fifth Generation Project (ICOT). However, the Prolog-like concurrent systems were based on message passing and consequently were subject to the same indeterminacy as other concurrent message-passing systems, such as Actors.

Consequently, the ICOT languages were not based on logic in the sense that computational steps could not be logically deduced [Hewitt and Agha, 1988]. Concurrent constraint logic programming combines concurrent logic programming and constraint logic programming, using constraints to control concurrency. A clause can contain a guard, which is a set of constraints that may block the applicability of the clause. When the guards of several clauses are satisfied, concurrent constraint logic programming makes a committed choice to the use of only one.

Inductive Logic Programming

Inductive logic programming is concerned with generalizing positive and negative examples in the context of background knowledge. Generalizations, as well as the examples and background knowledge, are expressed in logic programming syntax. Recent work in this area, combining logic programming, learning and probability, has given rise to the new field of statistical relational learning and probabilistic inductive logic programming.

Higher-Order Logic Programming

Several researchers have extended logic programming with higher-order programming features derived from higher-order logic, such as predicate variables. Such languages include the Prolog extensions HiLog and ëProlog.

Linear Logic Programming

Basing logic programming within linear logic has resulted in the design of logic programming languages that are considerably more expressive than those based on classical logic. Horn clause programmes can only represent state change by the change in arguments to predicates. In linear logic programming, one can use the ambient linear logic to support state change. Some early designs of logic programming languages based on linear logic include LO [Andreoli & Pareschi, 1991], Lolli [Hodas & Miller, 1994], ACL [Kobayashi & Yonezawa, 1994], and Forum [Miller, 1996]. Forum provides a goal-directed interpretation of all of linear logic.

MODERN PROGRAMMING

Quality Requirements

Whatever the approach to software development may be, the final program must satisfy some fundamental properties. The following properties are among the most relevant:

- Efficiency/performance: the amount of system resources a program consumes (processor time, memory space, slow devices such as disks, network bandwidth and to some extent even user interaction): the less, the better. This also includes correct disposal of some resources, such as cleaning up temporary files and lack of memory leaks.
- Reliability: how often the results of a program are correct. This depends on conceptual correctness of algorithms, and minimization of programming mistakes, such as mistakes in resource management (e.g., buffer overflows and race conditions) and logic errors (such as division by zero or off-by-one errors).
- Robustness: how well a program anticipates problems not due to programmer error. This includes situations such as incorrect, inappropriate or corrupt data, unavailability of needed resources such as memory,

operating system services and network connections, and user error.

- Usability: the ergonomics of a program: the ease with which a person can use the program for its intended purpose, or in some cases even unanticipated purposes. Such issues can make or break its success even regardless of other issues. This involves a wide range of textual, graphical and sometimes hardware elements that improve the clarity, intuitiveness, cohesiveness and completeness of a program's user interface.
- Portability: the range of computer hardware and operating system platforms on which the source code of a program can be compiled/interpreted and run. This depends on differences in the programming facilities provided by the different platforms, including hardware and operating system resources, expected behaviour of the hardware and operating system, and availability of platform specific compilers (and sometimes libraries) for the language of the source code
- Maintainability: the ease with which a program can be modified by its present or future developers in order to make improvements or customizations, fix bugs and security holes, or adapt it to new environments. Good practices during initial development make the difference in this regard. This quality may not be directly apparent to the end user but it can significantly affect the fate of a program over the long term.

Algorithmic Complexity

The academic field and the engineering practice of computer programming are both largely concerned with discovering and implementing the most efficient algorithms for a given class of problem. For this purpose, algorithms are classified into *orders* using so-called Big O notation, $O(n)$, which expresses resource use, such as execution time or memory consumption, in terms of the size of an input. Expert programmers are familiar with a variety of well-established algorithms and their respective complexities and use this knowledge to choose algorithms that are best suited to the circumstances.

Methodologies

The first step in most formal software development projects is requirements analysis, followed by testing to determine value modelling, implementation, and failure elimination (debugging). There exist a lot of differing approaches for each of those tasks. One approach popular for requirements analysis is Use Case analysis.

Popular modelling techniques include Object-Oriented Analysis and Design (OOAD) and Model-Driven Architecture (MDA). The Unified Modelling Language (UML) is a notation used for both the OOAD and MDA. A similar technique used for database design is Entity-Relationship Modelling (ER Modelling). Implementation techniques include imperative languages (object-oriented or procedural), functional languages, and logic languages.

Measuring Language Usage

It is very difficult to determine what are the most popular of modern programming languages. Some languages are very popular for particular kinds of applications (e.g., COBOL is still strong in the corporate data centre, often on large mainframes, FORTRAN in engineering applications, scripting languages in web development, and C in embedded applications), while some languages are regularly used to write many different kinds of applications. Methods of measuring programming language popularity include: counting the number of job advertisements that mention the language, the number of books teaching the language that are sold (this overestimates the importance of newer languages), and estimates of the number of existing lines of code written in the language (this underestimates the number of users of business languages such as COBOL).

Debugging

Debugging is a very important task in the software development process, because an incorrect program can have significant consequences for its users. Some languages are more prone to some kinds of faults because their specification does not require compilers to perform as much checking as other languages. Use of a static analysis tool can help detect some possible problems. Debugging is often done with IDEs like Eclipse, Kdevelop, NetBeans, and Visual Studio. Standalone debuggers like gdb are also used, and these often provide less of a visual environment, usually using a command line.

Programming Languages

Different programming languages support different styles of programming (called *programming paradigms*). The choice of language used is subject to many considerations, such as company policy, suitability to task, availability of third-party packages, or individual preference. Ideally, the programming language best suited for the task at hand will be selected. Trade-offs from this ideal involve finding enough programmers who know the language to build a team, the availability of compilers for that language, and the efficiency with which programs written in a given language execute. Languages form an approximate spectrum from "low-level" to "high-level"; "low-level" languages are typically more machine-oriented and faster to execute, whereas "high-level" languages are more abstract and easier to use but execute less quickly.

Allen Downey, in his book *How To Think Like A Computer Scientist*, writes:

The details look different in different languages, but a few basic instructions appear in just about every language:

- input: Get data from the keyboard, a file, or some other device.
- output: Display data on the screen or send data to a file or other device.
- arithmetic: Perform basic arithmetical operations like addition and multiplication.
- conditional execution: Check for certain conditions and execute the appropriate sequence of statements.

- repetition: Perform some action repeatedly, usually with some variation.

Many computer languages provide a mechanism to call functions provided by libraries. Provided the functions in a library follow the appropriate run time conventions (e.g., method of passing arguments), then these functions may be written in any other language.

Concept programming is initially a very simple idea: *Your code should reflect the concepts in your application.*

As simple as this idea is, it is not easy to implement, nor is it easy to fully understand the implications. As a matter of fact, we believe that this would give well enough material for an entire book. But we will try to quickly brush over the subject here.

7

Computational Creativity

Computational creativity (also known as artificial creativity, mechanical creativity or creative computation) is a multidisciplinary endeavour that is located at the intersection of the fields of artificial intelligence, cognitive psychology, philosophy, and the arts.

The goal of computational creativity is to model, simulate or replicate creativity using a computer, to achieve one of several ends:

- to construct a programme or computer capable of human-level creativity
- to better understand human creativity and to formulate an algorithmic perspective on creative behaviour in humans
- to design programmes that can enhance human creativity without necessarily being creative themselves

The field of computational creativity concerns itself with theoretical and practical issues in the study of creativity. Theoretical work on the nature and proper definition of creativity is performed in parallel with practical work on the implementation of systems that exhibit creativity, with one strand of work informing the other.

Theoretical Issues

As measured by the amount of activity in the field (e.g., publications, conferences and workshops), computational creativity is a growing area of research. But the field is still hampered by a number of fundamental problems:

- Creativity is very difficult, perhaps even impossible, to define in objective terms.
- Creativity takes many forms in human activity, some *eminent* (meaning "recognized" or "ingenious", e.g., Einstein's creativity; sometimes referred to as "Creativity" with a capital C) and some *mundane*.
- Creativity can mean different things in different contexts: Is it a state of mind, a talent or ability, or a process? Does it describe a person, an activity or an end-product? Can collaborative work in which exceptional products emerge from simple interactions be considered creative?

These are problems that complicate the study of creativity in general, but certain problems attach themselves specifically to *computational* creativity:

- Can creativity be hard-wired? In existing systems to which creativity is attributed, is the creativity that of the system or that of the system's programmer or designer?
- How do we evaluate computational creativity? What counts as creativity in a computational system? Are natural language generation systems creative? Are machine translation systems creative? What distinguishes research in computational creativity from research in artificial intelligence generally?
- If eminent creativity is about rule-breaking or the disavowal of convention, how is it possible for an algorithmic system to be creative? In essence, this is a variant of the Ada Lovelace objection to machine intelligence, as recapitulated by modern theorists such as Teresa Amabile: If a machine can do only what it was programmed to do, how can its behaviour ever be called *creative*?

LINGUISTIC CREATIVITY

Language provides continuous opportunity for creativity, evident in the generation of novel sentences, phrasings, puns, neologisms, rhymes, allusions, sarcasm, irony, similes, metaphors, analogies, witticisms, and jokes. Native speakers of morphologically rich languages (including all Slavic languages) frequently create new word-forms that are easily understood, although they will never find their way to the dictionary. The area of natural language generation has been well studied, but these creative aspects of everyday language have yet to be incorporated with any robustness or scale.

Story Generation

Substantial work has been conducted in this area of linguistic creation since the 1970s, with the development of James Meehan's TALE-SPIN system. TALE-SPIN viewed stories as narrative descriptions of a problem-solving effort, and created stories by first establishing a goal for the story's characters so that their search for a solution could be tracked and recorded. The MINSTREL system represents a complex elaboration of this basis approach, distinguishing a range of character-level goals in the story from a range of author-level goals for the story.

Systems like Bringsjord's BRUTUS elaborate these ideas further to create stories with complex inter-personal themes like betrayal. Nonetheless, MINSTREL explicitly models the creative process with a set of Transform Recall Adapt Methods (TRAMs) to create novel scenes from old. The MEXICA model of Rafael Pérez y Pérez and Mike Sharples is more explicitly interested in the creative process of storytelling, and implements a version of the engagement-reflection cognitive model of creative writing.

Metaphor and Simile

Example of a metaphor: *"She was an ape."*

Example of a simile: *"Felt like a tiger-fur blanket."* The computational study of these phenomena has mainly focused on interpretation as a knowledge-based process. Computationalists such as Yorick Wilks, James Martin, Dan Fass, John Barnden, and Mark Lee have developed knowledge-based approaches to the processing of metaphors, either at a linguistic level or a logical level. Tony Veale and Yanfen Hao have developed a system, called Sardonicus, that acquires a comprehensive database of explicit similes from the web; these similes are then tagged as bona-fide (e.g., "as hard as steel") or ironic (e.g., "as hairy as a bowling ball", "as pleasant as a root canal"); similes of either type can be retrieved on demand for any given adjective. They use these similes as the basis of an on-line metaphor generation system called Aristotle that can suggest lexical metaphors for a given descriptive goal (e.g., to describe a supermodel as skinny, the source terms "pencil", "whip", "whippet", "rope", "stick-insect" and "snake" are suggested).

Analogy

The process of analogical reasoning has been studied from both a mapping and a retrieval perspective, the latter being key to the generation of novel analogies. The dominant school of research, as advanced by Dedre Gentner. views analogy as a structure-preserving process; this view has been implemented in the structure mapping engine or SME, the MAC/FAC retrieval engine (Many Are Called, Few Are Chosen), ACME (Analogical Constraint Mapping Engine) and ARCS (Analogical Retrieval Constraint System).

Other mapping-based approaches include Sapper, which situates the mapping process in a semantic-network model of memory. Analogy is a very active sub-area of creative computation and creative cognition; active figures in this sub-area include Douglas Hofstadter, Paul Thagard, and Keith Holyoak. Also worthy of note here is Peter Turney and Michael Littman's machine learning approach to the solving of SAT-style analogy problems; their approach achieves a score that compares well with average scores achieved by humans on these tests.

Joke Generation

Humour is an especially knowledge-hungry process, and the most successful joke-generation systems to date have focussed on pun-generation, as exemplified by the work of Kim Binsted and Graeme Ritchie. This work includes the JAPE system, which can generate a wide range of puns that are consistently evaluated as novel and humorous by young children. An improved version of JAPE has been developed in the guise of the STANDUP system, which has been experimentally deployed as a means of enhancing linguistic interaction with children with communication disabilities. Some limited progress has been made in generating humour that involves other aspects of natural language, such as the deliberate misunderstanding of pronominal reference (in the work of Hans Wim Tinholt and Anton Nijholt), as well as in the generation of humorous acronyms in the HAHAcronym system of Oliviero Stock and Carlo Strapparava.

Neologisms

The blending of multiple word forms is a dominant force for new word creation in language; these new words are commonly called "blends" or "portmanteau words" (after Lewis Carroll). Tony Veale has developed a system called ZeitGeist that harvests neological headwords from Wikipedia and interprets them relative to their local context in Wikipedia and relative to specific word senses in WordNet. ZeitGeist has been extended to generate neologisms of its own; the approach combines elements from an inventory of word parts that are harvested from WordNet, and simultaneously determines likely glosses for these new words (e.g., "food traveller" for "gastronaut" and "time traveller" for "chrononaut"). It then uses Web search to determine which glosses are meaningful and which neologisms have not been used before; this search identifies the subset of generated words that are both novel ("H-creative") and useful. Neurolinguistic inspirations have been used to analyze the process of novel word creation in the brain, understand neurocognitive processes responsible for intuition, insight, imagination and creativity and to create a server that invents novel names for products, based on their description.

Poetry

More than iron, more than lead, more than gold I need electricity. I need it more than I need lamb or pork or lettuce or cucumber. I need it for my dreams. Racter, from *The Policeman's Beard Is Half Constructed* Like jokes, poems involve a complex interaction of different constraints, and no general-purpose poem generator adequately combines the meaning, phrasing, structure and rhyme aspects of poetry. Nonetheless, Pablo Gervás has developed a noteworthy system called ASPERA that employs a case-based reasoning (CBR) approach to generating poetic formulations of a given input text via a composition of poetic fragments that are retrieved from a case-base of existing poems. Each poem fragment in the ASPERA case-base is annotated with a prose string that expresses the meaning of the fragment, and this prose string is used as the retrieval key for each fragment. Metrical rules are then used to combine these fragments into a well-formed poetic structure. Example software projects include:

- Racter
- Flowerewolf automatic poetry generator

And poetry collections include:

- *The Policeman's Beard Is Half Constructed*

MUSICAL CREATIVITY

Computational creativity in the music domain has focussed both on the generation of musical scores for use by human musicians, and on the generation of music for performance by computers. The domain of generation has included classical music (with software that generates music in the style of Mozart and Bach) and jazz. Most notably, David Cope has written a software system called "Experiments in Musical Intelligence" (or "EMI") that is capable of analyzing and generalizing from existing music by a human composer to generate novel musical compositions in the same style. EMI's output is convincing enough to persuade human listeners that its music is human-generated to a high level of competence. Creativity research in jazz has focussed on the process of improvisation and the cognitive demands that this places on a musical agent: reasoning about time, remembering and conceptualizing what has already been played, and planning ahead for what might be played next. The robot Shimon, developed by Gil Weinberg of Georgia Tech, has demonstrated jazz improvisation.

Visual and Artistic Creativity

Computational creativity in the generation of visual art has had some notable successes in the creation of both abstract art and representational art. The most famous programme in this domain is Harold Cohen's AARON, which has been continuously developed and augmented since 1973. Though formulaic, Aaron exhibits a range of outputs, generating black-and-white drawings or colour paintings that incorporate human figures (such as dancers), potted plants, rocks, and other elements of background imagery. These images are of a sufficiently high quality to be displayed in reputable galleries. Other software artists of note include the NEvAr system (for "Neuro-Evolutionary Art") of Penousal Machado. NEvAr uses a genetic algorithm to derive a mathematical function that is then used to generate a coloured three-dimensional surface. A human user is allowed to select the best pictures after each phase of the genetic algorithm, and these preferences are used to guide successive phases, thereby pushing NEvAr's search into pockets of the search space that are considered most appealing to the user. The Painting Fool, developed by Simon Colton originated as a system for overpainting digital images of a given scene in a choice of different painting styles, colour palettes and brush types. Given its dependence on an input source image to work with, the earliest iterations of the Painting Fool raised as questions about the extent of, or lack of, creativity in a computational art system. Nonetheless, in more recent work, The Painting Fool has been extended to create novel images, much as AARON does, from its own limited imagination. Images in this vein include cityscapes and forests, which are generated by a process of constraint satisfaction from some basic scenarios provided by the user (e.g., these scenarios allow the system to infer that objects closer to the viewing plane should be larger and more color-saturated, while those further away should be less saturated and appear smaller). Artistically, the images now created by the Painting Fool appear on a par with those created by Aaron, though the extensible mechanisms employed by the former (constraint satisfaction, etc.) may well allow it to develop into a more elaborate and sophisticated painter.

DEFINING CREATIVITY IN COMPUTATIONAL TERMS

Since no single perspective or definition seems to offer a complete picture of creativity, the AI researchers Newell, Shaw and Simon developed the combination of novelty and usefulness into the corner-stone of a multi-pronged view of creativity, one that uses the following four criteria to categorize a given answer or solution as creative:

1. The answer is novel and useful (either for the individual or for society)
2. The answer demands that we reject ideas we had previously accepted
3. The answer results from intense motivation and persistence
4. The answer comes from clarifying a problem that was originally vague

Notice how these criteria touch on many of the stereotypical themes that are typically associated with creativity: newness and value (1), transformation and revolution (2), passion and drive (3), vision and insight (4).

These four criteria also combine elements of the producer-perspective and the product-perspective described earlier: criterion (1) characterizes the two most important qualities of a creative product, while criteria (2) – (4) characterize the attitude and actions of the producer of such a product. A given product may satisfy all or none of these criteria, but we should expect products that exhibit all four to be widely perceived as creative, while products that exhibit just some of these criteria will be judged with greater subjectivity and variation. Though no criterion is likely to be either necessary or sufficient, criterion (1) is perhaps the most common hallmark of creativity and thus serves to anchor the others. From a computational perspective, then, one can consider (1) to be a *must-have* feature, and (2) – (4) as desirable extras.

Newell and Simon are best known for their contribution to the search-in-a-state-space paradigm of AI, sometimes caricatured as Good Old Fashioned AI (GOFAI), and it is interesting to consider how the GOFAI paradigm can incorporate these criteria.

From a search perspective, criterion (1) characterizes the goal or end-state of a computational search, criterion (4) characterizes the starting state from which the search is launched, criterion (3) characterizes the scale of the search, suggesting that many dead-ends are likely to be encountered, while criterion (2) suggests that well-worn pathways through the search space are best avoided if a creative end-state is to be reached.

Key Ideas

Some high-level and philosophical themes recur throughout the field of computational creativity.

P-creativity and H-creativity

Margaret Boden refers to creativity that is novel *merely to the agent that produces it* as "P-creativity" (or "psychological creativity"), and refers to creativity that is recognized as novel *by society at large* as "H-creativity" (or "historical creativity").

Exploratory and Transformational Creativity

Boden also distinguishes between the creativity that arises from an exploration within an established conceptual space, and the creativity that arises from a deliberate transformation or transcendence of this space. She labels the former as "exploratory creativity" and the latter as "transformational creativity", seeing the latter as a form of creativity far more radical, challenging, and rarer than the former. Following Newell and Simon's criteria, we can see that both forms of creativity should produce results that are appreciably novel and useful (criterion 1), but exploratory creativity is more likely to arise from a thorough and persistent search of a well-understood space (criterion 3) while transformational creativity should involve the rejection of some of the constraints that define this space (criterion 2) or some of the assumptions that define the problem itself (criterion 4).

Boden's insights have guided work in computational creativity at a very general level, providing more an inspirational touchstone for development work than a technical framework of algorithmic substance. However, Boden's insights are the subject of formalization, most notably in the work by Geraint Wiggins.

GENERATION AND EVALUATION

The criterion that creative products should be novel and useful means that creative computational systems are typically structured into two phases, generation and evaluation. In the first phase, novel (to the system itself, thus P-Creative) constructs are generated; unoriginal constructs that are already known to the system are filtered at this stage. This body of potentially creative constructs are then evaluated, to determine which are meaningful and useful and which are not. This two-phase structure conforms to the Geneplore model of Finke, Ward and Smith, which is a psychological model of creative generation based on empirical observation of human creativity.

Combinatorial Creativity

A great deal, perhaps all, of human creativity can be understood as a novel combination of pre-existing ideas or objects. Common strategies for combinatorial creativity include:

- placing a familiar object in an unfamiliar setting (e.g., Marcel Duchamp's *Fountain*) or an unfamiliar object in a familiar setting (e.g., a fish-out-of-water story such as *The Beverly Hillbillies*)

- Blending two superficially different objects or genres (e.g., a sci-fi story set in the Wild West, with robot cowboys, as in *Westworld*, or the reverse, as in *Firefly*; Jewish haiku poems, etc.)
- Comparing a familiar object to a superficially unrelated and semantically distant concept (e.g., "Makeup is the Western burka"; "A zoo is a gallery with living exhibits")
- Adding a new and unexpected feature to an existing concept (e.g., adding a scalpel to a Swiss Army knife; adding a camera to a mobile phone)
- Compressing two incongruous scenarios into the same narrative to get a joke (e.g., the Emo Philips joke "Women are always using me to advance their careers. Damned anthropologists!")
- Using an iconic image from one domain in a domain for an unrelated or incongruous idea or product (e.g., using the Marlboro Man image to sell cars, or to advertise the dangers of smoking-related impotence).

The combinatorial perspective allows us to model creativity as a search process through the space of possible combinations. The combinations can arise from composition or concatenation of different representations, or through a rule-based or stochastic transformation of initial and intermediate representations. Genetic algorithms and neural networks can be used to generate blended or crossover representations that capture a combination of different inputs.

Bisociation

Arthur Koestler proposes a very general model of creative combination in his 1964 book *The Act of Creation,* claiming that scientific discovery, art and humour are all linked by a common mechanism called "bisociation". Koestler lacked a formal, computational vocabulary for describing bisociation, which he defined as a reconciliation of two orthogonal matrices of thought (conceptual structures, mental spaces).

Conceptual Blending

Mark Turner and Gilles Fauconnier propose a model called Conceptual Integration Networks that elaborates upon the ideas of Koestler by synthesizing ideas from Cognitive Linguistic research into mental spaces and conceptual metaphors. Their basic model defines an integration network as four connected spaces:

- A first input space (contains one conceptual structure or mental space)
- A second input space (to be blended with the first input)
- A *generic space* of stock conventions and image-schemas that allow the input spaces to be understood from an integrated perspective
- A *blend space* in which a selected projection of elements from both input spaces are combined; inferences arising from this combination also reside here, sometimes leading to emergent structures that conflict with the inputs.

Fauconnier and Turner describe a collection of optimality principles that are claimed to guide the construction of a well-formed integration network. In essence, they see blending as a compression mechanism in which two or more input structures are compressed into a single blend structure.

This compression operates on the level of conceptual relations. For example, a series of similarity relations between the input spaces can be compressed into a single identity relationship in the blend. Blending theory is an elaborate framework that provides a rich terminology for describing the products of creative thinking, from metaphors to jokes to neologisms to adverts.

It is most typically applied retrospectively, to describe how a blended conceptual structure could have arisen from a particular pair of input structures. These conceptual structures are often good examples of human creativity, but blending theory is not a theory of creativity, nor – despite its authors' claims – does it describe a mechanism for creativity. The theory lacks an explanation for how a creative individual chooses the input spaces that should be blended to generate a desired result.

Nonetheless, some computational success has been achieved with the blending model by extending pre-existing computational models of analogical mapping that are compatible by virtue of their emphasis on connected semantic structures. More recently, Francisco Câmara Pereira presented an implementation of blending theory that employs ideas both from GOFAI and from genetic algorithms to realize some aspects of blending theory in a practical form; his example domains range from the linguistic to the visual, and the latter most notably includes the creation of mythical monsters by combining 3-D graphical models.

8

Speech Recognition

Speech recognition (also known as automatic speech recognition or computer speech recognition) converts spoken words to text. The term "voice recognition" is sometimes used to refer to recognition systems that must be trained to a particular speaker—as is the case for most desktop recognition software. Recognizing the speaker can simplify the task of translating speech. Speech recognition is a broader solution which refers to technology that can recognize speech without being targeted at single speaker—such as a call system that can recognize arbitrary voices. Speech recognition applications include voice user interfaces such as voice dialing (e.g., "Call home"), call routing (e.g., "I would like to make a collect call"), domotic appliance control, search (e.g., find a podcast where particular words were spoken), simple data entry (e.g., entering a credit card number), preparation of structured documents (e.g., a radiology report), speech-to-text processing (e.g., word processors or emails), and aircraft (usually termed Direct Voice Input).

HISTORY

The first speech recognizer appeared in 1952 and consisted of a device for the recognition of single spoken digits Another early device was the IBM Shoebox, exhibited at the 1964 New York World's Fair. One of the most notable domains for the commercial application of speech recognition in the United States has been health care and in particular the work of the medical transcriptionist (MT). According to industry experts, at its inception, speech recognition (SR) was sold as a way to completely eliminate transcription rather than make the transcription process more efficient, hence it was not accepted. It was also the case that SR at that time was often technically deficient. Additionally, to be used effectively, it required changes to the ways physicians worked and documented clinical encounters, which many if not all were reluctant to do. The biggest limitation to speech recognition automating transcription, however, is seen as the software. The nature of narrative dictation is highly interpretive and often requires judgment that may be provided by a real human but not yet by an automated system. Another limitation has been the extensive amount of time required by the user and/or system provider to train the software. A distinction in ASR is often made between "artificial syntax systems" which are usually domain-specific and "natural language processing" which is usually language-specific. Each of these types of application presents its own particular goals and challenges.

SPEECH RECOGNITION AND NATURAL MODE

Speech is a natural mode of communication for people. We learn all the relevant skills during early childhood, without instruction, and we continue to rely on speech communication throughout our lives. It comes so naturally to us that we don't realise how complex a phenomenon speech is. The human vocal tract and articulators are biological organs with nonlinear properties, whose operation is not just under conscious control but also affected by factors ranging from gender to upbringing to emotional state.

As a result, vocalizations can vary widely in terms of their accent, pronunciation, articulation, roughness, nasality, pitch, volume, and speed; moreover, during transmission, our irregular speech patterns can be further distorted by background noise and echoes, as well as electrical characteristics (if telephones or other electronic equipment are used). All these sources of variability make speech recognition, even more than speech generation, a very complex problem. What makes people so good at recognizing speech? Intriguingly, the human brain is known to be wired differently than a conventional computer; in fact it operates under a radically different computational paradigm. While conventional computers use a very fast and complex central processor with explicit programme instructions and locally addressable memory, by contrast the human brain uses a massively parallel collection of slow and simple processing elements (neurons), densely connected by weights (synapses) whose strengths are modified with experience, directly supporting the integration of multiple constraints, and providing a distributed form of associative memory. The brain's impressive superiority at a wide range of cognitive skills, including speech recognition, has motivated research into its novel computational paradigm since the 1940's, on the assumption that brainlike models may ultimately lead to brainlike performance on many complex tasks.

This fascinating research area is now known as connectionism, or the study of artificial neural networks. What is the current state of the art in speech recognition? This is a complex question, because a system's accuracy depends on the conditions under which it is evaluated: under sufficiently narrow conditions almost any system can attain human-like accuracy, but it's much harder to achieve good accuracy under general conditions. The conditions of evaluation - and hence the accuracy of any system - can vary along the following dimensions:

Vocabulary Size and Confusability

As a general rule, it is easy to discriminate among a small set of words, but error rates naturally increase as the vocabulary size grows. For example, the 10 digits 'zero' to 'nine' can be recognized essentially perfectly, but vocabulary sizes of 200, 5000, or 100000 may have error rates of 3%, 7%, or 45%.

On the other hand, even a small vocabulary can be hard to recognize if it contains confusable words. For example, the 26 letters of the English alphabet (treated as 26 'words') are very difficult to discriminate because they contain so many confusable words (most notoriously, the E-set: 'B, C, D, E, G, P, T, V, Z'); an 8% error rate is considered good for this vocabulary

Speaker Dependence vs. Independence

By definition, a speaker dependent system is intended for use by a single speaker, but a speaker independent system is intended for use by any speaker. Speaker independence is difficult to achieve because a system's parametres become tuned to the speaker(s) that it was trained on, and these parametres tend to be highly speaker-specific.

Isolated, Discontinuous, or Continuous Speech

Isolated speech means single words; discontinuous speech means full sentences in which words are artificially separated by silence; and continuous speech means naturally spoken sentences. Isolated and discontinuous speech recognition is relatively easy because word boundaries are detectable and the words tend to be cleanly pronounced.

Task and Language Constraints

Even with a fixed vocabulary, performance will vary with the nature of constraints on the word sequences that are allowed during recognition. Some constraints may be task-dependent (for example, an airlinequerying application may dismiss the hypothesis 'The apple is red'); other constraints may be semantic (rejecting 'The apple is angry'), or syntactic (rejecting 'Red is apple the').

Constraints are often represented by a grammar, which ideally filters out unreasonable sentences so that the speech recognizer evaluates only plausible sentences. Grammars are usually rated by their perplexity, a number that indicates the grammar's average branching factor (*i.e.*, the number of words that can follow any given word). The difficulty of a task is more reliably measured by its perplexity than by its vocabulary size.

Read vs. Spontaneous Speech

Systems can be evaluated on speech that is either read from prepared scripts, or speech that is uttered spontaneously.

Spontaneous speech is vastly more difficult, because it tends to be peppered with disfluencies like 'uh' and 'um', false starts, incomplete sentences, stuttering, coughing, and laughter; and moreover, the vocabulary is essentially unlimited, so the system must be able to deal intelligently with unknown words (*e.g.*, detecting and flagging their presence, and adding them to the vocabulary, which may require some interaction with the user).

Adverse Conditions

A system's performance can also be degraded by a range of adverse conditions. These include environmental noise (*e.g.*, noise in a car or a factory); acoustical distortions (*e.g*, echoes, room acoustics); different microphones (*e.g.*, close-speaking, omnidirectional, or telephone); limited frequency bandwidth (in telephone transmission); and altered speaking manner (shouting, whining, speaking quickly, etc.).

In order to evaluate and compare different systems under well-defined conditions, a number of standardized databases have been created with particular characteristics.

For example, one database that has been widely used is the DARPA Resource Management database - a large vocabulary (1000 words), speaker-independent, continuous speech database, consisting of 4000 training sentences in the domain of naval resource management, read from a script and recorded under benign environmental conditions; testing is usually performed using a grammar with a perplexity of 60.

Under these controlled conditions, state-of-the-art performance is about 97% word recognition accuracy (or less for simpler systems).

FUNDAMENTALS OF SPEECH RECOGNITION

Speech recognition is a multileveled pattern recognition task, in which acoustical signals are examined and structured into a hierarchy of subword units (*e.g.*, phonemes), words, phrases, and sentences. Each level may provide additional temporal constraints, *e.g.*, known word pronunciations or legal word sequences, which can compensate for errors or uncertainties at lower levels. This hierarchy of constraints can best be exploited by combining decisions probabilistically at all lower levels, and making discrete decisions only at the highest level.

The elements are as follows:

- *Raw speech:* Speech is typically sampled at a high frequency, *e.g.*, 16 KHz over a microphone or 8 KHz over a telephone. This yields a sequence of amplitude values over time.
- *Signal analysis*: Raw speech should be initially transformed and compressed, in order to simplify subsequent processing. Many signal analysis techniques are available which can extract useful features and compress the data by a factor of ten without losing any important information. Among the most popular:
- – Fourier analysis (FFT) yields discrete frequencies over time, which can be interpreted visually. Frequencies are often distributed using a Mel scale, which is linear in the low range but logarithmic in the high range, corresponding to physiological characteristics of the human ear.
- – Perceptual Linear Prediction (PLP) is also physiologically motivated, but yields coefficients that cannot be interpreted visually.
- – Linear Predictive Coding (LPC) yields coefficients of a linear equation that approximate the recent history of the raw speech values.
- – Cepstral analysis calculates the inverse Fourier transform of the logarithm of the power spectrum of the signal.

In practice, it makes little difference which technique is used1. Afterwards, procedures such as Linear Discriminant Analysis (LDA) may optionally be applied to further reduce the dimensionality of any representation, and to decorrelate the coefficients.

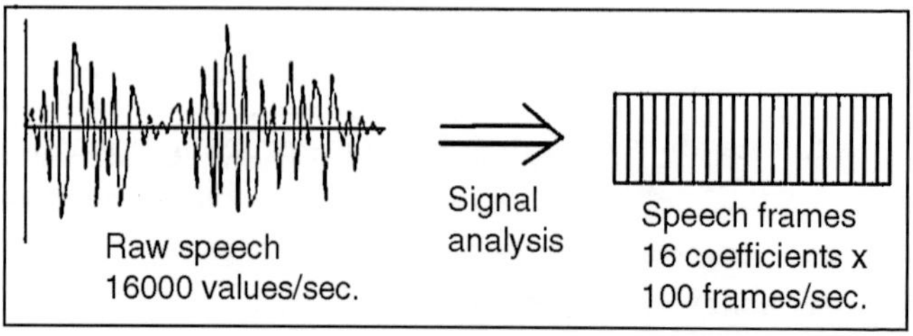

- *Speech frames:* The result of signal analysis is a sequence of speech frames, typically at 10 msec intervals, with about 16 coefficients per frame. These frames may be augmented by their own first and/or second derivatives, providing explicit information about speech dynamics; this typically leads to improved performance. The speech frames are used for acoustic analysis.
- *Acoustic models*: In order to analyse the speech frames for their acoustic content, we need a set of acoustic models. There are many kinds of acoustic models, varying in their representation, granularity, context dependence, and other properties.

It shows two popular representations for acoustic models. The simplest is a template, which is just a stored sample of the unit of speech to be modeled, *e.g.*, a recording of a word. An unknown word can be recognized by simply comparing it against all known templates, and finding the closest match. Templates have two major drawbacks:–

- They cannot model acoustic variabilities, except in a coarse way by assigning multiple templates to each word; and
- In practice they are limited to whole-word models, because it's hard to record or segment a sample shorter than a word - so templates are useful only in small systems which can afford the luxury of using whole-word models.

A more flexible representation, used in larger systems, is based on trained acoustic models, or states. In this approach, every word is modeled by a sequence of trainable states, and each state indicates the sounds that are likely to be heard in that segment of the word, using a probability distribution over the acoustic space. Probability distributions can be modeled parametrically, by assuming that they have a simple shape (*e.g.*, a Gaussian distribution) and then trying to find the parametres that describe it; or non-parametrically, by representing the distribution directly (*e.g.*, with a histogram over a quantization of the acoustic space, or, as we shall see, with a neural network).

Time Warping

In this we motivate and explain the Dynamic Time Warping algorithm, one of the oldest and most important algorithms in speech recognition. The simplest way to recognize an isolated word sample is to compare it against a number of stored word templates and determine which is the 'best match'.

This goal is complicated by a number of factors. First, different samples of a given word will have somewhat different durations. This problem can be eliminated by simply normalizing the templates and the unknown speech so that they all have an equal duration. However, another problem is that the rate of speech may not be constant throughout the word; in other words, the optimal alignment between a template and the speech sample may be nonlinear. Dynamic Time Warping (DTW) is an efficient method for finding this optimal nonlinear alignment.

DTW is an instance of the general class of algorithms known as dynamic programming. Its time and space complexity is merely linear in the duration of the speech sample and the vocabulary size. The algorithm makes a single pass through a matrix of frame scores while computing locally optimized segments of the global alignment path.

If D(x,y) is the Euclidean distance between frame x of the speech sample and frame y of the reference template, and if C(x,y) is the cumulative score along an optimal alignment path that leads to (x,y), then

$$C(x, y) = \text{MIN}(C(x - 1,y), C(x - 1,y - 1), C(x, y - 1)) + D(x, y)$$

The resulting alignment path may be visualized as a low valley of Euclidean distance scores, meandering through the hilly landscape of the matrix, beginning at (0, 0) and ending at the final point (X, Y).

By keeping track of backpointers, the full alignment path can be recovered by tracing backwards from (X, Y). An optimal alignment path is computed for each reference word template, and the one with the lowest cumulative score is considered to be the best match for the unknown speech sample.

There are many variations on the DTW algorithm. For example, it is common to vary the local path constraints, *e.g.*, by introducing transitions with slope 1/2 or 2, or weighting the transitions in various ways, or applying other kinds of slope constraints. While the reference word models are usually templates, they may be state-based models (as shown previously in Figure). When using states, vertical transitions are often disallowed (since there are fewer states than frames), and often the goal is to maximize the cumulative score, rather than to minimize it.

A particularly important variation of DTW is an extension from isolated to continuous speech. This extension is called the One Stage DTW algorithm. Here the goal is to find the optimal alignment between the speech sample and the best sequence of reference words.

The complexity of the extended algorithm is still linear in the length of the sample and the vocabulary size. The only modification to the basic DTW algorithm is that at the beginning of each reference word model (*i.e.*, its first frame or state), the diagonal path is allowed to point back to the end of all reference word models in the preceding frame.

Local backpointers must specify the reference word model of the preceding point, so that the optimal word sequence can be recovered by tracing backwards from the final point of the word W with the best final score. Grammars can be imposed on continuous speech recognition by restricting the allowed transitions at word boundaries.

APPLICATIONS

Health Care

In the health care domain, even in the wake of improving speech recognition technologies, medical transcriptionists (MTs) have not yet become obsolete. The services provided may be redistributed rather than replaced. Speech recognition can be implemented in front-end or back-end of the medical documentation process. Front-End SR is where the provider dictates into a speech-recognition engine, the recognized words are displayed right after they are spoken, and the dictator is responsible for editing and signing off on the document. It never goes through an MT/editor. Back-End SR or Deferred SR is where the provider dictates into a digital dictation system, and the voice is routed through a speech-recognition machine and the recognized draft document is routed along with the original voice file to the MT/editor, who edits the draft and finalizes the report. Deferred SR is being widely used in the industry currently. Many Electronic Medical Records (EMR) applications can be more effective and may be performed more easily when deployed in conjunction with a speech-recognition engine. Searches, queries, and form filling may all be faster to perform by voice than by using a keyboard. Healthcare solutions are usually very state-specific, however some companies adjust their solutions to the needs of concreete markets (p.e. Speech Technology Center in Russia has a Finnish partner Vitim OY with a "Terve Elama" project).

Military

High-Performance Fighter Aircraft

Substantial efforts have been devoted in the last decade to the test and evaluation of speech recognition in fighter aircraft. Of particular note is the U.S. programme in speech recognition for the Advanced Fighter Technology Integration (AFTI)/F-16 aircraft (F-16 VISTA), and a programme in France installing speech recognition systems on Mirage aircraft, and also programmes in the UK dealing with a variety of aircraft platforms. In these programmes, speech recognizers have been operated successfully in fighter aircraft, with applications including: setting radio frequencies, commanding an autopilot system, setting steer-point coordinates and weapons release parameters, and controlling flight displays. Working with Swedish pilots flying in the JAS-39 Gripen cockpit, Englund (2004) found recognition deteriorated with increasing G-loads. It was also concluded that adaptation greatly improved the results in all cases and introducing models for breathing was shown to improve recognition scores significantly. Contrary to what might be expected, no effects of the broken English of the speakers were found.

It was evident that spontaneous speech caused problems for the recognizer, as could be expected. A restricted vocabulary, and above all, a proper syntax, could thus be expected to improve recognition accuracy substantially. The Eurofighter Typhoon currently in service with the UK RAF employs a speaker-dependent system, i.e. it requires each pilot to create a template. The system is not used for any safety critical or weapon critical tasks, such as weapon release or lowering of the undercarriage, but is used for a wide range of other cockpit functions. Voice commands are confirmed by visual and/or aural feedback. The system is seen as a major design feature in the reduction of pilot workload, and even allows the pilot to assign targets to himself with two simple voice commands or to any of his wingmen with only five commands. Speaker independent systems are also being developed and are in testing for the F35 Lightning II (JSF) and the Alenia Aermacchi M-346 Master lead-in fighter trainer. These systems have produced word accuracies in excess of 98%.

Helicopters

The problems of achieving high recognition accuracy under stress and noise pertain strongly to the helicopter environment as well as to the fighter environment. The acoustic noise problem is actually more severe in the helicopter environment, not only because of the high noise levels but also because the helicopter pilot generally does not wear a facemask, which would reduce acoustic noise in the microphone. Substantial test and evaluation programmes have been carried out in the past decade in speech recognition systems applications in helicopters, notably by the U.S. Army Avionics Research and Development Activity (AVRADA) and by the Royal Aerospace Establishment (RAE) in the UK. Work in France has included speech recognition in the Puma helicopter.

There has also been much useful work in Canada. Results have been encouraging, and voice applications have included: control of communication radios; setting of navigation systems; and control of an automated target handover system. As in fighter applications, the overriding issue for voice in helicopters is the impact on pilot effectiveness. Encouraging results are reported for the AVRADA tests, although these represent only a feasibility demonstration in a test environment. Much remains to be done both in speech recognition and in overall speech recognition technology, in order to consistently achieve performance improvements in operational settings.

Battle Management

Battle Management command centres generally require rapid access to and control of large, rapidly changing information databases. Commanders and system operators need to query these databases as conveniently as possible, in an eyes-busy environment where much of the information is presented in a display format. Human-machine interaction by voice has the potential to be very useful in these environments. A number of efforts have been undertaken to interface commercially available isolated-word recognizers into battle management environments. In one feasibility study speech recognition equipment was tested in conjunction with an integrated information display for naval battle management applications. Users were very optimistic about the potential of the system, although capabilities were limited. Speech understanding programmes sponsored by the Defense Advanced Research

Projects Agency (DARPA) in the U.S. has focused on this problem of natural speech interface. Speech recognition efforts have focused on a database of continuous speech recognition (CSR), large-vocabulary speech which is designed to be representative of the naval resource management task. Significant advances in the state-of-the-art in CSR have been achieved, and current efforts are focused on integrating speech recognition and natural language processing to allow spoken language interaction with a naval resource management system.

Training Air Traffic Controllers

Training for air traffic controllers (ATC) represents an excellent application for speech recognition systems. Many ATC training systems currently require a person to act as a "pseudo-pilot", engaging in a voice dialog with the trainee controller, which simulates the dialog which the controller would have to conduct with pilots in a real ATC situation. Speech recognition and synthesis techniques offer the potential to eliminate the need for a person to act as pseudo-pilot, thus reducing training and support personnel. In theory, Air controller tasks are also characterized by highly structured speech as the primary output of the controller, hence reducing the difficulty of the speech recognition task should be possible. In practice this is rarely the case. The FAA document 7110.65 details the phrases that should be used by air traffic controllers. While this document gives less than 150 examples of such phrases, the number of phrases supported by one of the simulation vendors speech recognition systems is in excess of 500,000. The USAF, USMC, US Army,US Navy and FAA as well as a number of international ATC training organizations such as the Royal Australian Air Force and Civil Aviation Authorities in Italy, Brazil, Canada are currently using ATC simulators with speech recognition from a number of different vendors.

Telephony and Other Domains

ASR in the field of telephony is now commonplace and in the field of computer gaming and simulation is becoming more widespread. Despite the high level of integration with word processing in general personal computing, however, ASR in the field of document production has not seen the expected increases in use. The improvement of mobile processor speeds made feasible the speech-enabled Symbian and Windows Mobile Smartphones. Speech is used mostly as a part of User Interface, for creating pre-defined or custom speech commands. Leading software vendors in this field are: Microsoft Corporation (Microsoft Voice Command), Digital Syphon (Sonic Extractor), Nuance Communications (Nuance Voice Control), Speech Technology Center, Vito Technology (VITO Voice2Go), Speereo Software (Speereo Voice Translator and SVOX.

PERFORMANCE

The performance of speech recognition systems is usually specified in terms of accuracy and speed. Accuracy is usually rated with word error rate (WER), whereas speed is measured with the real time factor. Other measures of accuracy include Single Word Error Rate (SWER) and Command Success Rate (CSR). In 1982, Kurzweil Applied Intelligence and Dragon Systems released speech recognition products. By 1985, Kurzweil's software had a vocabulary of 1,000 words—if uttered one word at a time. Two years later, in 1987, its lexicon reached 20,000 words, entering the realm of human vocabularies, which range from 10,000 to 150,000 words. But recognition accuracy was only 10% in 1993. Two years later, the error rate crossed below 50%. Dragon Systems released "Naturally Speaking" in 1997 which recognized normal human speech. Progress mainly came from improved computer performance and larger source text databases. The Brown Corpus was the first major database available, containing several million words. In 2006, Google published a trillion-word corpus, while Carnegie Mellon University researchers found no significant increase in recognition accuracy.

Algorithms

Both acoustic modeling and language modeling are important parts of modern statistically-based speech recognition algorithms. Hidden Markov models (HMMs) are widely used in many systems. Language modeling has many other applications such as smart keyboard and document classification.

Hidden Markov Models

Modern general-purpose speech recognition systems are based on Hidden Markov Models. These are statistical models which output a sequence of symbols or quantities. HMMs are used in speech recognition because a speech signal can be viewed as a piecewise stationary signal or a short-time stationary signal. In a short-time (e.g., 10 milliseconds)), speech can be approximated as a stationary process. Speech can be thought of as a Markov model for many stochastic purposes. Another reason why HMMs are popular is because they can be trained automatically and are simple and computationally feasible to use. In speech recognition, the hidden Markov model would output a sequence of n-dimensional real-valued vectors (with n being a small integer, such as 10), outputting one of these every 10 milliseconds.

The vectors would consist of cepstral coefficients, which are obtained by taking a Fourier transform of a short time window of speech and decorrelating the spectrum using a cosine transform, then taking the first (most significant) coefficients. The hidden Markov model will tend to have in each state a statistical distribution that is a mixture of diagonal covariance Gaussians which will give a likelihood for each observed vector. Each word, or (for more general speech recognition systems), each phoneme, will have a different output distribution; a hidden Markov model for a sequence of words or phonemes is made by concatenating the individual trained hidden Markov models for the separate words and phonemes.

Described above are the core elements of the most common, HMM-based approach to speech recognition. Modern speech recognition systems use various combinations of a number of standard techniques in order to improve results over the basic approach described above. A typical large-vocabulary system would need context dependency for the phonemes (so phonemes with different left and right context have different realizations as HMM states); it would use cepstral normalization to normalize for different speaker and recording conditions; for further speaker normalization it might use vocal tract length normalization (VTLN) for male-female normalization and maximum likelihood linear regression (MLLR) for more general speaker adaptation. The features would have so-called delta and delta-delta coefficients to capture speech dynamics and in addition might use heteroscedastic linear discriminant analysis (HLDA); or might skip the delta and delta-delta coefficients and use splicing and an LDA-based projection followed perhaps by heteroscedastic linear discriminant analysis or a global semitied covariance transform (also known as maximum likelihood linear transform, or MLLT). Many systems use so-called discriminative training techniques which dispense with a purely statistical approach to HMM parameter estimation and instead optimize some classification-related measure of the training data. Examples are maximum mutual information (MMI), minimum classification error (MCE) and minimum phone error (MPE).

Decoding of the speech (the term for what happens when the system is presented with a new utterance and must compute the most likely source sentence) would probably use the Viterbi algorithm to find the best path, and here there is a choice between dynamically creating a combination hidden Markov model which includes both the acoustic and language model information, or combining it statically beforehand (the finite state transducer, or FST, approach). A possible improvement to decoding is to keep a set of good candidates instead of just keeping the best candidate, and to use a better scoring function (rescoring) to rate these good candidates so that we may pick the best one according to this refined score. The set of candidates can either be kept as a list (the N-best list approach) or as a subset of the models (a lattice). Rescoring is usually done by trying to minimize the Bayes risk (or an approximation thereof): instead of taking the source sentence with maximal probability, we try to take the sentence which minimizes the expectancy of a given loss function with regards to all possible transcriptions (ie. we take the sentence which minimizes the average distance to other possible sentences weighted by their estimated probability). The loss function is usually the Levenshtein distance, though it can be different distances for specific tasks; the set of possible transcriptions is of course pruned to maintain tractability. Efficient algorithms have been devised to rescore lattices represented as weighted finite state transducers with edit distances represented themselves as a finite state transducer verifying certain assumptions.

Dynamic Time Warping (DTW)-Based Speech Recognition

Dynamic time warping is an approach that was historically used for speech recognition but has now largely been displaced by the more successful HMM-based approach. Dynamic time warping is an algorithm for measuring similarity between two sequences which may vary in time or speed. For instance, similarities in walking patterns would be detected, even if in one video the person was walking slowly and if in another they were walking more quickly, or even if there were accelerations and decelerations during the course of one observation. DTW has been applied to video, audio, and graphics – indeed, any data which can be turned into a linear representation can be analyzed with DTW. A well known application has been automatic speech recognition, to cope with different speaking speeds. In general, it is a method that allows a computer to find an optimal match between two given sequences (e.g. time series) with certain restrictions, i.e. the sequences are "warped" non-linearly to match each other. This sequence alignment method is often used in the context of hidden Markov models.

Further Information

Popular speech recognition conferences held each year or two include SpeechTEK and SpeechTEK Europe, ICASSP, Eurospeech/ICSLP (now named Interspeech) and the IEEE ASRU. Conferences in the field of Natural language processing, such as ACL, NAACL, EMNLP, and HLT, are beginning to include papers on speech processing. Important journals include the IEEE Transactions on Speech and Audio Processing (now named IEEE Transactions on Audio, Speech and Language Processing), Computer Speech and Language, and Speech Communication. Books like "Fundamentals of Speech Recognition" by Lawrence Rabiner can be useful to acquire basic knowledge but may not be fully up to date (1993). Another good source can be "Statistical Methods for Speech Recognition" by Frederick Jelinek and "Spoken Language Processing (2001)" by Xuedong Huang etc. More up to date is "Computer Speech", by Manfred R. Schroeder, second edition published in 2004. The recently updated textbook of "Speech and Language Processing (2008)" by Jurafsky and Martin presents the basics and the state of the art for ASR. A good insight into the techniques used in the best modern systems can be gained by paying attention to government sponsored evaluations such as those organized by DARPA (the largest speech recognition-related project ongoing as of 2007 is the GALE project, which involves both speech recognition and translation components).

In terms of freely available resources, Carnegie Mellon University's SPHINX toolkit is one place to start to both learn about speech recognition and to start experimenting. Another resource (free as in free beer, not free software) is the HTK book (and the accompanying HTK toolkit). The AT&T libraries GRM library, and DCD library are also general software libraries for large-vocabulary speech recognition.

People with Disabilities

People with disabilities can benefit from speech recognition programmes. Speech recognition is especially useful for people who have difficulty using their hands, ranging from mild repetitive stress injuries to involved disabilities that preclude using conventional computer input devices. In fact, people who used the keyboard a lot and developed RSI became an urgent early market for speech recognition. Speech recognition is used in deaf telephony, such as voicemail to text, relay services, and captioned telephone. Individuals with learning disabilities who have problems with thought-to-paper communication (essentially they think of an idea but it is processed incorrectly causing it to end up differently on paper) can benefit from the software.

Current Research and Funding

Measuring progress in speech recognition performance is difficult and controversial. Some speech recognition tasks are much more difficult than others. Word error rates on some tasks are less than 1%.

On others they can be as high as 50%. Sometimes it even appears that performance is going backwards as researchers undertake harder tasks that have higher error rates.

Because progress is slow and is difficult to measure, there is some perception that performance has plateaued and that funding has dried up or shifted priorities. Such perceptions are not new. In 1969, John Pierce wrote an open letter that did cause much funding to dry up for several years. In 1993 there was a strong feeling that performance had plateaued and there were workshops dedicated to the issue. However, in the 1990s funding continued more or less uninterrupted and performance continued slowly but steadily to improve.

For the past thirty years, speech recognition research has been characterized by the steady accumulation of small incremental improvements. There has also been a trend continually to change focus to more difficult tasks due both to progress in speech recognition performance and to the availability of faster computers.

In particular, this shifting to more difficult tasks has characterized DARPA funding of speech recognition since the 1980s. In the last decade it has continued with the EARS project, which undertook recognition of Mandarin and Arabic in addition to English, and the GALE project, which focused solely on Mandarin and Arabic and required translation simultaneously with speech recognition. Commercial research and other academic research also continue to focus on increasingly difficult problems. One key area is to improve robustness of speech recognition performance, not just robustness against noise but robustness against any condition that causes a major degradation in performance. Another key area of research is focused on an opportunity rather than a problem.

This research attempts to take advantage of the fact that in many applications there is a large quantity of speech data available, up to millions of hours. It is too expensive to have humans transcribe such large quantities of speech, so the research focus is on developing new methods of machine learning that can effectively utilize large quantities of unlabeled data. Another area of research is better understanding of human capabilities and to use this understanding to improve machine recognition performance.

9

Artificial Neural Network

An artificial neural network (ANN), usually called neural network (NN), is a mathematical model or computational model that is inspired by the structure and/or functional aspects of biological neural networks. A neural network consists of an interconnected group of artificial neurons, and it processes information using a connectionist approach to computation. In most cases an ANN is an adaptive system that changes its structure based on external or internal information that flows through the network during the learning phase. Modern neural networks are non-linear statistical data modeling tools. They are usually used to model complex relationships between inputs and outputs or to find patterns in data.

Qualities

- A neural network can perform tasks that a linear programme can not.
- When an element of the neural network fails, it can continue without any problem by their parallel nature.
- A neural network learns and does not need to be reprogrammed.
- It can be implemented in any application.
- It can be implemented without any problem.

Drawbacks

- The neural network needs training to operate.

- The architecture of a neural network is different from the architecture of microprocessors therefore needs to be emulated.
- Requires high processing time for large neural networks.

Another aspect of the artificial neural networks is that there are different architectures, which consequently requires different types of algorithms, but despite to be an apparently complex system, a neural network is relatively simple.Artificial neural networks (ANN) are among the newest signal-processing technologies in the engineer's toolbox.

The field is highly interdisciplinary, but our approach will restrict the view to the engineering perspective. In engineering, neural networks serve two important functions: as pattern classifiers and as nonlinear adaptive filters.

We will provide a brief overview of the theory, learning rules, and applications of the most important neural network models. Definitions and Style of Computation An Artificial Neural Network is an adaptive, most often nonlinear system that learns to perform a function (an input/output map) from data. Adaptive means that the system parametres are changed during operation, normally called the training phase.

After the training phase the Artificial Neural Network parametres are fixed and the system is deployed to solve the problem at hand (the testing phase). The Artificial Neural Network is built with a systematic step-by-step procedure to optimize a performance criterion or to follow some implicit internal constraint, which is commonly referred to as the learning rule.

The input/output training data are fundamental in neural network technology, because they convey the necessary information to 'discover' the optimal operating point. The nonlinear nature of the neural network processing elements (PEs) provides the system with lots of flexibility to achieve practically any desired input/output map, *i.e.*, some Artificial Neural Networks are universal mappers. There is a style in neural computation that is worth describing.

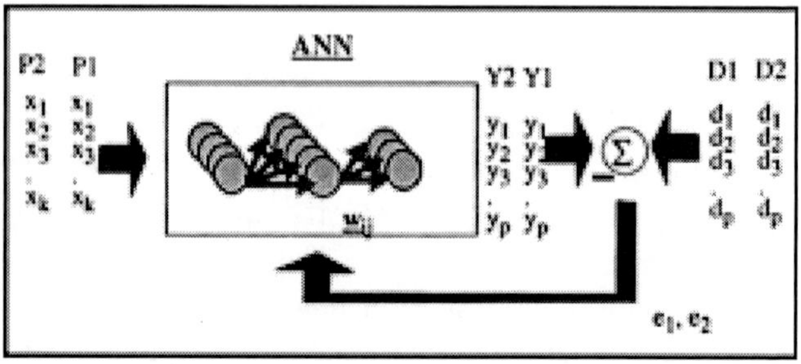

An input is presented to the neural network and a corresponding desired or target response set at the output (when this is the case the training is called supervised). An error is composed from the difference between the desired response and the system output.

This error information is fed back to the system and adjusts the system parametres in a systematic fashion (the learning rule). The process is repeated until the performance is acceptable. It is clear from this description that the performance hinges heavily on the data.

If one does not have data that cover a significant portion of the operating conditions or if they are noisy, then neural network technology is probably not the right solution. On the other hand, if there is plenty of data and the problem is poorly understood to derive an approximate model, then neural network technology is a good choice.

This operating procedure should be contrasted with the traditional engineering design, made of exhaustive subsystem specifications and intercommunication protocols. In artificial neural networks, the designer chooses the network topology, the performance function, the learning rule, and the criterion to stop the training phase, but the system automatically adjusts the parametres.

So, it is difficult to bring a priori information into the design, and when the system does not work properly it is also hard to incrementally refine the solution. But ANN-based solutions are extremely efficient in terms of development time and resources, and in many difficult problems artificial neural networks provide performance that is difficult to match with other technologies. Denker 10 years ago said that 'artificial neural networks are the second best way to implement a solution' motivated by the simplicity of their design and because of their universality, only shadowed by thc traditional design obtained by studying the physics of the problem.

At present, artificial neural networks are emerging as the technology of choice for many applications, such as pattern recognition, prediction, system identification, and control.

BACKGROUND

The original inspiration for the term *Artificial Neural Network* came from examination of central nervous systems and their neurons, axons, dendrites, and synapses, which constitute the processing elements of biological neural networks investigated by neuroscience. In an artificial neural network, simple artificial nodes, variously called "neurons", "neurodes", "processing elements" (PEs) or "units", are connected together to form a network of nodes mimicking the biological neural networks — hence the term "artificial neural network". Because neuroscience is still full of unanswered questions, and since there are many levels of abstraction and therefore many ways to take inspiration from the brain, there is no single formal definition of what an artificial neural network is. Generally, it involves a network of simple processing elements that exhibit complex global behaviour determined by connections between processing elements and element parameters. While an artificial neural network does not have to be adaptive per se, its practical use comes with algorithms designed to alter the strength (weights) of the connections in the network to produce a desired signal flow.

These networks are also similar to the biological neural networks in the sense that functions are performed collectively and in parallel by the units, rather than there being a clear delineation of subtasks to which various units are assigned. Currently, the term Artificial Neural Network (ANN) tends to refer mostly to neural network models employed in statistics, cognitive psychology and artificial intelligence. Neural network models designed with emulation of the central nervous system (CNS) in mind are a subject of theoretical neuroscience and computational neuroscience.

In modern software implementations of artificial neural networks, the approach inspired by biology has been largely abandoned for a more practical approach based on statistics and signal processing.

In some of these systems, neural networks or parts of neural networks (such as artificial neurons) are used as components in larger systems that combine both adaptive and non-adaptive elements.

While the more general approach of such adaptive systems is more suitable for real-world problem solving, it has far less to do with the traditional artificial intelligence connectionist models. What they do have in common, however, is the principle of non-linear, distributed, parallel and local processing and adaptation.

BACKPROPAGATION NEURAL NETWORK

A single-layer network has severe restrictions: the class of tasks that can be accomplished is very limited. In this chapter we will focus on feed-forward networks with layers of processing units. Minsky and Papert showed in 1969 that a two layer feed-forward network can overcome many restrictions, but did not present a solution to the problem of how to adjust the weights from input to hidden units.

An answer to this question was presented by Rumelhart, Hinton and Williams similar solutions appeared to have been published earlier. The central idea behind this solution is that the errors for the units of the hidden layer are determined by back-propagating the errors of the units of the output layer. For this reason the method is often called the back-propagation learning rule. Back-propagation can also be considered as a generalisation of the delta rule for non-linear activation functions1 and multilayer networks.

Multi-layer feed-forward networks

A feed-forward network has a layered structure. Each layer consists of units which receive their input from units from a layer directly below and send their output to units in a layer directly above the unit. There are no connections within a layer. The Ni inputs are fed into the first layer of Nh;1 hidden units. The input units are merely 'fan-out' units; no processing takes place in these units. The activation of a hidden unit is a function Fi of the weighted inputs plus a bias, as given in in eq.

$$y_k(t+1) = F_k\left(S_k(t)\right) = F_k\left(\sum_j w_{jk}(t)y_j(t) + \theta_k(t)\right),$$

The output of the hidden units is distributed over the next layer of Nh;2 hidden units, until the last layer of hidden units, of which the outputs are fed into a layer of No output units.

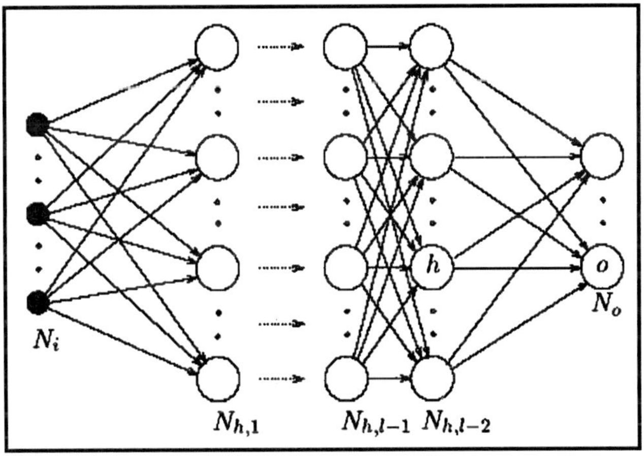

Although backpropagation can be applied to networks with any number of layers, just as for networks with binary units it has been shown that only one layer of hidden units suces to approximate any function with finitely many discontinuities to arbitrary precision, provided the activation functions of the hidden units are non-linear. In most applications a feed-forward network with a single layer of hidden units is used with a sigmoid activation function for the units.

Delta Rule

Since we are now using units with nonlinear activation functions, we have to generalise the delta rule:

The activation is a differentiable function of the total input, given by

$$y_k^p = F\left(S_k^p\right)$$

in which

$$\left(S_k^p\right) = \sum_j w_{jk} y_j^p + \theta_k$$

to get the correct generalisation of the delta rule as presented in the previous chapter, we must set

$$\Delta_p w_{jk} = -\gamma \frac{\delta E^p}{\delta w_{jk}}$$

The error measure Ep is defined as the total quadratic error for pattern p at the output units:

$$E^p = \frac{1}{2} \sum_{0=1}^{N_0} \left(d_0^p - y_0^p\right),$$

where dpo is the desired output for unit o when pattern p is clamped. We further set

$$E = \sum_p E^p$$

as the summed squared error. We can write

$$\frac{\delta E^p}{\delta w_{jk}} = \frac{\delta E^p}{\delta S_k^p} \frac{\delta S_k^p}{\delta w_{jk}}$$

By equation

$$S_k^p = \sum_j w_{jk} y_j^p + \theta_k$$

we see that the second factor is

$$\frac{\delta S_k^p}{\delta w_{jk}} = y_j^p$$

When we define

$$\delta_k^p = -\frac{\delta E^p}{\delta S_k^p}$$

wc will get an update rule which is equivalent to the delta rule as described in the previous chapter, resulting in a gradient descent on the error surface if we make the weight changes according to:

$$\Delta_p w_{jk} = \gamma \delta_k^p y_j^p$$

The trick is to figure out what δp k should be for each unit k in the network. The interesting result, which we now derive, is that there is a simple recursive computation of these δ's which can be implemented by propagating error signals backward through the network.

To compute δp k we apply the chain rule to write this partial derivative as the product of two factors, one factor reflecting the change in error as a function of the output of the unit and one re ecting thc change in the output as a function of changes in the input. Thus, we have

$$\delta_k^p = -\frac{\delta E^p}{\delta s_k^p} = -\frac{\delta E^p}{\delta y_k^p}\frac{\delta y_k^p}{\delta s_k^p}$$

Let us compute the second factor.

By equation,

$$y_k^p = F\left(S_k^p\right)$$

we see that,

$$\frac{\delta y_k^p}{\delta s_k^p} = F'\left(s_k^p\right)$$

which is the same result as we obtained with the standard delta rule. Substituting this and equation

$$\delta_k^p = -\frac{\delta E^p}{\delta s_k^p} = -\frac{\delta E^p}{\delta y_k^p}\frac{\delta y_k^p}{\delta s_k^p}$$

in equation, we get $\delta_0^p = (d_0^p - y_0^p)F_0'(s_0^p)$ for any output unit o. Secondly, if k is not an output unit but a hidden unit k = h, we do not readily know the contribution of the unit to the output error of the network.

However, the error measure can be written as a function of the net inputs from hidden to output layer; Ep = Ep(sp 1,sp 2,....... sp j.....) and we use the chain rule to write substituting this in equation yields. Equations and give a recursive procedure for computing the δ's for all units in the network, which are then used to compute the weight changes according to equation. This procedure constitutes the generalised delta rule for a feed-forward network of non-linear units.

Understanding backpropagation

The equations derived in the previous section may be mathematically correct, but what do they actually mean? Is there a way of understanding back-propagation other than reciting the necessary equations? In fact, the whole back-propagation process is intuitively very clear.

When a learning pattern is clamped, the activation values are propagated to the output units, and the actual network output is compared with the desired output values, we usually end up with an error in each of the output units. Let's call this error eo for a particular output unit o. We have to bring eo to zero.

The simplest method to do this is the greedy method: we strive to change the connections in the neural network in such a way that, next time around, the error eo will be zero for this particular pattern. We know from the delta rule that, in order to reduce an error, we have to adapt its incoming weights according to.

$$\Delta w_{ho} = (d_0 - y_0)y_h$$

That's step one. But it alone is not enough: when we only apply this rule, the weights from input to hidden units are never changed, and we do not have the full representational power of the feed-forward network as promised by the universal approximation theorem. In order to adapt the weights from input to hidden units, we again want to apply the delta rule. This is solved by the chain rule which does the following: distribute the error of an output unit o to all the hidden units that is it connected to, weighted by this connection.

Differently put, a hidden unit h receives a delta from each output unit o equal to the delta of that output unit weighted with (=multiplied by)the weight of the connection between those units.

Working with back-propagation

The application of the generalised delta rule thus involves two phases: During the first phase the input x is presented and propagated forward through the network to compute the output values yp o for each output unit. This output is compared with its desired value do, resulting in an error signal δp o for each output unit. The second phase involves a backward pass through the network during which the error signal is passed to each unit in the network and appropriate weight changes are calculated.Weight adjustments with sigmoid activation function.

The weight of a connection is adjusted by an amount proportional to the product of an error signal on the unit k receiving the input and the output of the unit j sending this signal along the connection.If the unit is an output unit, the error signal is given by Take as the activation function F the 'sigmoid' function as definedIn this case the derivative is equal to such that the error signal for an output unit can be written as the error signal for a hidden unit is determined recursively in terms of error signals of the units to which it directly connects and the weights of those connections. For the sigmoid activation function:

$$\delta_h^p = F'\left(s_h^p\right)\sum_{0=1}^{N_0}\delta_0^p w_{ho} = y_h^p\left(1-y_h^p\right)\sum_{0=1}^{N_0}\delta_0^p w_{ho}$$

Learning Rate and Momentum

The learning procedure requires that the change in weight is proportional to $\delta E^p / \delta w$ True gradient descent requires that in nitesimal steps are taken. The constant of proportionality is the learning rate. For practical purposes we choose a learning rate that is as large as possible without leading to oscillation. One way to avoid oscillation at large, is to make the change in weight dependent of the past weight change by adding a momentum term. Where indexes the presentation number and F is a constant which determines the efect of the previous weight change. Although, theoretically, the back-propagation algorithm performs gradient descent on the total error only if the weights are adjusted after the full set of learning patterns has been presented, more often than not the learning rule is applied to each pattern separately, *i.e.*, a pattern p is applied, Ep is calculated, and the weights are adapted (p = 1, 2,..... P). There exists empirical indication that this results in faster convergence. Care has to be taken, however, with the order in which the patterns are taught. For example, when using the same sequence over and over again the network may become focused on the few patterns. This problem can be overcome by using a permuted training method.

NEURAL NETWORKS

Robot Control

An important area of application of neural networks is in the field of robotics. Usually, these networks are designed to direct a manipulator, which is the most important form of the industrial robot, to grasp objects, based on sensor data. Another applications include the steering and path-planning of autonomous robot vehicles.

In robotics, the major task involves making movements dependent on sensor data. There are four, related, problems to be distinguished.

Forward kinematics

Kinematics is the science of motion which treats motion without regard to the forces which cause it. Within this science one studies the position, velocity, acceleration, and all higher order derivatives of the position variables. A very basic problem in the study of mechanical manipulation is that of forward kinematics.

This is the static geometrical problem of computing the position and orientation of the end-efector ('hand') of the manipulator. Specifi- cally, given a set of joint angles, the forward kinematic problem is to compute the position and orientation of the tool frame relative to the base frame.

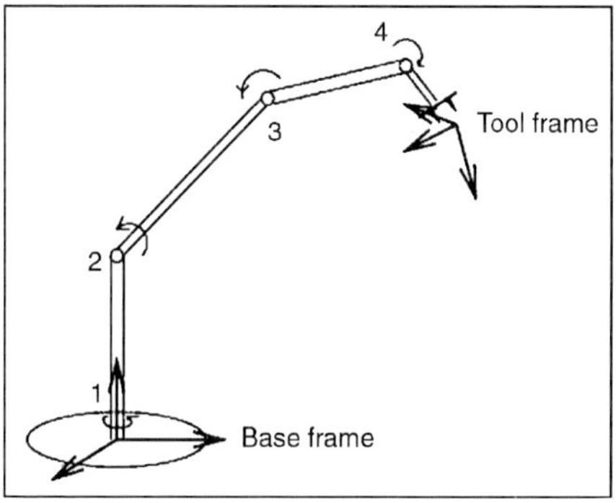

Fig. ***An Exemplar Robot Manipulator***

Inverse kinematics

This problem is posed as follows: given the position and orientation of the end-efector of the manipulator, calculate all possible sets of joint angles which could be used to attain this given position and orientation. This is a fundamental problem in the practical use of manipulators. The inverse kinematic problem is not as simple as the forward one. Because the kinematic equations are nonlinear, their solution is not always easy or even possible in a closed form. Also, the questions of existence of a solution, and of multiple solutions, arise. Solving this problem is a least requirement for most robot control systems.

Dynamics

Dynamics is a field of study devoted to studying the forces required to cause motion. In order to accelerate a manipulator from rest, glide at a constant end-efector velocity, and finally decelerate to a stop, a complex set of torque functions must be applied by the joint actuators.

In dynamics not only the geometrical properties (kinematics) are used, but also the physical properties of the robot are taken into account. Take for instance the weight (inertia) of the robotarm, which determines the force required to change the motion of the arm. The dynamics introduces two extra problems to the kinematic problems.

- The robot arm has a 'memory'. Its responds to a control signal depends also on its history (*e.g.* previous positions, speed, acceleration).
- If a robot grabs an object then the dynamics change but the kinematics don't. This is because the weight of the object has to be added to the weight of the arm (that's why robot arms are so heavy, making the relative weight change very small).

Trajectory Generation

To move a manipulator from here to there in a smooth, controlled fashion each joint must be moved via a smooth function of time. Exactly how to compute these motion functions is the problem of trajectory generation.

In the first section of this chapter we will discuss the problems associated with the positioning of the end-efector (in efect, representing the inverse kinematics in combination with sensory transformation).

End-efector positioning

The final goal in robot manipulator control is often the positioning of the hand or end-effector in order to be able to, *e.g.*, pick up an object. With the accurate robot arm that are manufactured, this task is often relatively simple, involving the following steps:

- Determine the target coordinates relative to the base of the robot. Typically, when this position is not always the same, this is done with a number of fixed cameras or other sensors which observe the work scene, from the image frame determine the position of the object in that frame, and perform a pre-determined coordinate transformation;

- With a precise model of the robot (supplied by the manufacturer), calculate the joint angles to reach the target (*i.e.*, the inverse kinematics). This is a relatively simple problem;
- Move the arm (dynamics control) and close the gripper.

Involvement of neural networks. So if these parts are relatively simple to solve with a high accuracy, why involve neural networks? The reason is the applicability of robots. When 'traditional' methods are used to control a robot arm, accurate models of the sensors and manipulators (in some cases with unknown parametres which have to be estimated from the system's behaviour; yet still with accurate models as starting point) are required and the system must be calibrated.

Also, systems which suffer from wear-and-tear (and which mechanical systems don't?) need frequent recalibration or parametre determination. Finally, the development of more complex (adaptive!) control methods allows the design and use of more exible (*i.e.*, less rigid) robot systems, both on the sensory and motory side.

Camera-robot Coordination

The system we focus on in this section is a work oor observed by a fixed cameras, and a robot arm. The visual system must identify the target as well as determine the visual position of the end-effector. The target position Xtarget together with the visual position of the hand Xhand are input to the neural controller N(.).

This controller then generates a joint position θ for the robot:

$$\theta = N(Xtarget, Xhand)$$

We can compare the neurally generated θ with the optimal $\theta 0$ generated by a fictitious perfect controller R(.):

$$\theta 0 = R(Xtarget, Xhand):$$

The task of learning is to make the N generate an output 'close enough' to θ0 There are two problems associated with teaching N(.):

- Generating learning samples which are in accordance with eq. θ0 = R(Xtarget,Xhand). This is not trivial, since in useful applications R(.) is an unknown function. Instead, a form of self-supervised or unsupervised learning is required. Some examples to solve this problem are given below;
- Constructing the mapping N(.)from the available learning samples. When the (usually randomly drawn) learning samples are available, a neural network uses these samples to represent the whole input space over which the robot is active. This is evidently a form of interpolation, but has the problem that the input space is of a high dimensionality, and the samples are randomly distributed.

Approach 1: Feed-forward Networks

When using a feed-forward system for controlling the manipulator, a self-supervised learning system must be used. One such a system has been reported by Psaltis, Sideris and Yamamura.

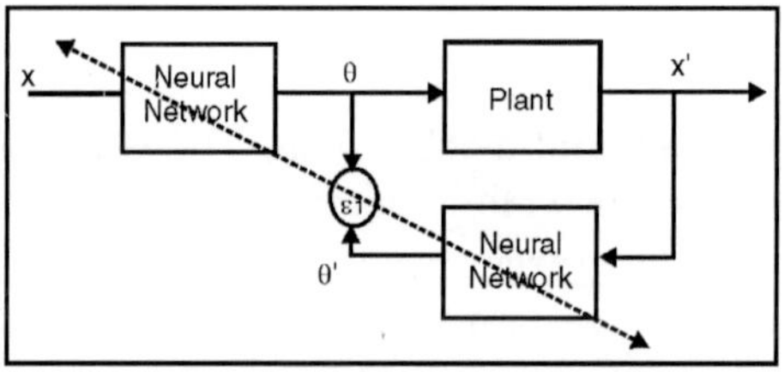

Here, the network, which is constrained to two-dimensional positioning of the robot arm, learns by experimentation. Three methods are proposed: Indirect learning.In indirect learning, a Cartesian target point x in world coordinates is generated, *e.g.*, by a two cameras looking at an object. This target point is fed into the network, which generates an angle vector θ. The manipulator moves to position θ, and the cameras determine the new position x' of the end-effector in world coordinates.

This x' again is input to the network, resulting in θ'. The network is then trained on the error $\varepsilon 1 = \theta - \theta'$

Indirect learning system for robotics. In each cycle, the network is used in two different places: first in the forward step, then for feeding back the error.

However, minimisation of ε1 does not guarantee minimisation of the overall error $\varepsilon = x - x'$. For example, the network often settles at a 'solution' that maps all x's to a single θ (*i.e.*, the mapping).

General Learning

The method is basically very much like supervised learning, but here the plant input θ must be provided by the user. Thus the network can directly minimise $|\theta - \theta'|$. The success of this method depends on the interpolation capabilities of the network. Correct choice of θ may pose a problem.

Specialised Learning

Keep in mind that the goal of the training of the network is to minimise the error at the output of the plant: $\varepsilon = x - x'$. We can also train the neural network by 'backpropagating' this error trough the plant (compare this with the back propagation of the error).

This method requires knowledge of the Jacobian matrix of the plant. A Jacobian matrix of a multidimensional function F is a matrix of partial derivatives of F, *i.e.*, the multidimensional form of the derivative. For example, if we have Y = F(X), *i.e.*,

$$y_1 = f_1(x_1, x_2, \ldots, x_n),$$
$$y_2 = f_2(x_1, x_2, \ldots, x_n),$$
$$\vdots$$
$$y_m = f_m(x_1, x_2, \ldots, x_n)$$

then,

$$\delta y_1 = \frac{\delta f_1}{\delta x_1}\delta x_1 + \frac{\delta f_1}{\delta x_2}\delta x_2 + \ldots + \frac{\delta f_1}{\delta x_n}\delta x_n,$$

$$\delta y_2 = \frac{\delta f_2}{\delta x_1}\delta x_1 + \frac{\delta f_2}{\delta x_2}\delta x_2 + \ldots + \frac{\delta f_2}{\delta x_n}\delta x_n,$$

$$\vdots$$

$$\delta y_m = \frac{\delta f_m}{\delta x_1}\delta x_1 + \frac{\delta f_m}{\delta x_2}\delta x_2 + \ldots + \frac{\delta f_m}{\delta x_n}\delta x_n$$

or,

$$\delta Y = \frac{\delta F}{\delta X}\delta X$$

also written as,

$$\delta Y = J(X)\delta X$$

where J is the Jacobian matrix of F. So, the Jacobian matrix can be used to calculate the change in the function when its parametres change. Now, in this case we have,

$$J_{ij} = \left[\frac{\delta Pi}{\delta \theta j}\right]$$

where $Pi(\theta)$ the ith element of the plant output for input θ. The learning rule applied here regards the plant as an additional and unmodiable layer in the neural network. The total error $\varepsilon = x - x'$ is propagated back through the plant by calculating the δ as in eq.

$$\delta_j = F'(s_j)\sum_i \delta_i \frac{\delta Pi(\theta)}{\delta \theta_j}$$

$$\delta_i = x_i - x_{i,}$$

where i iterates over the outputs of the plant. When the plant is an unknown function, where,

$$\frac{\delta Pi(\theta)}{\delta \theta_j}$$

can be approximated by

$$\frac{\delta Pi(\theta)}{\delta \theta_j} \approx \frac{Pi(\theta + h\theta_j e_j) - Pi(\theta)}{h}$$

where ej is used to change the scalar θj into a vector.

This approximate derivative can be measured by slightly changing the input to the plant and measuring the changes in the output.Again a two-layer feed-forward network is trained with back-propagation.

However, instead of calculating a desired output vector the input vector which should have invoked the current output vector is reconstructed, and back-propagation is applied to this new input vector and the existing output vector.

The configuration used consists of a monocular manipulator which has to grasp objects. Due to the fact that the camera is situated in the hand of the robot, the task is to move the hand such that the object is in the centre of the image and has some predetermined size (in a later article, a biologically inspired system is proposed in which the visual flow-field is used to account for the monocularity of the system, such that the dimensions of the object need not to be known anymore to the system).

One step towards the target consists of the following operations:

- Measure the distance from the current position to the target position in camera domain, x.
- Use this distance, together with the current state ? of the robot, as input for the neural network. The network then generates a joint displacement vector $\Delta\theta$.
- Send $\Delta\theta$ to the manipulator.
- Again measure the distance from the current position to the target position in camera domain, x'.
- Calculate the move made by the manipulator in visual domain, $x - {}_{t}^{t+1}Rx'$ where ${}_{t}^{t+1}R$
- The rotation matrix of the second camera image with respect to the First camera image;
- Teach the learning pair $\left(x - {}_{t}^{t+1}Rx', \theta; \Delta\theta\right)$ to the neural network.

This system has shown to learn correct behaviour in only tens of iterations, and to be very adaptive to changes in the sensor or manipulator. By using a feed-forward network, the available learning samples are approximated by a single, smooth function consisting of a summation of sigmoid functions. As mentioned in section 4, a feed-forward network with one layer of sigmoid units is capable of representing practically any function. But how are the optimal weights determined in finite time to obtain this optimal representation? Experiments have shown that, although a reasonable representation can be obtained in a short period of time, an accurate representation of the function that governs the learning samples is often not feasible or extremely dificult.

The reason for this is the global character of the approximation obtained with a feed-forward network with sigmoid units: every weight in the network has a global effect on the final approximation that is obtained. Building local representations is the obvious way out: every part of the network is responsible for a small subspace of the total input space. Thus accuracy is obtained locally. This is typically obtained with a Kohonen neural network.

Approach 2: Topology Conserving Maps

The system described consists of a robot manipulator with three degrees of freedom (orientation of the end-effector is not included) which has to grab objects in 3D-space. The system is observed by two fixed cameras which output their (x; y) coordinates of the object and the end effector

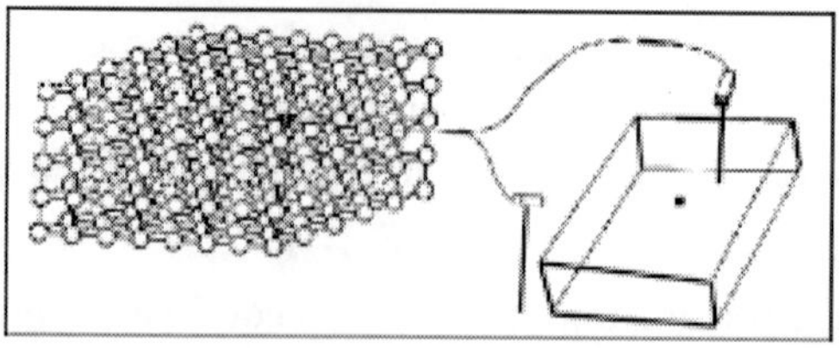

A Kohonen network merging the output of two cameras. Each run consists of two movements. In the gross move, the observed location of the object x (a four-component vector) is input to the network.

As with the Kohonen neural network, the neuron k with highest activation value is selected as winner, because its weight vector Wk is nearest to x. The neurons, which are arranged in a 3-dimensional lattice, correspond in a 1-1 fashion with subregions of the 3D workspace of the robot, *i.e.*, the neuronal lattice is a discrete representation of the workspace.

With each neuron a vector θ and Jacobian matrix A are associated. During gross move θk is fed to the robot which makes its move, resulting in retinal coordinates X g of the end-effector. To correct for the discretisation of the working space, an additional move is made which is dependent of the distance between the neuron and the object in space wk - x; this small displacement in Cartesian space is translated to an angle change using the Jacobian Ak:

$$\theta^{\text{final}} = \theta_k + A_k(x - w_k)$$

which is a first-order Taylor expansion of θ^{final}. The final retinal coordinates of the end-effector after this fine move are in xf. Learning proceeds as follows: when an improved estimate (θ,A) has been found, the following adaptations are made for all neurons j:

$$w_j^{\text{new}} = w_j^{\text{old}} + \gamma(t) g_{jk}(t)\left(x - w_j^{\text{old}}\right),$$

$$(\theta, A)_j^{\text{new}} = (\theta, A)_j^{\text{old}} + \gamma(t) g'_{jk}(t)\left((\theta, A)_j^* - (\theta, A)_j^{\text{old}}\right.$$

If gjk(t) = g'jk(t) = δjk, this is similar to perceptron learning. Here, as with the Kohonen learning rule, a distance function is used such that gjk(t) and g'jk(t) are Gaussians depending on the distance between neurons j and k with a maximum at j = k. An improved estimate (θ,A)* is obtained as follows.

$$\theta^* = \theta_k + A_k(x - x_f),$$

$$A^* = A_k + A_k\left(x - w_k - x_f + x_g\right) \times \frac{\left(x_f - x_g\right)^T}{\| x_f - x_g \|^2}$$

$$= A_k + \left(\Delta\theta - A_k \Delta x\right) \frac{\Delta x^T}{\| \Delta x \|^2}$$

NEURAL NETWORK APPROACHES

Because speech recognition is basically a pattern recognition problem, and because neural networks are good at pattern recognition, many early researchers naturally tried applying neural networks to speech recognition. The earliest attempts involved highly simplified tasks, *e.g.*, classifying speech segments as voiced/unvoiced, or nasal/fricative/plosive.

Success in these experiments encouraged researchers to move on to phoneme classification; this task became a proving ground for neural networks as they quickly achieved world-class results.

There are two basic approaches to speech classification using neural networks: static and dynamic, as illustrated in Figure.

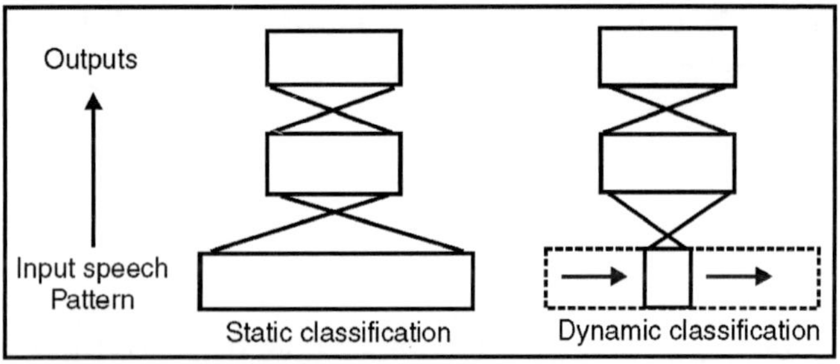

Fig. ***Static and Dynamic Approaches to Classification***

In static classification, the neural network sees all of the input speech at once, and makes a single decision. By contrast, in dynamic classification, the neural network sees only a small window of the speech, and this window slides over the input speech while the network makes a series of local decisions, which have to be integrated into a global decision at a later time.

Static classification works well for phoneme recognition, but it scales poorly to the level of words or sentences; dynamic classification scales better. Either approach may make use of recurrent connections, although recurrence is more often found in the dynamic approach.

Phoneme Classification

Phoneme classification can be performed with high accuracy by using either static or dynamic approaches. Here we review some typical experiments using each approach.

Static Approaches

A simple but elegant experiment was performed by Huang and Lippmann, demonstrating that neural networks can form complex decision surfaces from speech data. They applied a multilayer perceptron with only 2 inputs, 50 hidden units, and 10 outputs, to Peterson and Barney's collection of vowels produced by men, women, and children, using the first two formants of the vowels as the input speech representation. After 50,000 iterations of training, the network produced the decision regions.

These decision regions are nearly optimal, resembling the decision regions that would be drawn by hand, and they yield classification accuracy comparable to that of more conventional algorithms, such as k-nearest neighbour and Gaussian classification. In a more complex experiment, Elman and Zipser trained a network to classify the vowels/a,i,u/and the consonants/ b,d,g/as they occur in the utterances ba,bi,bu; da,di,du; and ga,gi,gu.

Their network input consisted of 16 spectral coefficients over 20 frames (covering an entire 64 msec utterance, centered by hand over the consonant's voicing onset); this was fed into a hidden layer with between 2 and 6 units, leading to 3 outputs for either vowel or consonant classification. This network achieved error rates of roughly 0.5% for vowels and 5.0% for consonants.

An analysis of the hidden units showed that they tend to be feature detectors, discriminating between important classes of sounds, such as consonants versus vowels. Among the most difficult of classification tasks is the so-called E-set, *i.e.*, discriminating between the rhyming English letters 'B, C, D, E, G, P, T, V, Z'. Burr applied a static network to this task, with very good results. His network used an input window of 20 spectral frames, automatically extracted from the whole utterance using energy information. These inputs led directly to 9 outputs representing the E-set letters. The network was trained and tested using 180 tokens from a single speaker. When the early portion of the utterance was oversampled, effectively highlighting the disambiguating features, recognition accuracy was nearly perfect.

Dynamic Approaches

In a seminal paper, Waibel *et al* demonstrated excellent results for phoneme classification using a Time Delay Neural Network (TDNN), shown in Figure.

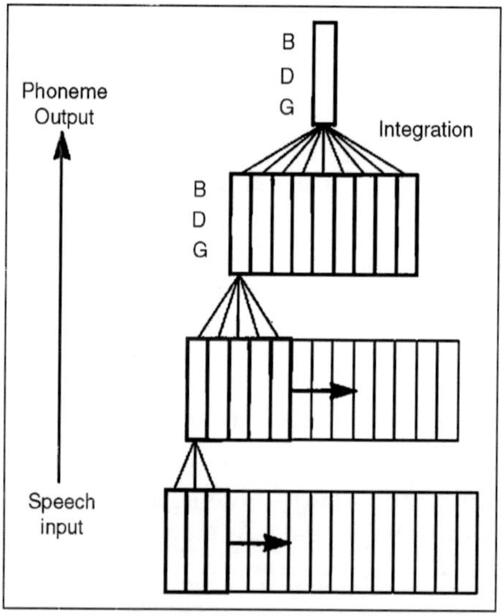

This architecture has only 3 and 5 delays in the input and hidden layer, respectively, and the final output is computed by integrating over 9 frames of phoneme activations in the second hidden layer.

The TDNN's design is attractive for several reasons: its compact structure economizes on weights and forces the network to develop general feature detectors; its hierarchy of delays optimizes these feature detectors by increasing their scope at each layer; and its temporal integration at the output layer makes the network shift invariant (*i.e.*, insensitive to the exact positioning of the speech). The TDNN achieved an error rate of 1.5%, compared to 6.5% achieved by a simple HMM-based recognizer.

Neural Networks

It is nowadays a common notion that vast amounts of capital are traded through the Stock Markets all around the world. National economies are strongly linked and heavily influenced of the performance of their Stock Markets. Moreover, recently the Markets have become a more accessible investment tool, not only for strategic investors but for common people as well.

Consequently they are not only related to macroeconomic parametres, but they influence everyday life in a more direct way. Therefore they constitute a mechanism which has important and direct social impacts. The characteristic that all Stock Markets have in common is the uncertainty, which is related with their short and long-term future state. This feature is undesirable for the investor but it is also unavoidable whenever the Stock Market is selected as the investment tool. The best that one can do is to try to reduce this uncertainty. Stock Market Prediction (or Forecasting) is one of the instruments in this process.

The Stock Market prediction task divides researchers and academics into two groups those who believe that we can devise mechanisms to predict the market and those who believe that the market is efficient and whenever new information comes up the market absorbs it by correcting itself, thus there is no space for prediction (EMH). Furthermore they believe that the Stock Market follows a Random Walk, which implies that the best prediction you can have about tomorrow's value is today's value.

In literature a number of different methods have been applied in order to predict Stock Market returns. These methods can be grouped in four major categories: i) Technical Analysis

Methods, ii) Fundamental Analysis Methods, iii) Traditional Time Series Forecasting and iv) Machine Learning Methods. Technical analysts, known as chartists, attempt to predict the market by tracing patterns that come from the study of charts which describe historic data of the market.

Fundamental analysts study the intrinsic value of an stock and they invest on it if they estimate that its current value is lower that its intrinsic value. In Traditional Time Series forecasting an attempt to create linear prediction models to trace patterns in historic data takes place.

These linear models are divided in two categories: the univariate and the multivariate regression models, depending on whether they use one of more variables to approximate the Stock Market time series.

Finally a number of methods have been developed under the common label Machine Learning these methods use a set of samples and try to trace patterns in it (linear or non-linear) in order to approximate the underlying function that generated the data.

Investments

Investment Theories:An investment theory suggests what parametres one should take into account before placing his (or her) capital on the market. Traditionally the investment community accepts two major theories: the Firm Foundation and the Castles in the Air. Reference to these theories allows us to understand how the market is shaped, or in other words how the investors think and react. It is this sequence of 'thought and reaction' by the investors that defines the capital allocation and thus the level of the market.

There is no doubt that the majority of the people related to stock markets is trying to achieve profit. Profit comes by investing in stocks that have a good future (short or long term future). Thus what they are trying to accomplish one way or the other is to predict 16 the future of the market. But what determines this future? The way that people invest their money is the answer; and people invest money based on the information they hold. Therefore we have the following schema:

Information→Investor→Market Level

The factors that are under discussion on this schema are: the content of the 'Information' component and the way that the 'Investor' reacts when having this info.

On the other hand, according to the Castles in the Air theory the investors are triggered by information that is related to other investors' behaviour. So for this theory the only concern that the investor should have is to buy today with the price of 20 and sell tomorrow with the price of 30, no matter what the intrinsic value of the firm he (or she) invests on is.

Prediction Methods:The prediction of the market is without doubt an interesting task. In the literature there are a number of methods applied to accomplish this task. These methods use various approaches, ranging from highly informal ways (*e.g.* the study of a chart with the fluctuation of the market) to more formal ways (*e.g.* linear or non-linear regressions).

We have categorized these techniques as follows:

- Technical Analysis Methods
- Fundamental Analysis Methods
- Traditional Time Series Prediction Methods
- Machine Learning Methods

The criterion to this categorization is the type of tools and the type of data that each method is using in order to predict the market. What is common to these techniques is that they are used to predict and thus benefit from the market's future behaviour.

Technical Analysis

'Technical analysis is the method of predicting the appropriate time to buy or sell a stock used by those believing in the castles-in-the-air view of stock pricing'. The idea behind technical analysis is that share prices move in trends dictated by the constantly changing attributes of investors in response to different forces.

Using technical data such as price, volume, highest and lowest prices per trading period the technical analyst uses charts to predict future stock movements. Price charts are used to detect trends, these trends are assumed to be based on supply and demand issues which often have cyclical or noticeable patterns. From the study of these charts trading rules are extracted and used in the market environment. The technical analysts are known and as 'chartists'. Most chartists believe that the market is only 10 per cent logical and 90 per cent psychological. The chartist's belief is that a careful study of what the other investors are doing will shed light on what the crowed is likely to do in the future.

This is a very popular approach used to predict the market, which has been heavily criticized. The major point of criticism is that the extraction of trading rules from the study of charts is highly subjective therefore different analysts might extract different trading rules by studying the same charts. Although it is possible to use this methodology to predict the market on daily basis we will not follow this approach on this study due to its subjective character.

Fundamental Analysis

'Fundamental analysis is the technique of applying the tenets of the firm foundation theory to the selection of individual stocks". The analysts that use this method of prediction use fundamental data in order to have a clear picture of the firm (industry or market) they will choose to invest on. They are aiming to compute the 'real' value of the asset that they will invest in and they determine this value by studying variables such as the growth, the dividend payout, the interest rates, the risk of investment, the sales level, the tax rates an so on.

Their objective is to calculate the intrinsic value of an asset (*e.g.* of a stock). Since they do so they apply a simple trading rule. If the intrinsic 21 value of the asset is higher than the value it holds in the market, invest in it. If not, consider it a bad investment and avoid it. The fundamental analysts believe that the market is defined 90 per cent by logical and 10 per cent by physiological factors. This type of analysis is not possible to fit in the objectives of our study. The reason for this is that the data it uses in order to determine the intrinsic value of an asset does not change on daily basis. Therefore fundamental analysis is helpful for predicting the market only in a long-term basis.

Traditional Time Series Prediction

The Traditional Time Series Prediction analyses historic data and attempts to approximate future values of a time series as a linear combination of these historic data. In econometrics there are two basic types of time series forecasting: univariate (simple regression) and multivariate (multivariate regression).

These types of regression models are the most common tools used in econometrics to predict time series. The way they are applied in practice is that firstly a set of factors that influence (or more specific is assumed that influence) the series under prediction is formed. These factors are the explanatory variables xi of the prediction model. Then a mapping between their values xit and the values of the time series yt (y is the to-be explained variable) is done, so that pairs {xit, yt} are formed. These pairs are used to define the importance of each explanatory variable in the formulation of the to-be explained variable. In other words the linear combination of xi that approximates in an optimum way y is defined. Univariate models are based on one explanatory variable (I=1) while multivariate models use more than one variable (I>1). Regression models have been used to predict stock market time series. A good example of the use of multivariate regression is the work of Pesaran and Timmermann (1994).

They attempted prediction of the excess returns time series of S&P 500 and the Dow Jones on monthly, quarterly and annually basis. The data they used was from Jan 1954 until Dec 1990. Initially they used the subset from Jan 1954 until Dec 1959 to adjust the coefficients of the explanatory variables of their models, and then applied the models to predict the returns for the next year, quarter and month respectively.

Machine Learning Methods

Several methods for inductive learning have been developed under the common label 'Machine Learning'. All these methods use a set of samples to generate an approximation of the underling function that generated the data. The aim is to draw conclusions from these samples in such way that when unseen data are presented to a model it is possible to infer the to-be explained variable from these data.

The methods we discuss here are: The Nearest Neighbour and the Neural Networks Techniques. Both of these methods have been applied to market prediction; particularly for Neural Networks there is a rich literature related to the forecast of the market on daily basis.

NETWORK FUNCTION

The word *network* in the term 'artificial neural network' refers to the inter–connections between the neurons in the different layers of each system. The most basic system has three layers.

The first layer has input neurons, which send data via synapses to the second layer of neurons, and then via more synapses to the third layer of output neurons. More complex systems will have more layers of neurons with some having increased layers of input neurons and output neurons.

The synapses store parameters called "weights" that manipulate the data in the calculations. Networks such as the previous one are commonly called feedforward, because their graph is a directed acyclic graph. Networks with cycles are commonly called recurrent. Such networks are commonly depicted in the manner shown at the top of the figure, where is shown as being dependent upon itself. However, an implied temporal dependence is not shown. ANN depends on three basic criteria:

- Interconnection between different Layers of Neurons;
- Learning process of ANN;
- Activation Function;

Interconnection shows the relationship between single layer, multiple layers of input output parameters of Neurons it shows the relationship of One to Many .it means same input can perform many outputs for different layer of architecture.

Choosing a Cost Function

While it is possible to define some arbitrary, ad hoc cost function, frequently a particular cost will be used, either because it has desirable properties (such as convexity) or because it arises naturally from a particular formulation of the problem (e.g., in a probabilistic formulation the posterior probability of the model can be used as an inverse cost). Ultimately, the cost function will depend on the desired task. An overview of the three main categories of learning tasks is provided below.

Learning Paradigms

There are three major learning paradigms, each corresponding to a particular abstract learning task. These are supervised learning, unsupervised learning and reinforcement learning.

Supervised Learning

A commonly used cost is the mean-squared error, which tries to minimize the average squared error between the network's output, f(x), and the target value y over all the example pairs. When one tries to minimize this cost using gradient descent for the class of neural networks called multilayer perceptrons, one obtains the common and well-known backpropagation algorithm for training neural networks. Tasks that fall within the paradigm of supervised learning are pattern recognition (also known as classification) and regression (also known as function approximation). The supervised learning paradigm is also applicable to sequential data (e.g., for speech and gesture recognition). This can be thought of as learning with a "teacher," in the form of a function that provides continuous feedback on the quality of solutions obtained thus far. Basically supervised learning are classified in two types.These are error connection gradient descent and stochastic.

Error connection gradient descent are also classified into least mean square and backpropagation.

Learning Algorithms

Training a neural network model essentially means selecting one model from the set of allowed models (or, in a Bayesian framework, determining a distribution over the set of allowed models) that minimizes the cost criterion. There are numerous algorithms available for training neural network models; most of them can be viewed as a straightforward application of optimization theory and statistical estimation. Recent developments in this field use particle swarm optimization and other swarm intelligence techniques. Most of the algorithms used in training artificial neural networks employ some form of gradient descent. This is done by simply taking the derivative of the cost function with respect to the network parameters and then changing those parameters in a gradient-related direction. Evolutionary methods, simulated annealing, expectation-maximization and non-parametric methods are some commonly used methods for training neural networks. Temporal perceptual learning relies on finding temporal relationships in sensory signal streams. In an environment, statistically salient temporal correlations can be found by monitoring the arrival times of sensory signals. This is done by the perceptual network.

KOHONEN NEURAL NETWORK

The cerebral cortex is arguably the most fascinating structure in all of human physiology. Although vastly complex on a microscopic level, the cortex reveals a consistently uniform structure on a macroscopic scale, from one brain to another. Centres for such diverse activities as thought, speech, vision, hearing, and motor functions lie in specific areas of the cortex, and these areas are located consistently relative to one another. Moreover, individual areas exhibit a logical ordering of their functionality.

An example is the so-called tonotopic map of the auditory regions, where neighbouring neurons respond to similar sound frequencies in an orderly sequence from high pitch to low pitch. Another example is the somatotopic map of motor nerves. Regions such as the tonotopic map and the somatotopic map can be referred to as ordered feature maps. The purpose of this chapter is to investigate a mechanism by which these ordered feature maps might develop naturally.

It appears likely that our genetic makeup predestines our neural development to a large extent. Whether the mechanisms that we shall describe here play a major or a minor role in the organization of neural tissue is not an issue for us. It was, however, an interest in discovering how such an organization might be learned that led Kohonen. The cortex is essentially a large (approximately 1-metre-square, in adult humans) thin (2-to-4-millimetre thick) sheet consisting of six layers of neurons of varying type and density. It is folded into its familiar shape to maximize packing density in the cranium. Since we are not so much concerned with the details of anatomy here, we shall consider an adequate model of the cortex to be a two-dimensional sheet of processing elements. As a simplified definition, we can say that, in a topology-preserving map, units located physically next to each other will respond to classes of input vectors that are likewise next to each other.

Although it is easy to visualize units next to each other in a two-dimensional array, it is not so easy to determine which classes of vectors are next to each other in a high-dimensional space. Large-dimensional input vectors are, in a sense, projected down on the twodimensional map in a way that maintains the natural order of the input vectors.

This dimensional reduction could allow us to visualize easily important relationships among the data that otherwise might go unnoticed. In the next section, we shall formalize some of the definitions presented in this section, and shall look at the mathematics of the topology-preserving map. Henceforth, we shall refer to the topology-preserving map as a self-organizing map (SOM).

The Kohonen network can be seen as an extension to the competitive learning network, although this is chronologically incorrect. Also, the Kohonen network has a diferent set of applications.In the Kohonen network, the output units in S are ordered in some fashion, often in a twodimensional grid or array, although this is application-dependent. The ordering, which is chosen by the user1, determines which output neurons are neighbours.

Now, when learning patterns are presented to the network, the weights to the output units are thus adapted such that the order present in the input space $\Re N$ is preserved in the output, *i.e.*, the neurons in S.

This means that learning patterns which are near to each other in the input space (where 'near' is determined by the distance measure used in finding the winning unit) must be mapped on output units which are also near to each other, *i.e.*, the same or neighbouring units. Thus, if inputs are uniformly distributed in $\Re N$ and the order must be preserved, the dimensionality of S must be at least $\Re N$. The mapping, which represents a discretisation of the input space, is said to be topology preserving.

However, if the inputs are restricted to a subspace of $\Re N$, a Kohonen network can be used of lower dimensionality. For example: data on a twodimensional manifold in a high dimensional input space can be mapped onto a two-dimensional Kohonen network, which can for example be used for visualisation of the data. Usually, the learning patterns are random samples from ?N. At time t, a sample x(t) is generated and presented to the network. Using the same formulas as in section 6.1, the winning unit k is determined. Next, the weights to this winning unit as well as its neighbours are adapted using the learning rule

$$w_0(t+1) = w_0(t) + \gamma g(0,k)(x(t) - w_0(t)) \; \forall_0 \in S$$

Here, g(o,k) is a decreasing function of the grid-distance between units o and k, such that g(k,k) = 1. For example, for g() a Gaussian function can be used, such that (in one dimension!) g(o,k) = exp -(-(o - k)2).Due to this collective learning scheme, input signals.

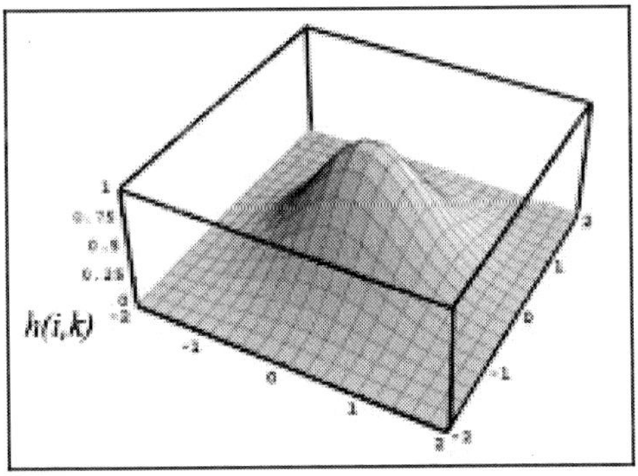

Gaussian neuron distance function g(). In this case, g() is shown for a two-dimensional grid because it looks nice. which are near to each other will be mapped on neighbouring neurons. A topology-conserving map converging. The weight vectors of a network with two inputs and 8x8 output neurons arranged in a planar grid are shown. A line in each figure connects weight wi(o1,o2) with weights wi(o1+1,o2) and wi(i1,i2+1). The left most gure shows the initial weights; the rightmost when the map is almost completely formed. If the intrinsic dimensionality of S is less than N, the neurons in the network are 'folded' in the input space, such as depicted in figure.

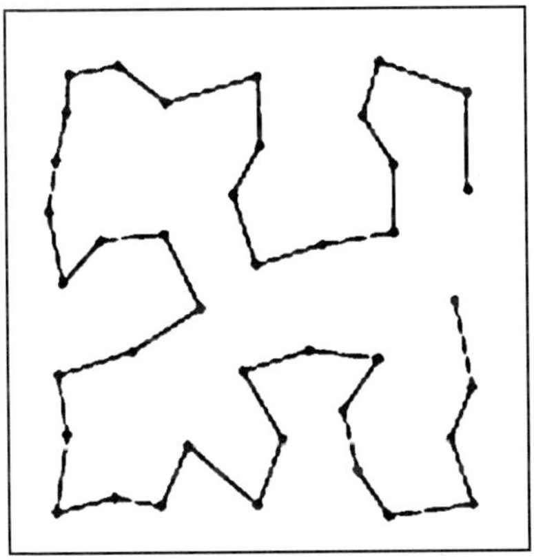

The topology-conserving quality of this network has many counterparts in biological brains. The brain is organised in many places so that aspects of the sensory environment are represented in the form of two-dimensional maps. For example, in the visual system, there are several topographic mappings of visual space onto the surface of the visual cortex. There are organised mappings of the body surface onto the cortex in both motor and somatosensory areas, and tonotopic mappings of frequency in the auditory cortex.

The use of topographic representations, where some important aspect of a sensory modality is related to the physical locations of the cells on a surface, is so common that it obviously serves an important information processing function.It does not come as a surprise, therefore, that already many applications have been devised of the Kohonen topology-conserving maps. Kohonen himself has successfully used the network for phoneme-recognition (Kohonen, Makisara, and Saramaki, 1984). Also, the network has been used to merge sensory data from dierent kinds of sensors, such as auditory and visual, 'looking' at the same scene. To explain the plausibility of a similar structure in biological networks, Kohonen remarks that the lateral inhibition between the neurons could be obtained via e erent connections between those neurons. In one dimension, those connection strengths form a 'Mexican hat'

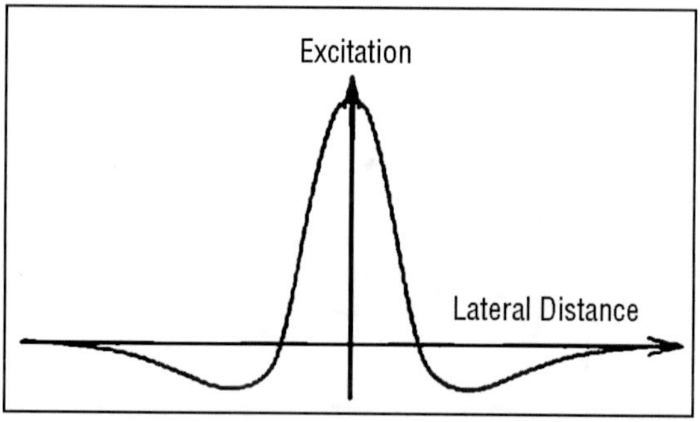

Mexican hat. Lateral interaction around the winning neuron as a function of distance: excitation to nearby neurons, inhibition to farther of neurons.

SOM Learning Algorithm

During the training period, each unit with a positive activity within the neighbourhood of the winning unit participates in the learning process.We can describe the learning process by the equations:

$$wi = (t)(x - wi,)U(Yi)$$

where w, is the weight vector of the ith unit and x is the input vector. The function U(yi) is zero unless yi > 0 in which case U(yi) = 1, ensuring that only those units with positive activity participate in the learning process. The factor ?(t) is written as a function of time to anticipate our desire to change it as learning progresses.To demonstrate the formation of an ordered feature map, we shall use an example in which units are trained to recognize their relative positions in two-dimensional space.

Each processing element is identified by its coordinates, (u,v), in two-dimensional space. Weight vectors for this example are also two dimensional and are initially assigned to the processing elements randomly. As with other competitive structures, a winning processing element is determined for each input vector based on the similarity between the input vector and the weight vector. For an input vector x, the winning unit can be determined by,

$$||xwc||=\min\{||x-wi||\}$$

where the index c refers to the winning unit. To keep subscripts to a minimum, we identify each unit in the two-dimensional array by a single subscript. Instead of updating the weights of the winning unit only, we define a physical neighbourhood around the unit, and all units within this neighbourhood participate in the weight-update process. As learning proceeds, the size of the neighbourhood is diminished until it encompasses only a single unit.If c is the winning unit, and N,. is the list of unit indices that make up the neighbourhood, then the weight-update equations are

$$w_i(t+1) = \begin{cases} w_i(t) + \alpha(t)(x - w_i(t)) i \in N \\ 0 \quad \text{otherwise} \end{cases}$$

Each weight vector participating in the update process rotates slightly towards the input vector, x. Once training has progressed sufficiently, the weight vector on each unit will converge to a value that is representative of the coordinates of the points near the physical location of the unit.

Hopfield Neural Network

One of the earliest recurrent neural networks reported in literature was the auto-associator independently described by Anderson and Kohonen in 1977. It consists of a pool of neurons with connections between each unit i and j, i 6= j.

The auto-associator network. All neurons are both input and output neurons, *i.e.*, a pattern is clamped, the network iterates to a stable state, and the output of the network consists of the new activation values of the neurons.All connections are weighted. In 1982, Hopfield brings together several earlier ideas concerning these networks and presents a complete mathematical analysis based on Ising spin models. It is therefore that this network, which we will describe in this chapter, is generally referred to as the Hopfield network. The Hopfield network consists of a set of N interconnected neurons which update their activation values asynchronously and independently of other neurons. All neurons are both input and output neurons.

The activation values are binary. Originally, Hopfield chose activation values of 1 and 0, but using values +1 and -1 presents some advantages discussed below. We will therefore adhere to the latter convention. The state of the system is given by the activation values1 y = (yk). The net input sk(t+1) of a neuron k at cycle t+1 is a weighted sum

$$s_k(t+1) = \sum_{j \neq k} y_j(t) w_{jk} + \theta_k$$

A simple threshold function is applied to the net input to obtain the new activation value yi(t + 1) at time t + 1:

$$y_k(t+1) = \begin{cases} +1 & \text{if } s_k(t+1) > U_k \\ -1 & \text{if } s_k(t+1) < U_k \\ y_k(t) & \text{otherwise} \end{cases}$$

Hopfield Network as Associative Memory

A primary application of the Hopfield network is an associative memory. In this case, the weights of the connections between the neurons have to be thus set that the states of the system corresponding with the patterns which are to be stored in the network are stable. These states can be seen as 'dips' in energy space. When the network is cued with a noisy or incomplete test pattern, it will render the incorrect or missing data by iterating to a stable state which is in some sense 'near' to the cued pattern.

$$w_{jk} = \begin{cases} \sum_{p=1}^{P} x_j^p x_k^p & \text{if } j \neq k \\ 0 & \end{cases}$$

i.e., if xp j and xp k are equal, wjk is increased, otherwise decreased by one (note that, in the original Hebb rule, weights only increase). It appears, however, that the network gets saturated very quickly, and that about 0:15N memories can be stored before recall errors become severe. There are two problems associated with storing too many patterns:

- The stored patterns become unstable;
- Spurious stable states appear (*i.e.*, stable states which do not correspond with stored patterns).

The first of these two problems can be solved by an algorithm proposed by Bruce *et al.*

Algorithm 1 Given a starting weight matrix for each pattern xp to be stored and each element xp k in xp de ne a correction εk such that

$$\in_k = \begin{cases} 0 & \text{if } y_k \text{ is stable and } x^p \text{ is clamped;} \\ 1 & \text{otherwise} \end{cases}$$

Now modify wjk by $\Delta w_{jk} = y_j y_k \left(\in_j + \in_k \right)$ if $j \neq k$ Repeat this procedure until all patterns are stable.

It appears that, in practice, this algorithm usually converges. There exist cases, however, where the algorithm remains oscillatory.

EMPLOYING ARTIFICIAL NEURAL NETWORKS

Perhaps the greatest advantage of ANNs is their ability to be used as an arbitrary function approximation mechanism that 'learns' from observed data. However, using them is not so straightforward and a relatively good understanding of the underlying theory is essential.

- Choice of model: This will depend on the data representation and the application. Overly complex models tend to lead to problems with learning.
- Learning algorithm: There are numerous trade-offs between learning algorithms. Almost any algorithm will work well with the *correct hyperparameters* for training on a particular fixed data set. However selecting and tuning an algorithm for training on unseen data requires a significant amount of experimentation.
- Robustness: If the model, cost function and learning algorithm are selected appropriately the resulting ANN can be extremely robust.

With the correct implementation, ANNs can be used naturally in online learning and large data set applications. Their simple implementation and the existence of mostly local dependencies exhibited in the structure allows for fast, parallel implementations in hardware.

Applications

The utility of artificial neural network models lies in the fact that they can be used to infer a function from observations. This is particularly useful in applications where the complexity of the data or task makes the design of such a function by hand impractical.

Real-Life Applications

The tasks artificial neural networks are applied to tend to fall within the following broad categories:

- Function approximation, or regression analysis, including time series prediction, fitness approximation and modeling.
- Classification, including pattern and sequence recognition, novelty detection and sequential decision making.
- Data processing, including filtering, clustering, blind source separation and compression.
- Robotics, including directing manipulators, Computer numerical control.

Application areas include system identification and control (vehicle control, process control), quantum chemistry, game-playing and decision making (backgammon, chess, racing), pattern recognition (radar systems, face identification, object recognition and more), sequence recognition (gesture, speech, handwritten text recognition), medical diagnosis, financial applications (automated trading systems), data mining (or knowledge discovery in databases, "KDD"), visualization and e-mail spam filtering.

Neural Networks and Neuroscience

Theoretical and computational neuroscience is the field concerned with the theoretical analysis and computational modeling of biological neural systems. Since neural systems are intimately related to cognitive processes and behaviour, the field is closely related to cognitive and behavioural modeling. The aim of the field is to create models of biological neural systems in order to understand how biological systems work. To gain this understanding, neuroscientists strive to make a link between observed biological processes (data), biologically plausible mechanisms for neural processing and learning (biological neural network models) and theory (statistical learning theory and information theory).

Types of Models

Many models are used in the field defined at different levels of abstraction and modeling different aspects of neural systems. They range from models of the short-term behaviour of individual neurons, models of how the dynamics of neural circuitry arise from interactions between individual neurons and finally to models of how behaviour can arise from abstract neural modules that represent complete subsystems. These include models of the long-term, and short-term plasticity, of neural systems and their relations to learning and memory from the individual neuron to the system level.

Current Research

While initial research had been concerned mostly with the electrical characteristics of neurons, a particularly important part of the investigation in recent years has been the exploration of the role of neuromodulators such as dopamine, acetylcholine, and serotonin on behaviour and learning.

Biophysical models, such as BCM theory, have been important in understanding mechanisms for synaptic plasticity, and have had applications in both computer science and neuroscience.

Research is ongoing in understanding the computational algorithms used in the brain, with some recent biological evidence for radial basis networks and neural backpropagation as mechanisms for processing data. Computational devices have been created in CMOS for both biophysical simulation and neuromorphic computing. More recent efforts show promise for creating nanodevices for very large scale principal components analyses and convolution. If successful, these effort could usher in a new era of neural computing that is a step beyond digital computing, because it depends on learning rather than programming and because it is fundamentally analog rather than digital even though the first instantiations may in fact be with CMOS digital devices.

Neural Network Software

Neural network software is used to simulate, research, develop and apply artificial neural networks, biological neural networks and in some cases a wider array of adaptive systems.

Types of Artificial Neural Networks

Artificial neural network types vary from those with only one or two layers of single direction logic, to complicated multi–input many directional feedback loop and layers. On the whole, these systems use algorithms in their programming to determine control and organization of their functions. Some may be as simple, one neuron layer with an input and an output, and others can mimic complex systems such as dANN, which can mimic chromosomal DNA through sizes at cellular level, into artificial organisms and simulate reproduction, mutation and population sizes. Most systems use "weights" to change the parameters of the throughput and the varying connections to the neurons. Artificial neural networks can be autonomous and learn by input from outside "teachers" or even self-teaching from written in rules.

TOPOLOGIES

The properties of the basic processing unit in an artificial neural network. This section focuses on the pattern of connections between the units and the propagation of data. As for this pattern of connections, the main distinction we can make is between:

Feed-forward neural networks

Where the data ow from input to output units is strictly feedforward. The data processing can extend over multiple (layers of) units, but no feedback connections are present, that is, connections extending from outputs of units to inputs of units in the same layer or previous layers.

Recurrent neural networks

That do contain feedback connections. Contrary to feed-forward networks, the dynamical properties of the network are important. In some cases, the activation values of the units undergo a relaxation process such that the neural network will evolve to a stable state in which these activations do not change anymore. In other applications, the change of the activation values of the output neurons are significant, such that the dynamical behaviour constitutes the output of the neural network.Classical examples of feed-forward neural networks are the Perceptron and Adaline. Examples of recurrent networks have been presented.

Training of artifcial neural networks

A neural network has to be configured such that the application of a set of inputs produces (either 'direct' or via a relaxation process) the desired set of outputs. Various methods to set the strengths of the connections exist. One way is to set the weights explicitly, using a priori knowledge. Another way is to'train' the neural network by feeding it teaching patterns and letting it change its weights according to some learning rule We can categorise the learn.ing situations in two distinct sorts.

These are:

- Supervised learning or Associative learning in which the network is trained by providing it with input and matching output patterns. These input-output pairs can be provided by an external teacher, or by the system which contains the neural network
- Unsupervised learning or Self-organisation in which an (output) unit is trained to respond to clusters of pattern within the input. In this paradigm the system is supposed to discover statistically salient features of the input population. Unlike the supervised learning paradigm, there is no a priori set of categories into which the patterns are to be classified; rather the system must develop its own representa-tion of the input stimuli.
- Reinforcement Learning This type of learning may be considered as an intermediate form of the above two types of learning. Here the learning machine does some action on the environment and gets a feedback response from the environment. The learning system grades its action good (rewarding) or bad (punishable) based on the environmental response and accordingly adjusts its

parametres. Generally, parametre adjustment is continued until an equilibrium state occurs, following which there will be no more changes in its parametres. The selforganizing neural learning may be categorized under this type of learning.

Patterns of Connectivity of Neural Networks

Both learning paradigms supervised learning and unsupervised learning result in an adjustment of the weights of the connections between units, according to some modification rule. The basic idea is that if two units j and k are active simultaneously, their interconnection must be strengthened. If j receives input from k, the simplest version of Hebbian learning prescribes to modify the weight wjk with

$$\Delta w_{jk} = \gamma y_j y_k$$

where γ is a positive constant of proportionality representing the learning rate. Another common rule uses not the actual activation of unit k but the difference between the actual and desired activation for adjusting the weights:

$\Delta w_{jk} = \gamma y_j (d_k - y_k)$ in which dk is the desired activation provided by a teacher. This is often called the Widrow-Hoff rule or the delta rule, and will be discussed in the next chapter. Many variants (often very exotic ones) have been published the last few years.

BIOLOGICAL MODEL

Artificial neural networks emerged after the introduction of simplified neurons by McCulloch and Pitts in 1943. These neurons were presented as models of biological neurons and as conceptual components for circuits that could perform computational tasks. The basic model of the neuron is founded upon the functionality of a biological neuron. 'Neurons are the basic signaling units of the nervous system' and 'each neuron is a discrete cell whose several processes arise from its cell body'.

The neuron has four main regions to its structure. The cell body, or soma, has two offshoots from it, the dendrites, and the axon, which end in presynaptic terminals. The cell body is the heart of the cell, containing the nucleus and maintaining protein synthesis. A neuron may have many dendrites, which branch out in a treelike structure, and receive signals from other neurons.

A neuron usually only has one axon which grows out from a part of the cell body called the axon hillock. The axon conducts electric signals generated at the axon hillock down its length. These electric signals are called action potentials. The other end of the axon may split into several branches, which end in a presynaptic terminal.

Action potentials are the electric signals that neurons use to convey information to the brain. All these signals are identical. Therefore, the brain determines what type of information is being received based on the path that the signal took. The brain analyses the patterns of signals being sent and from that information it can interpret the type of information being received.

Myelin is the fatty tissue that surrounds and insulates the axon. Often short axons do not need this insulation. There are uninsulated parts of the axon. These areas are called Nodes of Ranvier. At these nodes, the signal traveling down the axon is regenerated. This ensures that the signal traveling down the axon travels fast and remains constant (*i.e.* very short propagation delay and no weakening of the signal). The synapse is the area of contact between two neurons. The neurons do not actually physically touch. They are separated by the synaptic cleft, and electric signals are sent through chemical 13 interaction. The neuron sending the signal is called the presynaptic cell and the neuron receiving the signal is called the postsynaptic cell.

The signals are generated by the membrane potential, which is based on the differences in concentration of sodium and potassium ions inside and outside the cell membrane. Neurons can be classified by their number of processes (or appendages), or by their function. If they are classified by the number of processes, they fall into three categories. Unipolar neurons have a single process (dendrites and axon are located on the same stem), and are most common in invertebrates. In bipolar neurons, the dendrite and axon are the neuron's two separate processes. Bipolar neurons have a subclass called pseudo-bipolar neurons, which are used to send sensory information to the spinal cord. Finally, multipolar neurons are most common in mammals. Examples of these neurons are spinal motor neurons, pyramidal cells and Purkinje cells (in the cerebellum). If classified by function, neurons again fall into three separate categories. The first group is sensory, or afferent, neurons, which provide information for perception and motor coordination.

The second group provides information (or instructions) to muscles and glands and is therefore called motor neurons. The last group, interneuronal, contains all other neurons and has two subclasses. One group called relay or projection interneurons have long axons and connect different parts of the brain. The other group called local interneurons are only used in local circuits.

MATHEMATICAL MODEL

When creating a functional model of the biological neuron, there are three basic components of importance. First, the synapses of the neuron are modeled as weights. The strength of the connection between an input and a neuron is noted by the value of the weight. Negative weight values reflect inhibitory connections, while positive values designate excitatory connections. The next two components model the actual activity within the neuron cell. An adder sums up all the inputs modified by their respective weights. This activity is referred to as linear combination. Finally, an activation function controls the amplitude of the output of the neuron. An acceptable range of output is usually between 0 and 1, or -1 and 1.Mathematically, this process is described in the figure

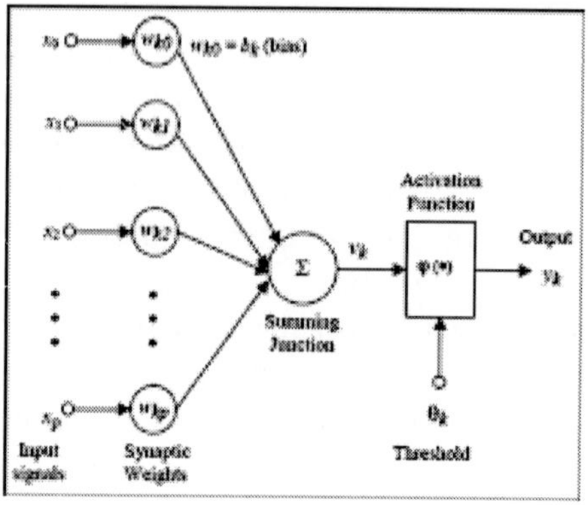

From this model the interval activity of the neuron can be shown to be:

$$v_k = \sum_{j=1}^{p} w_{kj} x_j$$

The output of the neuron, yk, would therefore be the outcome of some activation function on the value of vk.

Activation Functions

As mentioned previously, the activation function acts as a squashing function, such that the output of a neuron in a neural network is between certain values. In general, there are three types of activation functions, denoted. First, there is the Threshold Function which takes on a value of 0 if the summed input is less than a certain threshold value (v), and the value 1 if the summed input is greater than or equal to the threshold value.

$$\varphi(v) = \begin{cases} 1 \text{if } v \geq 0 \\ 0 \text{if } v < 0 \end{cases}$$

Secondly, there is the Piecewise-Linear function. This function again can take on the values of 0 or 1, but can also take on values between that depending on the amplification factor in a certain region of linear operation.

$$\varphi(v) = \begin{cases} 1 & v \geq 1/2 \\ v & -1/2 > v > 1/2 \\ 0 & v \leq -1/2 \end{cases}$$

Thirdly, there is the sigmoid function. This function can range between 0 and 1, but it is also sometimes useful to use the -1 to 1 range. An example of the sigmoid function is the hyperbolic tangent function.

$$\varphi(v) = \tanh\left(\frac{v}{2}\right) = \frac{1-\exp(-v)}{1+\exp(-v)}$$

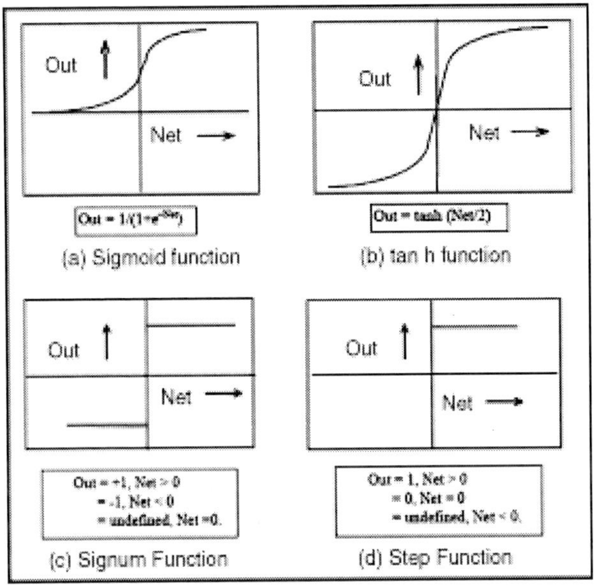

(a) Sigmoid function

(b) tan h function

(c) Signum Function

(d) Step Function

The artifcial neural networks are all variations on the parallel distributed processing (PDP) idea. The architecture of each neural network is based on very similar building blocks which perform the processing. In this chapter we first discuss these processing units and discuss diferent neural network topologies. Learning strategies as a basis for an adaptive system

distributed representation

An artifcial neural network consists of a pool of simple processing units which communicate by sending signals to each other over a large number of weighted connections. A set of major aspects of a parallel distributed model can be distinguished:

- A set of processing units ('neurons,' 'cells');

- A state of activation yk for every unit, which equivalent to the output of the unit;
- Connections between the units. Generally each connection is defined by a weight wjk which determines the effect which the signal of unit j has on unit k;
- A propagation rule, which determines the effective input sk of a unit from its external inputs;
- An activation function Fk, which determines the new level of activation based on the efective input sk(t) and the current activation yk(t) (*i.e.*, the update);
- An external input (aka bias, offset) øk for each unit;
- A method for information gathering (the learning rule);
- An environment within which the system must operate, providing input signals and | if necessary | error signals.

Processing Units

Each unit performs a relatively simple job: receive input from neighbours or external sources and use this to compute an output signal which is propagated to other units. Apart from this processing, a second task is the adjustment of the weights.

The system is inherently parallel in the sense that many units can carry out their computations at the same time.

Within neural systems it is useful to distinguish three types of units: input units (indicated by an index i) which receive data from outside the neural network, output units (indicated by an index o) which send data out of the neural network, and hidden units (indicated by an index h) whose input and output signals remain within the neural network.

During operation, units can be updated either synchronously or asynchronously.

With synchronous updating, all units update their activation simultaneously; with asynchronous updating, each unit has a (usually fixed) probability of updating its activation at a time t, and usually only one unit will be able to do this at a time. In some cases the latter model has some advantages.

THEORETICAL PROPERTIES

Computational Power

The multi-layer perceptron (MLP) is a universal function approximator, as proven by the Cybenko theorem. However, the proof is not constructive regarding the number of neurons required or the settings of the weights. Work by Hava Siegelmann and Eduardo D. Sontag has provided a proof that a specific recurrent architecture with rational valued weights (as opposed to full precision real number-valued weights) has the full power of a Universal Turing Machine using a finite number of neurons and standard linear connections. They have further shown that the use of irrational values for weights results in a machine with super-Turing power.

Capacity

Artificial neural network models have a property called 'capacity', which roughly corresponds to their ability to model any given function. It is related to the amount of information that can be stored in the network and to the notion of complexity.

Convergence

Nothing can be said in general about convergence since it depends on a number of factors. Firstly, there may exist many local minima. This depends on the cost function and the model. Secondly, the optimization method used might not be guaranteed to converge when far away from a local minimum. Thirdly, for a very large amount of data or parameters, some methods become impractical. In general, it has been found that theoretical guarantees regarding convergence are an unreliable guide to practical application.

Generalization and Statistics

In applications where the goal is to create a system that generalizes well in unseen examples, the problem of over-training has emerged. This arises in convoluted or over-specified systems when the capacity of the network significantly exceeds the needed free parameters. There are two schools of thought for avoiding this problem: The first is to use cross-validation and similar techniques to check for the presence of overtraining and optimally select hyperparameters such as to minimize the generalization error. The second is to use some form of *regularization*. This is a concept that emerges naturally in a probabilistic (Bayesian) framework, where the regularization can be performed by selecting a larger prior probability over simpler models; but also in statistical learning theory, where the goal is to minimize over two quantities: the 'empirical risk' and the 'structural risk', which roughly corresponds to the error over the training set and the predicted error in unseen data due to overfitting.

Dynamic Properties

Various techniques originally developed for studying disordered magnetic systems (i.e., the spin glass) have been successfully applied to simple neural network architectures, such as the Hopfield network. Influential work by E. Gardner and B. Derrida has revealed many interesting properties about perceptrons with real-valued synaptic weights, while later work by W. Krauth and M. Mezard has extended these principles to binary-valued synapses.

Criticism

A common criticism of artificial neural networks, particularly in robotics, is that they require a large diversity of training for real-world operation. Dean Pomerleau, in his research presented in the paper "Knowledge-based Training of Artificial Neural Networks for Autonomous Robot Driving," uses a neural network to train a robotic vehicle to drive on multiple types of roads (single lane, multi-lane, dirt, etc.). A large amount of his research is devoted to (1) extrapolating multiple training scenarios from a single training experience, and (2) preserving past training diversity so that the system does not become overtrained (if, for example, it is presented with a series of right turns – it should not learn to always turn right). These issues are common in neural networks that must decide from amongst a wide variety of responses. A. K. Dewdney, a former *Scientific American* columnist, wrote in 1997, "Although neural nets do solve a few toy problems, their powers of computation are so limited that I am surprised anyone takes them seriously as a general problem-solving tool." (Dewdney, p. 82)

Arguments for Dewdney's position are that to implement large and effective software neural networks, much processing and storage resources need to be committed. While the brain has hardware tailored to the task of processing signals through a graph of neurons, simulating even a most simplified form on Von Neumann technology may compel a NN designer to fill many millions of database rows for its connections - which can lead to abusive RAM and HD necessities. Furthermore, the designer of NN systems will often need to simulate the transmission of signals through many of these connections and their associated neurons - which must often be matched with incredible amounts of CPU processing power and time. While neural networks often yield *effective* programmes, they too often do so at the cost of time and money *efficiency*. Arguments against Dewdney's position are that neural nets have been successfully used to solve many complex and diverse tasks, ranging from autonomously flying aircraft to detecting credit card fraud. Technology writer Roger Bridgman commented on Dewdney's statements about neural nets: Neural networks, for instance, are in the dock not only because they have been hyped to high heaven, (what hasn't?) but also because you could create a successful net without understanding how it worked: the bunch of numbers that captures its behaviour would in all probability be "an opaque, unreadable table...valueless as a scientific resource". In spite of his emphatic declaration that science is not technology, Dewdney seems here to pillory neural nets as bad science when most of those devising them are just trying to be good engineers. An unreadable table that a useful machine could read would still be well worth having.

10

Nanocomputer Architecture Design

After looking at all of these different nanodevices and proposed networks and architectures, how can we determine what is the best direction to go in order to create the optimal computer architecture for the next generation? The first thing to look at is what will be the major issues and limitations with the devices we wish to use as the basic building blocks for our computer.

The focus will not necessarily be on how these devices will be built whether that is through lithography or self assembly, it is immaterial, and concern about cost will be factored in, but not necessarily a focal point.

Rather, we are more concerned with what qualities the finished product and the surrounding architecture will need to possess in order to be successful.

What are some qualities are interested in?:

- Fault Tolerance,
- Self testing/Re-configuration,
- Heat Tolerance and Power Dissipation,
- Independent and parallel processing,
- Improved communication, handling current pervasive bottlenecks in interconnections,
- Scalability.

We will use these important qualities as a guide to what each nanocomputer component will contain, as we lay out our proposed nanocomputer architecture from the bottom up.

NANO-COMPUTING

The history of computer technology has involved a sequence of changes from gears to relays to valves to transistors to integrated circuits and so on. Today's techniques can fit logic gates and wires a fraction of a micron wide onto a silicon chip. Soon the parts will become smaller and smaller until they are made up of only a handful of atoms. At this point the laws of classical physics break down and the rules of quantum mechanics take over, so the new quantum technology must replace and/ or supplement what we presently have.

It will support an entirely new kind of computation with new algorithms based on quantum principles. Presently our digital computers rely on bits, which, when charged, represent on, true, or 1. When not charged they become off, false, or 0. A register of 3 bits can represent at a given moment in time one of eight numbers (000,001,010,...,111). In the quantum state, an atom (one bit) can be in two places at once according to the laws of quantum physics, so 3 atoms (quantum bits or qubits) can represent all eight numbers at any given time.

So for x number of qubits, there can be 2^x numbers stored. (I will not go into the logic of all this or this paper would turn into a book!). Parallel processing can take place on the 2^x input numbers, performing the same task that a classical computer would have to repeat 2^x times or use 2^x processors working in parallel. In other words a quantum computer offers an enormous gain in the use of computational resources such as time and memory.

This becomes mind boggling when you think of what 32 qubits can accomplish. This all sounds like another purely technological process. Classical computers can do the same computations as quantum computers, only needing more time and more memory. The catch is that they need exponentially more time and memory to match the power of a quantum computer.

An exponential increase is really fast, and available time and memory run out very quickly. Quantum computers can be programed in a qualitatively new way using new algorithms. For example, we can construct new algorithms for solving problems, some of which can turn difficult mathematical problems, such as factorization, into easy ones. The difficulty of factorization of large numbers is the basis for the security of many common methods of encryption. RSA, the most popular public key cryptosystem used to protect electronic bank accounts gets its security from the difficulty of factoring very large numbers. This was one of the first potential uses for a quantum computer. "Experimental and theoretical research in quantum computation is accelerating world-wide.

New technologies for realising quantum computers are being proposed, and new types of quantum computation with various advantages over classical computation are continually being discovered and analysed and we believe some of them will bear technological fruit. From a fundamental standpoint, however, it does not matter how useful quantum computation turns out to be, nor does it matter whether we build the first quantum computer tomorrow, next year or centuries from now.

The quantum theory of computation must in any case be an integral part of the world view of anyone who seeks a fundamental understanding of the quantum theory and the processing of information."(Centre for Quantum Comput-ation)

POSSIBLE TYPES OF NANOCOMPUTERS

Several types of nanocomputers have been proposed to build the best nanocomputer. These include mechanical, chemical, quantum and electronic nanocomputers. Briefly, mechanical nanocomputers would use molecular-scale rods of rotating molecular-scale wheels. These wheels would spin on shafts and bearings. In this way, the mechanical nanocomputer could be used to calculate. Also, it may be possible to assemble mechanical nanocomputers using the mechanical positioning of atoms or other molecular building blocks one atom/molecule at a time. This process is known as "mechanosynthesis."

A chemical computer will process information by making and breaking chemical bonds. The resultant chemical will store the logic states or other information. A variation of this type of computer is a biochemical computer. Multicellular nervous systems demonstrate that this type of computer would be possible as this is the way in which animal nervous systems work. Every single action in an animal is mediated by biochemical reactions and pathways. This evinces that biochemical reactions and pathways could be used to store information. However, most biochemical pathways and mechanisms are not currently well understood.

A quantum computer would consist of many parallel computations performed by "natural" mechanism of interference among the quantum waves. These quantum waves are associated with the nanometre-scale elements of a multi-component, coherent quantum state. Each piece of information would be represented by a quantum state of some component in the computer.

Finally, there may be developments in electronic nanocomputers. This type of nanocomputer is the most likely because this is the way in which computers are currently developed, specifically through the use of electronic digital computers. As such, we should be able to expand on this knowledge and development in order to create a nanocomputer.

One noteworthy benefit is that this type of approach would not require a fundamental change in operating principles of the transistor. As mentioned, a change in the technology will need to happen to further decrease the size of computers. Fundamentally, an electronic nanocomputer will store and move electrons in order to represent information. This is the same way in which transistors work in modern computers. From here, we will discuss some theoretical technologies that will potential serve to build a nanocomputer.

Potential Technologies for use in NanoComputer

As discussed, transistors will need to be replaced by some form of nanotechnology in order to decrease the size of computers. Several replacement technologies have been suggested.

The technologies to be discussed include the resonant tunneling transistor, single electron transistor, and the quantum dot cell. Each of these devices is based upon the principles of quantum mechanics.

Resonant Tunneling Transistor

The resonant tunneling device (RTD) may be used to create a nanometre-scale two-state device. Often, RTDs are constructed from semiconductor heterostructures. The resonant tunneling diode consists of two insulating barriers in a semiconductor. This creates an island between the two insulators.

This centre island should be around 10 nanometres in width. In the event that electrons are confined between two closely spaced barriers, the quantum wave properties of the electrons restrict their energies to certain discrete levels that are closely spaced in energy. As a result of this energy restriction, the potential well contains only a finite, integral number of discrete "quantized" energy levels. Energy quantization is the way in which the resonant tunneling diode operates.

Electrons are able to pass through the device by tunneling through the two barriers. The probability that an electron will tunnel through the two barriers depends on the energy of the incoming electrons as compared to the device's internal energy level. Ultimately, current will only flow when the energy of the incoming electrons is the same as the energy levels that are allowed inside the potential well. When this is the case, current is allowed to flow through the device because the energy level of the electrons outside the well is in "resonance" with the energy level of the electrons inside the well. However, no current is able to flow when the energy of the electrons differs from the allowable levels inside the potential well. Again, the average energy of the incoming electrons must align with the internal energy level of the potential well in order for current to flow.

A resonant tunneling transistor can be made by incorporating an RTD into the emitter of a conventional bipolar junction transistors (BJTs), which is a microelectronic device. A BJT is a three terminal device that is similar to a MOSFET.

The difference is that a BJT is a current-controlled amplifier, rather than being a voltage-controlled amplifier. Also, the gate, source, and drain of the MOSFET are analogous to the three terminals of the BJT, referred to as the base, emitter, and collector.

In a BJT, the current that flows into the base determines the amount of current that flows between the emitter and collector. Small changes in the base current result in a large change in the collector current, allowing the BJT to be used as an amplifier.

The combination of an RTD and BJT is a resonant tunneling transistor (RTT) and this particular arrangement can allow the RTT to be a two-state device, which can be in an "on" or "off" mode. The way that this works is that the RTD is able to serve as a filter. The RTD will allow current to flow to the emitter of the BJT at certain base-emitter voltages. The voltages allowed correspond to the RTD's internal energy levels.

The "off" mode results when there is a low base-emitter voltage, which does not allow current to flow through the base-emitter RTD..

The transistor is "on" when the base-emitter voltage is increased so as to coincide with the first internal energy level of the RTD, thereby allowing the base current to pass through the RTD. Of note, the transistors can have multiple "on" and "off" states. What this allows for is multi-state transistors. These multi-state transistors enable for a reduction in the number of devices necessary to implement logic functions. Ultimately, the density of logic in integrated circuits will be increased. A problem with this RTT is that we have a nanometre device integrated into a microelectronic device.

This combination means that the size will decrease only so much, due to the presence of the microelectronic device. Hopefully, some combination of two nanodevices will be possible in the future in order for the size of computers to decrease.

Single Electron Transistor

A single electron transistor (SET) is another device that has the potential to be used in developing a nanocomputer. The SET does not experience quantum effects such as the interference among a few electrons. An SET operates by moving single electrons that have electrostatic interactions with a large number of surrounding electrons.

An SET consists of a source, an island, and a drain. The source and drains are wires. Electrons are able to enter the island only one at a time. The electrons tunnel onto the island from the source and then leave the island via the drain. This flow of electrons produces a flow of current. Very few electrons can remain on the island at the same time, due to the electrostatic repulsion of the electrons on the island. When extra electrons are prevented from tunneling, no current is able to flow. The phenomenon whereby electrons are prevented from tunneling is called a “Coulomb blockade.”

It is useful to control the number of electrons that enter and exit the island. This can be done by a metal gate electrode near the island. When the voltage of the gate electrode is increased, an additional electron is able to tunnel onto the island from the source. From there, the extra electron tunnels off the island onto the drain. This electron flow continues and creates a measurable current flow through the island.

An increase in the gate voltage will cause the number of electrons on the island to stabilize and no current will flow. However, a further increase in voltage will cause more electrons to migrate onto the island. This results in a step-wise function in the current flow. One limitation of the SET is the fact that at high temperatures, the thermal energy of the electrons may be able to overcome the Coulomb blockade. Ultimately, the thermal energy may be sufficient to allow the electrons to tunnel onto the island. In this case, current will flow regardless of the gate voltage. Ultimately, more work needs to be done in order for the SET to be fully operational at room temperatures. Once this occurs, SETs may be usable in the creation in nanocomputers.

Quantum Dot Cells

A final potential technology that may assist in the development of nanocomputers is a quantum dot cell. A quantum dot is a small potential well or box that is able to electrostatically isolate a single or few electrons. The electrostatic field of the quantum dot can be changed in order to determine the number of electrons in the quantum dot. Quantum dots are made from tiny insulated regions of conducting material. They are capable of holding zero to hundreds of electrons.

Quantum dots rely on specific quantum effects, unlike SETs. Another difference is that quantum dots cannot be used to store and retrieve information because the exact number of electrons in the device is unknown, due to the low resistivity of the device. However, interactions between quantum dots can retrieve and store information. Quantum dots can affect one another even if they are not wired together. Two dots can influence one another due to long-range electrostatic interactions. One dot's electric field of electrons can change the number of electrons in another nearby quantum dot.

The way that this works is that the addition of an electron to one quantum dot causes an electron to vacate a nearby dot. This is contingent on the electron having a vacancy to jump to. Quantum dots can be lined up to cause movement of electrons. The first quantum dot in this series must have an electron to start the movement of electrons in quantum dots. This electron will have to tunnel into the first quantum dot from a nearby reservoir. Since the quantum dots can be used this way, they can be two-state devices. The two states will correspond to occupancy of the dot by zero or one electron. When two devices are set next to each other, they will obtain opposite states due to the electrorepulsion between electrons. Quantum dots can be arranged in a certain series and can serve as electron reservoirs.

Quantum dot cells communicate through their electric field (exchange of photons), rather than through the flow of current (exchange of electrons). Since this is the case, quantum dots can give rise to wireless computation. The major obstacle in this type of technology is the fabrication of the quantum dot. It is also imperative that the location and size of the dots is precisely controlled. Finally, as with SETs, quantum dots have a maximum temperature of operation, especially as the size of the dot decreases. These are issues that need to be addressed before the use of quantum dots becomes a reality in the construction of nanocomputers.

DEVELOPMENTS IN NANOCOMPUTING

There have been countless approaches for handling the advent of molecular computing, and Computer scientists today have come up with several proposals to build components of nanocomputer. Some of these approaches will be summarized below, making note of the advantages and disadvantages in their implementation.

DNA Carbon Nanotubes and Nanowires

We know that a computer's building blocks can be a key component to system efficiency and speed. An organic carbon based nanowire structure has been proposed by a group of researchers from Duke, NC State, and The University of North Carolina. These researchers have focused on using the building block of the human body as the basis of building a computer. In this proposal, the top-down assembly approach of lithography would be replaced by DNA guided self-assembly. The DNA assembly uses strands of DNA to create tiles which in turn create a lattice structure.

They focus on a waffle-like lattice of 16x16 nanometre size, and they attach carbon nanotube devices to the DNA tile scaffolding through a process they call functionalization, which is the process of adding a molecule to another material through a chemical reaction. This circuit architecture does have a few shortcomings inherent in it. The self-assembly of the DNA lattices proposed does not produce a regular pattern which would insure a low level of defects.

They have found that by minimizing the number of tags and producing repetitive structures is desired. However, by minimizing the number of tags, there is a limit to the amount of complexity a circuit can then have. The DNA self assemblies will not be able to have as much complexity as a CMOS transistor as a result.

In a shift away from the CMOS circuit, the DNA self assemblies are designed to have some level of defect tolerance. This is mostly due to the fact that the error rate in photolithography is quite low. However, self-assemblies will inherently have a higher number of defects in production. This particular proposal does not outline a method for handling defects, and that is a shortcoming of this presentation. The proposed architecture for DNA self assemblies must handle limited node connectivity and random node placements. These limitations affect the performance in large scale control of the nodes. An accumulator based instruction set architecture is proposed to deal with the control and communications limitations.

The accumulator-based ISA reduces the need for widespread coordination and communication among many components, since the only data dependence involves the accumulator, and instructions are processed in order. Each instruction within the accumulator makes up an execution packet containing operands, operations, and the accumulator value to form a sequence.

This approach supports parallelism through the independence of data, and by initiating several execution packets at once. This proposal also puts forth a networking architecture for the execution packets. Three logical networks are proposed to handle three different types of information: memory requests, memory responses, and execution packets. Memory and execution are separated onto two different physical networks to avoid problems with deadlocking. This research has mapped out some of the major hurdles they must clear and are thinking ahead to putting their fabrication together to make a system, but they are still in the beginning phases.

Another paper produced by this group dealing with current research topics outline their experimental progress with carbon based nanotubes and nanowires. A 4x4 DNA tile has been produced for a variety of application computations, and they have demonstrated highly parallel computation via a set of DNA crossover tiles. [LABEAN] They hope to fashion a simple circuit with nanotube control in the near future.

Chemically Assembled Electronic Nanotechnology (CAEN)

This approach is presented by Seth Copen Goldstein at Carnegie Mellon University. Goldstein believes that CAEN devices will be the cornerstone of the nanocomputer and replace the dominant silicon transistor. The devices he proposes are small, dense, low power and reconfigurable. The proposed fabrication of these devices makes switches and wires using chemical self-assembly as opposed to the traditional lithography method which is currently used for CMOS chips. As stated by Goldstein, "The active devices are created where two appropriately functionalized wires intersect.

By choosing the molecules that coat the wires appropriately, the intersection points can be ohmic contacts, diodes, configurable switches, etc. The important point to note is that no precise alignment is required to create the devices." After proposing how these devices would be manufactured, Goldstein goes on to explain how a computer using these devices might be architected with his current fabrication plan.

Cost and fault tolerance is the most important aspects of CAEN devices, and Goldstein explains that the proposed manufacturing process will result in the following architectural characteristics:

- Transistors, or other three terminal devices, will probably not be part of CAEN devices.

- Any deterministic aperiodic circuit will have to be created after the device is fabricated through reconfiguration.
- Chips will have to work in the presence of a significant number of defects

Unfortunately these CAEN devices cannot create three terminal devices because precise alignment is required and this is not economically viable. CAEN devices would have to be limited to two terminals, and any processes which required three terminals (such as an inverter) would have to be built in conjunction with a CMOS device.

Goldstein believes that CAEN based devices can replace the silicon chip. These devices have the possibility of being reconfigurable, testable, and can be fault tolerant. A device called a negative differential resistance (NDR) can replace the traditional transistor circuit.

Unfortunately, current research requires a great deal of voltage in order for this device to work. Further study will be required in order to produce a low power and low static device. Despite its current limitations, the NDR is a key piece in Goldstein's proposed resonant tunneling diodes which are the building block of the molecular latch which will in his mind ultimately replace the transistor as we know it.

NanoBlocks and NanoFabrics

Goldstein has built upon the concept of Chemically Assembled Electronic Nanotechnology (CAEN) by outlining a reconfigurable architecture called a Nanofabric. This Nanofabric architecture could be used for factory-programmable devices configured by the manufacturer to emulate a processor or other computing device, or for reconfigurable computing devices.

A Nanofabric is a two dimensional mesh of interconnected NanoBlocks. A NanoBlock is a logic block that can be programmed to implement three-bit input to three-bit output Boolean function and its complement, as well as for switches to route signals.

This chapter outlines how to build an AND gate, an OR gate, and XOR gate, and an ADDER. These "gates" as we traditionally are used to calling them, exist in what they call the molecular logic array (MLA) where all of the functionality of the block is located. The upside to the method outlined in the paper is that it is similar to commercial Field Programmable Gate Arrays (FPGAs), allowing these nano-gates to leverage current FPGA tools.

The MLA would be created using "directed assembly", which means that the atoms are arranged one by one. While this would allow computer makers to place components in a precise manner, the signals, which are routed using diode-resistor logic, would be degraded every time it goes through a configurable switch.

While a plan for defect and fault tolerance is presented, the inherent problem is with the nanowires lacking resistance. Goldstein contends that while this is a problem, it is still easier to implement defect tolerance than with CMOS because wires can be swapped and rows can be moved anywhere within the NanoBlock without affecting the circuit. CMOS currently has little defect tolerance, and chips with a high error rate are discarded. The cost of directed assembly may be prohibitive as well and not economically viable. Testing the Nanofabric proved to be difficult because it is not possible for the components to be tested in isolation. After production of the fabric, a defect map is created to make the fabric into a viable circuit. The fabric is self-testing, and will provide fault free regions of the fabric.

Other researchers at the University of Massachusetts are looking to use Nanofabric to create integrated circuits which can be tailored towards the application domain. They are named NASICs, which stands for Nanoscale Application-Specific Integrated Circuits.

This research is built upon the Nanofabric proposal by Goldstein. In an effort to build these NASIC tiles, the researchers at UMass have presented a solution to a difficult problem. As they state, "A key issue when building NASIC tiles is the low effective density of latch circuits.

This is due to the difficulty of building sequential circuits on a nano-grid." In order to get around this limitation, they have developed a nano-latch, which allows for temporary storage along a nano-wire in a circuit. This research gives promise for improving nano-device density, scalability and reliability

Quantum Cellular Automata

A Quantum Cellular Automata (QCA) is another plausible nanodevice. This is a design which is based upon a theory of using electrons and their energy states for computing. This is a topic which has been studied for over 40 years, back to the work of von Neumann. Rather than being an individual device of a computer circuit scaled to a nanometre size, the QCA is a complete entity.

As described by researchers at Notre Dame, "quantum-dot cellular automata (QCA), parallels conventional computing in using a binary representation of information (not qubits) yet realises functionality in ways which are well-suited to the properties of single molecules - using molecules not as current switches but as structured charge containers."[LENT] The QCA is a single molecule which will contain a representation of the binary values 0 or 1 based upon the static electric charge of the electron. The cells have not been found at this point in time to be viable at room temperature, but rather only at very cold degrees in the Kelvin range. Needless to say, operating at such low temperatures is not practical for any working device, and this is a serious limitation to the usefulness of QCAs.

The QCA fabrication does differentiate from other devices that we have seen because the fabrication uses lithography. "Molecular QCA cells must be attached to surfaces in ordered arrays. We are using electron-beam lithography to burn narrow "tracks" along surfaces."

The temperature limitations of Quantum Cellular Automatas have been given a new perspective through a study of Magnetic QCA described by Cowburn and Welland. Their presentation uses interacting submicron magnetic dots to perform logic operations and propagate information.

[BEĊKETT] Although these devices will not be in the nanometre range, they will use less power than current CMOS.

CMOL

Some researchers are presenting a possible bridge from CMOS to the next generation of molecular computing by formulating a hybrid circuit. One such hybrid circuit is dubbed a CMOL, a play on the combination of CMOS and molecular. The CMOL is "a circuit [which] combines an advanced CMOS subsystem with two, mutually perpendicular, arrays of parallel nanowires and similar molecular devices formed at each crosspoint of the nanowires." [LIKHAREV]

This approach is important in several ways. First, it's unlikely that the computing industry will not be able to make the leap from its top-down lithography methodology to a bottom up approach using nanowires and integrating with some molecular components without some intermediate step. The CMOL maintains the stability of the silicon chip and takes a small step forward by using bottom up fabrication. The CMOS circuit maintains the level of functionality that we are used to. As mentioned, the system bus can be an area in which slowness can occur. Experiments with the CMOL circuits have operated faster than regular computers with better power dissipation.

The creator of the CMOL hybrid circuit claims, 'The development of CMOL technology (especially the high-yield molecular self-assembly) will certainly require a major industrial effort and substantial time period, probably not less than 10 to 15 years. However, this timing may be still acceptable to prevent the impending crisis of Moore's law, provided that we start right now."

Markov Random Network

Researchers at Brown University have a proposed architecture based on Markov Random Fields (MRF). A MRF is a concept based on Markov chain, which is a "graph of stochastic variables, where each variable has the property that is independent of all the others (future and past) given its two neighbors" A Markov Random Field network allows circuits to behave in a relatively independent fashion, allowing for re-configurability and a good level of fault tolerance.

The researchers feel that carbon nanotubes are one of the most promising devices which have been built at the Nanoscale. Some issues are inherent with these nanodevices though; these researchers point out that the use of carbon nanotubes circuits will increase failure rates and bring about heat dissipation issues.

In order to deal with possible failure rates upwards of 10% and heating issues at the thermal limit, it is necessary to configure a network of circuits which can handle a high fault level and can somehow dissipate heat throughout the circuit network.

It has been found through experiments that the use of a Markov Random Field Network in conjunction with the Gibbs formulation for dissipation of heat can be a viable solution, because as the authors state, "its operation does not depend o perfect devices or perfect connections. [...] Successful operation only requires that the energy of correct states is lower than the energy of errors"

Cell Matrix

The Cell Matrix architecture is presented by the Cell Matrix Corporation in Salt Lake City. This piece of research differs from the previous sections in the sense that this is a proposal of a true architecture as opposed to a design of a nano-sized component.

This architecture is currently being designed and tested in the silicon chip domain, but all research, configuration and design is for the coming of nanostructures. Currently, the Cell Matrix Corporation is developing an atomic cell unit, which is repeated to form a multidimensional matrix of cells to make a highly scalable architecture, which differs from other proposals discussed thus far.

The architecture is similar to the field programmable gate arrays (FPGAs) like the Nanofabric described in an earlier section, and it also has similarities to the cellular automaton proposed by Von Neumann. Several aspects of a cell matrix distinguish it from a Von Neumann cellular automaton. First, the cell matrix has the same three dimensional nature.

The cell matrix can only be in a certain number of states it can be in at any given time, just like a cellular automaton. Second, a cell matrix is fine grained and reconfigurable, and third it is programmed like a digital circuit, and not like a cellular automaton. The benefits which cell matrix architecture provides are many.

It can efficiently handle a large number of switches due to the fact that its controlling system is highly scalable, and can handle any addition of cells to the system. This architecture also promises to provide highly parallel large scale computing. This is the result of the fact that each cell contains all necessary functionality, and can compute across the matrix at any point in a parallel fashion.

This group has demonstrated this highly parallel computing ability through an experiment with a search space problem. The cell matrix architecture relies on a very simple hardware definition mixed with a complex programming of each individual cell. Simple logic functions can be handled by individual cells, whereas more complex functions are handled by a collection of cells, which are spatially close to each other. In these collections, cells are set up to perform a subset of the work of the entire circuit.

These cells communicate with one another in an asynchronous fashion. Each cell also has the ability to reconfigure itself, allowing for self-testing and fault tolerance, although experimentation and testing in this arena is still taking place.

The Cell Matrix Corporation believes that their design can provide dynamic circuitry, allowing each of the cells to change their original behaviour or the behaviour of cells around them, or to migrate into new areas within the matrix. They also see this as being a mechanism to handle faulty cells in order to make their circuits fault tolerant.

Defect tolerance is always an important issue with any computer architecture due to the cost which defects add to the final cost of a circuit. Due to the fact that silicon chips are discarded if their fail rate is too high, a new architecture can find cost savings in total manufacturing costs if the new circuitry can fin a way to be fault tolerant by working around bad cells. The Cell Matrix has implemented defect tolerance and self testing in their architecture.

They have designed a test driver which has the following goals:

- Permit reporting of faults with a high resolution
- Permit access to a region despite failed regions near it.
- It should be easy to extend to a decentralized, parallel, distributed fault testing process with as small a footprint as possible.
- Have a driver which can share the hardware with other tasks so it can perform its functions on subcomponents of a critical system while that system is running. [DURBECK01]

The Cell Matrix architecture outline is well planned and several experiments on digital circuits have been promising. However, no experiments have yet been performed on any microscopic components. In theory the layout may be scalable and successful; more incorporation of current nano-component research should be considered.

NanoPrism

It has already been determined that fault tolerance, while something not so prevalent in the construction of silicon chips, will need to be an important part of any architecture presented for a nanocomputer. One way in which many manufacturers provide better reliability is by implementing techniques to increase redundancy.

However, it is known that adding redundancy cannot always increase reliability of a device due to the fact that the redundant device can also contain faults. A paper from Virginia Tech is attempting to determine the level at which fault tolerance and redundancy can produce a reliable nano-architecture.

As stated by the researchers, "The questions we try to answer in this paper is, what level of granularity and what redundancy levels result in optimal reliability for specific architectures. In this paper, we extend previous work on evaluating reliability-redundancy trade-offs for NAND multiplexing to granularity vs. redundancy vs. reliability trade-offs for other redundancy mechanisms, and present our automation mechanism using the probabilistic model checking tool PRISM."

The NANOPRISM tool is based on another probabilistic model checking tool called PRISM built at the University of Binghamton, which is designed for conventional CMOS architectures. The NANOPRISM tool will be a valuable resource for building a new architecture for a nanocomputer. Redundancy can be a very important yet delicate technique to employ, due to the fact that employing too much can cause a lessening of reliability, not to mention the fact that there are several levels of granularity at which redundancy can be implemented. Because this tool automates the checking of a defect tolerant architecture, areas in which trade off levels are achieved can be identified much more quickly. The number of circuits and cells are going to increase exponentially as nanodevices scale up to the level they are supposed to be at. If we currently have almost 1 billion transistors on a single silicon chip, the number of devices we can just imagine the numbers present in a nanocomputer.

CURRENT ARCHITECTURE PARADIGMS

The last twenty years of computer hardware development have relied on the silicon chip, namely the CMOS integrated circuit. CMOS stands for a complementary metal-oxide semiconductor, and its invention is the cornerstone of digital integrated circuits. These transistors have been shrinking in size and increasing in speed each year as famously predicted by Gordon Moore.

Computer architects are now able to squeeze countless transistors on a single silicon chip. An article in PC Magazine state that "Intel estimates that it will offer chips that run at 20 GHz and contain 1 billion transistors by 2007." [METZ] While Moore's Law has held up for a significant amount of time, many foresee the end of the massive hardware improvements in the next decade.

The rising chorus calling for the demise of Moore's Law is almost deafening with every new nanotechnology proposal put forth. Below is an overview of the major components of today's computer, along with a brief description of their current design, and some conjecture as to what might become of these components in the future. Before we can propose a restructuring of a new nanocomputer, this overview will allow us to gauge where we are today so we can contrast it with the direction future computing trends are going.

Chip Manufacturing Techniques

Current CMOS chips are manufactured using lithographic-fabrication, which is a top-down approach to integrating circuits. Most of the expansion which has been made over the last 20 years took place by scaling down the size of transistors so that they can fit on top of the silicon chip. The CMOS design is centered on using a pair of transistors for logic functions which complement one another. These chips deal well with power usage and heat dissipation, and have been the central manufacturing technique on the market since the 1970s. [WIKI] Current sizes of the transistors on CMOS chips are reaching the nanometre size, and continued improvement has been proven to be limited.

Manufactures such as Intel see the end of the evolutionary path set out by Moore and have begun looking for alternatives to CMOS lithographic fabrication. [KANELLOS]. While lithography has been a big part of why we have seen such incredible improvements in size and speed of chips in the last 20-30 years, many are seeing that this current technique is not scaling well, and predicting the end of CMOS advancement.

In the computing industry, chip manufacturers outline a roadmap for their manufacturing each year called the International Technology Roadmap for SemiConductors. In their most recent meetings, they have stated, "Eventually, towards the end of the Roadmap or beyond, scaling of MOSFETs (metal-oxide semiconductor field effect transistor) will become ineffective and/or very costly, and advanced non-CMOS solutions will need to be implemented." [LEBECK]

While lithographic manufacturing of CMOS chips has been wildly successful, a new fabrication technique will be needed to continue the current pace of improvements in speed and size. However, changing the computing industry's reliance on CMOS will be a major paradigm shift. While Keyes argued in 1985 that no other device has matched silicon with respect to gain, voltage restoration, noise reduction, tolerance to variability in manufacturing, isolation of inputs from outputs, excellent fan-out, ability to invert a signal, tolerance to the high demands of a system environment, as well as a huge body of research and financial commitment, the end of the reign of the silicon chip is being predicted time and again.

Instruction Set Design

Instruction Set Design has moved from the very simple accumulator, to the advanced use of registers and load-store architecture. The most recent design shift for instruction sets was the move from CISC (Complex Instruction Set Computer) to RISC (Reduced Instruction Set Computer). CISC was used such machines as the DEC Alpha and the HP3000. Intel's x86 processor is the only remaining computer in production which still uses CISC. Most computers today have RISC architecture.

The RISC philosophy of design came into dominance due to the increasing complexity of CPU designs and the need to speed up instruction executions. It is also well known that RISC chips require fewer transistors to execute their instruction. All RISC instructions can be executed in a single clock cycle, and more complex instructions are handled by stringing simple instructions together.

In contrast, CISC has many more instructions, and relies less on the compiler to translate to assembly. RISC uses less RAM as well, and its simplicity was appropriate when hardware was very slow and very expensive. There has been a fair amount of debate in recent years regarding innovation in instruction set architectures in order to increase performance.

Previous performance gains have relied on improvements in instruction level parallelism and thread level parallelism. Most of the hesitation behind changing instruction sets has to do with the disruption it can cause to end users. The gains in speed and performance have been the driving force behind a design change.

It's likely that only a complete paradigm shift in the design and manufacturing of computers will cause any change in the basic instruction set design of the modern computer in place today, much akin to the movement from CISC to RISC. It is highly likely that a move into Nanocom-puting would be a catalyst for another shift in instruction set design, from RISC to perhaps an instruction set which relies less on software and takes advantage of significant gains in hardware speed and efficiency.

Multiprocessing and Instruction Level Parallelism

Multiprocessing came into being with the advent of the UNIX operating system, in which several computers could be networked together for computing power. CPUs can be linked in a tightly coupled fashion and connected by a bus, or loosely coupled by simply networking computers in a cluster. Either fashion is limited by what is known as Amdahl's Law. The law is a formula to measure the increase in speed gained by adding another CPU to an algorithm's computation.

There is a limit and an overhead associated with the addition of a new CPU, and the overall speedup increase will only be fraction of the true computing speed of the additional CPU. The use of multiprocessing does provide a significant benefit, but this benefit has a finite ceiling. Multiprocessing has been used in industry a great deal through the implementation of clusters.

Instruction level parallelism is the execution of instructions in parallel, by overlapping instructions which do not depend on one another in order to complete. While this provided a boost in processing speed initially, most CPUs simply do not have that many instructions which they can execute in parallel. According to an article in Embedded Systems Programming, "ILP becomes its own worst enemy. Even if you could find two, four, or 50 instructions to execute simultaneously, you probably couldn't access all the data at once. Data starvation becomes a real problem. For high-end systems, bandwidth is more important than ILP.

The processor in your Macintosh, SPARC station, or PC spends more cycles waiting on memory than it does processing instructions. Improving your "CPU efficiency" will simply increase the number of wait states." Perhaps the promise of speed and efficiency by parallelism will never reach the heights we had hoped within the current architecture paradigm, until the bottleneck in memory and bandwidth is corrected. Nanotechnology has promise in the area of multiprocessing and clustering, because adding more CPU processors and linking them will increase computing power. However, true computing increases will occur with changes in buses and memory.

Memory

Cheap and fast memory has become more readily available rather recently, but memory more often than not is the place where backlog begins. Computer scientists have focused a great deal on faster caching techniques and more efficient memory management algorithms, all while the cost of the hardware continued to get smaller and go down. It's presumed that nanocomputing will allow memory to move out of this position of bottleneck because caches can become smaller, faster and simpler, however it's not clear at this point if that will be true.

It's likely that computers will be faster and smaller all around, but the weakest links in any computer will still be the memory and interconnects. The biggest improvement in main memory bottlenecks in modern computing has come from the use of virtual memory, in which a computer can act as though it has much more RAM than it actually does by using the hard disk to copy data.

Virtual memory is used in all modern computers to run today's software, which tends to demand a great deal of space to run. Swapping algorithms and small caches have added to virtual memory by allowing programmes to run quickly enough to pick up the slack for when a disk write is necessary.

Interconnections

Current PCs use buses for the interconnection between devices. The bus is a commonly overlooked component to a computer's size, speed and efficiency. The bus ties almost everything together, including the hard disk, the CPU, the memory, and any other I/O components a computer might have. The PC generally has two main buses. The first, known as a system bus, connects the CPU and the memory. The second, which is a bit slower, is used to communicate with other devices such as the hard drive or sound/video cards. Modern PCs also usually offer a USB which stands for "Universal Serial Bus" to allow users to connect any number of peripherals to the computer. These peripherals can include extra memory or extra hard drives.

The system bus is an area in the computer which creates bottleneck between the hard drive and the CPU. As system buses have evolved, they have been able to deliver more data at a faster speed from the hard disk and into memory. This is an area in which research in nanotechnology can have a profound and marked effect.

Storage

Current technology trends have measured that disk capacity doubles approximately every 18 months. This increase is driven by the embedded computing market. Computers today can be found in everything from phones to music players to cars, and smaller disks are needed to run the software. The average computer has gone from having a 5 gigabyte hard drive in 1997 to an average 80 gigabyte hard drive in 2005. The costs of hard drives have decreased in almost the same proportions.

It is in this area that nanotechnology could also find its largest impact. As stated in the introduction, one of the main visions of nanotechnology is the ability to store data at the molecular level. Volumes of books can already be stored on a disk, and this improvement will continue with molecular storage of data.

CHIP DESIGN

The chip design of the nanocomputer would be best suited to have a carbon base which is both self-testing and reconfigurable. Because we know that faults will be at levels upwards of 10% for any chip built in the nanometre range, it will be necessary for these features to be part of any solution we choose. Also, it's important to remember the breadth of our failure rate. A Nanocomputer will contain not just one billion but several billion chips. If we have a computer with 5 billion chips, we will have 500 million chips which are defective with a 10% error rate. It will be an important cost factor to be able to repair these chips after they have been fabricated.

Of the research we have gone over thus far, the best proposed replacement for the CMOS chips is the NanoBlock, based on the FPGA, the Field Programmable Gate Array. These blocks are carbon based. These devices have been created from a bottom up assembly; they are fault tolerant and reconfigurable.

Bad devices or blocks of devices can be swapped out if necessary Another advantage to the NanoBlock is that it is chemically assembled, allowing more flexibility with reconfiguration. The devices can be manipulated so that changes can be made to improve any faults which may make an entire block unusable.

The argument for NanoBlocks also stems from the need to insure heat and power dissipation. The NanoBlocks are low power devices, and this makes it a good candidate as a base for building a nanocomputer.

Instruction Set Design

Very little research in nanotechnology has addressed the future of instruction set design. We know that our hardware systems will become more complex and more powerful. We can infer that the instruction set design should then move back from a reduced instruction set (RISC) design to a more powerful complex instruction set (CISC).

This way, we can take advantage of the improvements in the hardware and write less complex compilers. The instructions can also perform more work in a single clock cycle, improving the speed operations are performed in the system. However, the one architecture that we have looked at which took instruction set design into consideration only used a simple accumulator. One would think that a more complex design would be beneficial and more productive, but it is possible that a simple approach will be the best way to manage so many million components.

RISC was chosen as the instruction set for this generation of components due to cost, and it's conceivable that the next generation will choose a similarly simple instruction set due to size constraints and sheer numbers.

The instruction set will presumably be one of the last design components to consider, but designers must take it into consideration when building components.

Interconnections and Communication Points

Interconnections are another vital piece to consider. If there can be devices in the multi-billion in a nanocomputer, these nano-connectors will also number in the multi-billion and will need to be efficient and allow for both local and global communication.

The development of nanowires as communication pathways between neighboring cells is the most well developed form of nano-sized interconnects. The carbon based nanowires are the most promising format because of their stability.

These devices also allow for self-testing, reconfiguration, and self-assembly. Each of these qualities makes it an attractive component in terms of costs, reliability, and practicality. It is also presumed that the reduction in size of these wires can improve density and we can move more data through interconnections at a faster rate. This can reduce starvation which can sometimes occur in a system due to bus latency and lack of bandwidth.

While carbon nanowires have been produced in the lab, the nanowires which we must use in our nanocomputer must improve their resistance. Arranging these nanowires in a Markov Random Circuit as one group of researchers has proposed would be a valuable arrangement, and would be an important algorithm to employ in a nanocomputer.

Main Memory, Multiprocessing and Instruction Level Parallelism

Memory management is and will continue to be a very difficult topic facing all computer designers. Virtual memory demands which are currently limited by space will be unlimited in a nanocomputer architecture.

Memory will be more plentiful, cheaper and faster in a nanocomputer, and we can expect to move from the 1 gigabyte of memory standard on modern computers to numbers two to five times more powerful. However, these advantages will bring a new host of issues.

Instruction level parallelism may be more difficult because there will be so much more data to handle. Algorithms will need to be developed to insure that critical sections of code are executed properly. However, we do know that we will have many more CPUs which we can cluster together with much less space and cost requirements. It is likely that instruction level parallelism will fall away to a new paradigm of handling large scale multiprocessing.

Perhaps machines will be split apart so that certain CPUs are specifically for certain jobs, or certain tasks within a computer. Nanocomputer research has not reached the point of coming up with a memory management scheme, but the chances that it is exactly as we handle memory today is unlikely.

Storage

A nanocomputer will have the possibility of an unlimited amount of storage space. Currently we have computers which can hold up to 150 gigabytes of information. We expect a nanocomputer to be able to hold terabytes of information. These storage disks will also be easily searchable and can also be partitioned.Presumably we can hold volumes of data, and backup tapes or requiring repositories to be placed on a network of computers to make up a server can be a thing of the past. Smaller embedded devices will be able to hold much more data as well. Our entire medical history can exist on a key, or entire music collection can exist on a device the size of a credit card or smaller.

Conclusion

The future of nanotechnology will bring exciting change to the computing industry. We are promised machines which are faster, cheaper, and smaller. This promise will come with incredible challenges and sacrifice, and the computing industry must be flexible and agile enough to meet the demands of manufacturing these new devices and designing the machines which will contain them.

The industry must also change the current manufacturing processes and current design paradigms to meet the differences between this new generation of devices and our generation.

These new devices will require a completely new approach in manufacturing, moving from lithography top down design to bottom up design. It may also require self-assembly of components in order to be economically viable. This will require a new set of manufacturing tools and processes. Computer manufacturers will have to change their plants and assembly lines completely in order to build these new components.

A nanocomputer will also require a new instruction set, and innovative ways to handle the new challenges when dealing with molecular components must be considered. Hardware will be less reliable and self-testing and self-configuration must be built in to any nanocomputer. This may make manufacturing more expensive at first, and more time consuming.

COMPILING SCHEME TO NANO-COMPUTERS

Nano-computers

Our objective in these notes will be to identify some very simple machine models which are nevertheless powerful enough to run Scheme. Since even real RISC micro-processors are vastly more complex than the simple machines we consider, we'll refer to our machines as nano-computers. Of course even though in theory Scheme can be compiled into nano-computer code, we are not suggesting that this would be a sensible thing to do.

The resulting compiled code is spectacularly inefficient, and there would be no point in trying to run it. Rather, what we learn from this reduction of Scheme to a nano-computer is that apparently very limited nano-computers are as resistant to uniform analysis as much richer Scheme expressions. For example, the compilation process transforms the Halting Problem for Scheme into the Halting Problem for nano-computers. Hence the Nano-Computer Computer Halting Problem is "just as hard" as that for Scheme. In particular, the Nano-Computer Computer Halting Problem is undecidable. It is worth emphasizing that the definition of undecidability refers to

Scheme procedures. Undecidability of the Nano-Computer Halting Problem means that SCHEME programmes are incapable of deciding whether nano-computer programmes halt. So even using a richly featured language, it is not possible to predict the behaviour of extremely limited programmes.

Footnote

For certain kinds of "simple" machines, it is possible to show that the Halting Problem for Simple Machines cannot be decided BY "simple" machines. For example, we might choose simple machines to be the kind of "pushdown-store" machines used to parse inputs according to a BNF grammar.

These machines are too limited to include a decider for their own halting problem. But undecidability BY simple machines need not imply that a problem is really hard. For example, there is a rather efficient Scheme procedure which decides the Halting Problem for Pushdown-Store machines.)

End-footnote

A result like this provides some valuable guidance about where the "hard part" of programme analysis resides. For example, an important part of real compiler technology involves programme analyses which are far more detailed than just determining the halting property.

How can compilers do this analysis, since we know such analysis is undecidable? The answer is that compilers DON'T fully analyse ALL possible source programmes—they do the best they can. For some classes of programmes, compilers can use procedures which are guaranteed to provide complete analyses; for programmes which fall outside of the classes which the compiler can handle, there is no guarantee of the quality of analysis or of the resulting compiled code. It would be a waste of time for compiler designer to try developing perfect analysis methods for some unanalysable subclass of programmes.

From the compilation of Scheme to nano-computers, we learn, for example, that simply cutting down on the built-in operations in a language cannot be expected to yield an analysable class of programmes. In this way, identifying simple unanalysable/undecidable subclasses of programmes gives useful guidance on where NOT to waste time. The insight that even very simple programmes have undecidable properties plays an additional important role in the Theory of Computation.

It is a key technical fact used in establishing the pervasiveness of undecidability in subject areas far removed from Computer Science. So far we have seen only "incestuous" undecidable problems: problems about programmes which cannot be decided by programmes. Later we will discover undecidable problems about polynomials, simple algebras, and simple grammars, for example.

The proofs will be based on learning to "programme" with polynomials, algebraic equations, etc., so they simulate more familiar kinds of programmes. But these problems from outside Computer Science were not intended to embody programming, and it is generally very difficult to programme with them.

For example, writing algebraic equations which, in a suitable sense, "simulate," Scheme programmes would be an extremely cumbersome exercise. On the other hand, as should be expected, it is much easier to write equations which simulate nano-computer programmes. But simulating nano-computers is sufficient, since nano-computers in turn can simulate Scheme.

One of simplest nano-computers we consider is the n-Counter machine. This is a machine with n registers for some n > 0, each register capable of holding a nonnegative integer of arbitrary size. The only operations of the machine are to increment (add one) to any register, decrement any register (leaving it unchanged if the register contains zero), and branch on whether a register contains zero. The registers are called "counters" since in a single step they can only be incremented and decremented. *For example, in 2-counter machines, the only instructions are*:

Instruction	Informal meaning
Inc1	Increment first register
Inc2	Increment second register
Dec1	Decrement first register, except leave it alone if it is 0.
Dec2	Decrement second register, except leave it alone if it is 0.
Ifr1 n1 n2	If register 1 is zero, go to line n1, otherwise go to line n2.
Ifr2 n1 n2	If register 2 is zero, go to line n1, otherwise go to line n2.

A 2-counter machine, M, is a finite sequence of such instructions, numbered consecutively starting at zero. For example, the machine M1 below, adds the contents of its first counter to its second counter and then halts (by transfering to an instruction number larger than any in the programme).

2-counter Machine M1

0: ifr1 4 1	Line 4 means "halt"
1: dec1	
2: inc2	
3: ifr1 0 0	Goto line 0

The "configuration" of a 2-CM is defined to be a triple (k, l, m) of nonnegative integers. The intended interpretation of the triple is that k is the number of the next instruction to be executed, and l and m are the contents of counters 1 and 2.

Formally, we associate with 2-CM, M, a partial function step_M from configurations to configurations, where step_m(k, l, m) is the configuration, if any, after execution of M's k^th instruction when counter 1 contains l, and counter 2 contains m.

For example, for the machine above:

- Step_M1(0, 2, 0) = (1, 2, 0),
- Step_M1(1, 2, 0) = (2, 1, 0),
- Step_M1(2, 1, 0) = (3, 1, 1),
- Step_M1(3, 1, 1) = (0, 1, 1).

Exercise 1: Give a precise definition of the function step_M for an arbitrary 2-CM, M.

Now given the limited structure of counter machines, it is not even apparent what it would MEAN to compile Scheme onto one of them. Basic Scheme printable values such as symbols, lists or even negative integers are not available in counter machines, so we cannot expect a counter machine programme to produce the same printable values as a Scheme source programme.

The obvious thing to do would be to define some representation of Scheme values in terms of counter machine values, namely, nonnegative integers. We would then require that for any Scheme "source" expression, S, the compiled code—a counter machine we will call M_S—halts with the contents of some designated "output" counter equal to the nonnegative integer representation of the value of S.

However, for our purposes it is not necessary to develop such a representation of Scheme values. Namely, to conclude that the halting problem for various nano-computers is undecidable, it is enough to simulate halting behaviour only. We say a 2-CM HALTS iff it halts when started in the "standard" initial configuration (0, 0, 0). Our main result is:

Theorem

Scheme->2-CM) There is a procedure for translating any Scheme expression, S, into a 2-counter machine, M_S, such that S halts iff M_S halts. From this we immediately conclude

FUTURE OF TECHNOLOGY

It is exciting to look into the future of technology. In an age of continuous innovation and invention, when the discovery of today loses its sheen tomorrow, it is not easy to pinpoint technologies that will transform our future.

Engineering and technical developments are everyone's concern, as they will not be confined to industry, university classrooms, and R&D labs.

Instead, they will make a tremendous difference in our day-to-day lives. Here I will attempt to identify some of the technologies that will revolutionize our lives and our values in the coming years.

Quantum Computers

Unlike current PCs, quantum computers will have switches that can be in an on or off state simultaneously. The mechanism that will make this possible is known as superposition, and the switches are referred to as quantum bits. The system will make quantum computers operate very fast. A basic quantum computer is likely to be operational by 2020.

Bibliography

Allcock, R.S.: *Development Training: A Personal View*, Birmingham, Endeavour Training, 1988.

Augarten, Stan: *Bit By Bit, An Illustrated History of Computers,* New York, Ticknor & Fields, 1984.

Bandura, A.: *Social Learning and Personality Development,* New York, Holt, Rinehart, and Winston, 1963.

Baumann, P. R.: *Computer Assisted Instruction Programs in Geography: Five Climate Programs,* Oneonta, New York, 1970.

Bronstein, P. A.: *Teaching a Psychology of People,* Washington, American Psychological Association, 1988.

Burke, Colin: *Information and Secrecy, Vannevar Bush, Ultra, and the Other Memex,* Metuchen, NJ, Scarecrow Press, 1994.

Burke, Frank M., *Valuation and Valuation Planning for Closely Held Businesses,* Englewood Cliffs, NJ, Prentice Hall, 1981.

Campbell-Kelly, Martin and William Aspray: *Computer, A History of the Information Machine,* New York, Basic Books, 1996.

Charles R. Morris: *Computer Wars, The Fall of IBM and the Future of Global Technology,* New York, Times Books, 1993.

Charniak, Eugene: *Introduction to artificial intelligence,* page 2. Addison-Wesley, 1984.

Christopher D. Manning, Hinrich Schütze: *Foundations of Statistical Natural Language Processing,* MIT Press (1999).

Cox, Jr., T.: *Cultural Diversity in Organizations: Theory, Research & Practice,* San Francisco, Berrett-Koehler Publishers, 1993.

Damon, William: *Social and Personality Development: Infancy through Adolescence,* New York, Norton, 1983.

Dasgupta, Subrata: *Creativity in Invention and Design, Computational and Cognitive Explorations of Technological Originality,* New York, Cambridge University Press, 1994.

David J.: *The Machine Question: Critical Perspectives on AI, Robotics, and Ethics.* MIT Press, 2012.

David Post : *The Rise of Robots War in Cyberspace*, 48 Stan, L. Rev. 1367, 1996.

David S: *Understanding Information Age Warfare*, CCRP Publications, Washington DC, 2001.

Edwards, Paul N: *The Closed World: Computers and the Politics of Discourse in Cold War America,* Cambridge, MA, The MIT Press, 1996.

Eliot A Cohen,: *Supreme Command: Soldiers, Statesmen, and Leadership in Wartime*, Anchor Books, New York, 2003.

Feldman, Ronen; Sanger, James; *The Text Mining Handbook*, Cambridge University Press, 2007.

Garstka, J J and F P Stein: *Network Centric Warfare: Developing and Leveraging Information Superiority*, CCRP Publications, Washington DC, 1999.

Gast, A. P. : *The impact of Restricting Information Access on Science and Technology* Retrieved October 1, 2008.

Guala, F.: *The Methodology of Experimental Economics,* New York, Cambridge University Press, 2005.

Gusterson, Hugh. *Nuclear Rites: A Weapons Laboratory at the End of the Cold War*. Berkeley: University of California Press, 1996.

Han, Jiawei, Micheline Kamber, and Jian Pei: *Data mining: concepts and techniques*. Morgan kaufmann, 2006.

Hopkins, D. : *Personal Growth Through Adventure*, London, David Fulton Publishers, 1993.

Hsu, Jeffrey: *A Comprehensive Guide to Computer Bible Study. Up-to-Date Information on the Best Software and Techniques*, Dallas: Word, 1993.

James R.: *The Control Revolution: Technological and Economic Origins of the Information Society*, Cambridge, MA: Harvard University Press, 1986.

Katherine Davis: *The Computer Establishment*, New York: McGraw-Hill, 1981.

Kelly, G.A.: *Theory of Personality : The Psychology of Personal Constructs*. New York, W.W. Norton, 1955.

Kidder, Tracy: *Soul of a New Machine*, New York, Avon, 1981.

Lior Pachter and Bernd Sturmfels (2005). *Algebraic Statistics for Computational Biology*. Cambridge University Press.

Malone, Michael S.: *The Microprocessor, A Biography,* Santa Clara, CA, TELOS, 1995.

Maslow, A.: *Motivation and Personality,* New York, Harper and Row, 1987.

Minsky, Marvin (1967), *Computation: Finite and Infinite Machines,* Englewood Cliffs, N.J.: Prentice-Hall

Mooney, J. D., and Reiley, A. C.: *Onward Industry,* New York, 1931.

Moravec, Hans (1988), *Mind Children,* Harvard University Press.

Nick, Martin (2005), *Al Jazari: The Ingenious 13th Century Muslin Mechanic,* Al Shindagah.

Pearl, J. : *Probabilistic Reasoning in Intelligent Systems: Networks of Plausible Inference,* San Mateo, California: Morgan Kaufmann, 1988 .

Peirson, G., Bird, R., Brown, R., & Howard, P.: *Business Finance,* Roseville, 1990

Pournelle, Jerry: *The User's Guide to Small Computers,* New York, Baen, 1984.

Rodgers, William: *Think, A Biography of the Watsons and IBM,* New York, Stein and Day, 1969.

Rose, Frank: *West of Eden, The End of Innocence at Apple Computer,* New York, Penguin, 1989.

Rowan, John: *Subpersonalities: the People inside Us,* London, Routledge, 1990.

Russell, Stuart J.; Norvig, Peter: *Artificial Intelligence: A Modern Approach,* Upper Saddle River, New Jersey: Prentice Hall, 2003

Schuster, C.: *The Process of Human Development,* Boston, Little, Brown & Co., 1980.

Simon, H. A.: *The Shape of Automation for Men and Management,* New York: Harper & Row, 1965.

Slagmulder, R. : *Interorganizational Cost Management,* Productivity Press, 1999.

Stross, Randall: *The Microsoft Way, The Real Story of How the Company Outsmarts Its Competition,* New York: Addison-Wesley, 1996.

White, Stephen L.: *The Unity of the Self,* Cambridge, MIT Press, 1991.

Ye, Nong: *The Handbook of Data Mining,* Mahwah, NJ: Lawrence Erlbaum, 2003.

Index

❑❑❑